Angelo Mangiarotti
The Tectonics of Assembly

Edited by
Franz Graf
Francesca Albani

Angelo Mangiarotti
The Tectonics of Assembly

Original edition:
Angelo Mangiarotti. La tettonica dell'assemblaggio / The tectonics of Assembly,
Mendrisio Academy Press-Silvana Editoriale,
©2015 Accademia di architettura Università della Svizzera italiana, Mendrisio
This edition is published by ATELIER OPA - Opa Press, Tokyo
Under temporary license of Accademia di architettura-Università della Svizzera italiana,
Mendrisio Academy Press

All rights reserved. No part of this publication may be reproduced,
stored in retrieval systems, or transmitted, in any form or by any means,
electoric, mechanical, photocopying or recording or otherwise
without the prior permission of Accademia di architettura-Università
della Svizzera italiana, Mendrisio Academy Press.
We wish to thank Edoardo Nava Mangiarotti.

アンジェロ・マンジャロッティ
構築のリアリティ 組み立て工法による生成

フランツ・グラフ
フランチェスカ・アルバーニ 編

Opa Press

槇 文彦

Fumihiko Maki

マンジャロッティと私

Mangiarotti and I

　私は1958年に得たグラハム財団基金をもとに次の2年間アジア、中近東、ヨーロッパへの西方の旅を試みている。その2回目の旅は新婚旅行を兼ね、車でスイスの南、ティチノ（Ticino）の町を訪れた。理由はハーヴァード大学で親友であった、スイス人ドルフ・シェネブリ（Dolf Schnebli）が当時ここに居をかまえ、設計にいそしんでいたからである。この後、国境を超えてイタリアに行くなら、是非バランザーテ（Baranzate）という小さな町にあるアンジェロ・マンジャロッティの教会をみることを計画している。

　広い人気のない周縁の中にポツンとたつ教会は白い半透明の壁にPC（プレキャストコンクリート）のコンクリートの十字型の屋根板が空を鮮やかに区切り、清楚なモダニズムの建築の佇まいをみせていた。これが私の最初のマンジャロッティの建築との出会いであった。

　時はもう夕暮れに近く、丁度内部は小さな子供の葬式が終わった後だったのだろうか。人々が去ったあとの内部はこれも白い半透明の壁に囲まれた簡素な仕上げである。但し天井のPC梁とそれを支える柱の存在が際立っていた。

　私達はその翌日、近くのパドヴァ（Padova）の工場を訪れた。この工場もコンクリートの壁、金属の軒先の美しいシルエットが印象的なモダニズムの建築であった。それは勝れた構造エンジニア、精度の高いPCコンクリート業者とのレベルの高いコラボレーションの結晶でもあった。私が親しく彼の作品の内外をみる機会はこの2つに限られたが、次の数十年間、彼のデザインが私の心に深く残るものとなった。

I tried to travel westward to Asia, the Middle East and Europe for two years using the grant I obtained from Graham Foundation in 1958. My second travel was also a honeymoon, and we visited Ticino, south of Switzerland, by car because a close friend of mine at Harvard University, Swiss architect Dolf Schnebli, was living there and was diligent in design at that time. I made plans thinking that afterwards, if we were to cross the border to Italy, I would definitely like to visit a church designed by Angelo Mangiarotti that is located in a small town called Baranzate.

The church stood in a large deserted environment, showing a clean appearance of a modern building with cross-shaped roofing made of precast concrete (PC) on white translucent walls that sharply divide the sky. This was my first encounter with a Mangiarotti building.

It was already towards the evening; it might just have been after the funeral ceremony of a small child as people left. The interior also had a simple finishing surrounded by white translucent walls. However, the existence of PC beams in the ceiling and pillars supporting it stood out.

On the next day, we visited a factory near Padova. This factory was also a modernist building with concrete walls and metal eaves with beautiful silhouettes. It was the product of a high-level collaboration among excellent structural engineers and a highly precise PC concrete contractor. Although the opportunities of visiting both the inside and outside of his works were limited to these two instances, his designs have remained ingrained in my mind for the next few decades.

Since the beginning of the 20th century, one of the principles that modernism has advocated was the industrialisation and de-

20世紀の初頭以来、モダニズムが掲げてきた幾つかの建築生産の工業化と民主化があった。そして鉄、コンクリートとガラスは新時代の建築のイメージを確立していく上で欠かせない新素材として登場した。しかしコンクリートは新時代が要求する、より大きい、より高い空間の創造に寄与はするが、同時にその現場打ち生産方式は決して近代化を象徴するものではなかった。そうした情況の中からPC（プレキャストコンクリート）が登場し、建築家やエンジニア達の熱い視線が送られる。しかしひとりの建築家がその特質を徹底的に追求し、新しい建築美の創造にまで到達することは極めて稀であった。モダニズムの巨匠といわれるル・コルビュジエやミース・ファン・デル・ローエですら、理念としての建築の合理化、民主化を唱えながら、既に20年代の後半から芸術としての建築へと次第にスタンスを移行し、PCの追求に手を染めることはなかった。アメリカの産んだ偉大な建築家、フランク・ロイド・ライトは西海岸時代にPCに挑戦するが結局は装飾的な意匠への応用に終わってしまっている。

　このように見てくると、マンジャロッティが1957年につくったこの教会、そしてそれに続く一連の建築作品は、おそらくモダニズムの歴史の中で、新素材のもっている特質を追求しその結晶化として一つの建築に統合することに成功した最後のモダニズムの傑作として位置づけられよう。教会の後に続くパドヴァの工場、ミラノの中層のアパート、ジェノヴァの海岸に建つ展示パヴィリオン、更に彼が手掛けてきた数々の家具、或いはプロダクトデザインに至るまで、彼が一つ一つの素材に求める

mocratisation of construction production. Iron, concrete, and glass have appeared as indispensable new materials to establish an image of new-era architecture. Although the concrete contributed to the creation of larger and higher spaces that the new era demands, its on-site production method has never been a symbol of modernisation. From such a situation, PC emerged and caught the eye of architects and engineers. However, it was extremely rare for a single architect to thoroughly investigate the characteristics of concrete and produce a creation with a new architectural beauty. Even Le Corbusier and Mies van der Rohe, who were called great masters of modernism, gradually shifted their positions to architecture as art from the latter half of the twenties while advocating the idea of architectural rationalisation and democratisation and never touched PC exploration. Frank Lloyd Wright, a great American architect, challenged PC when he spent time at the United States West Coast but eventually ended up applying decorative designs.

To take these in consideration, this church that Mangiarotti created in 1957, and the series of architectural works hereafter, can be viewed as the last modernist masterpieces that pursued the characteristics of the new material and succeeded in their integration into one building as the crystallisation of the history of modernism. After church works, from a factory in Padova, a medium-rise apartment in Milan, an exhibition pavilion on the shore of Genoa and a great number of furniture he had worked on, or even products designed, his attitude towards every material in discovering their ultimate form was always consistent. With regard to being a true seeker of the principles of modernism, on the other hand, the rationality of scientists which was required for their discoveries and the sensitivity of artists have always been involved. We should not overlook that the foundation of such sensibility was

究極の形の発見に向かうその姿勢は常に一貫していた。それは一方において、あくまでモダニズムの原則に対する真摯な探究者でありながら、他方においてその発見に対して科学者に要求される合理性と、芸術家としての感性が常に参加した。そしてその感性の基盤には、イタリアという歴史的な風土と文化と密接な関係があったことを見逃してはならない。

彼にとって考えることと創ることは切り離せない一つの行為であり、そこにはものと、ものをつくる人間への愛情と期待が常に存在していた。

〈愛情と期待〉はこうした作業を支えるのに不可欠な人間の精神の所産であった。

マンジャロッティのように、第二次世界大戦直後に作家として人生の中で最も重要な創世の期を迎えた建築家達の数は決して少なくない。だがこれらの多くの建築家達は様々な理由、境遇の中で次第に去っていった。マンジャロッティのように強い精神と稀有の才能によって自身の小宇宙をつくりあげ得た作家は少ない。イタリアという風土と文化は、ローマの時代から今日まで多くの偉大な政治家、学者、芸術家達を輩出してきた。ある人の言によれば、偉大な人であればある程、彼等には常に孤高の影が存在していたという。

彼が1990年代、東京に来た時、私は「貴方は最後のモダニストではないか」と言ったが、彼は「いやいや私は多くのモダニストの一人に過ぎない」と言い、その謙虚さを隠さなかった。

当時東京のイタリア文化振興会が中心となって日本と

closely related to the history and culture of Italy. For Mangiarotti, thinking and creating are inseparable, in which love and an expectation for things and people who create things had always existed. 'Love and expectation' were the results of the human spirit that is essential to support these tasks.

There were a few architects who reached the age of the most important point in their lives as creators shortly after World War II, just like Mangiarotti. However, most of these architects have gradually left for various reasons and circumstances. A few of them achieved their own microcosm with a strong spirit and rare talent like Mangiarotti. Since the Roman period until now, the climate and culture of Italy have produced many great politicians, scholars and artists. In one's words, the greater they are, the larger their shadows of solitude.

When Mangiarotti came to Tokyo in the Nineties, I told him, «You seem to be the last modernist». He said, «No, I am just one of many modernists», not hiding his humility.

At that time, the Italian Culture Promotion Association in Tokyo led several cultural exchanges among architects in Japan and Italy. The last symposium took place near Carrara, Italy. Mangiarotti joined there as an Italian architect, and I had the opportunity to stay with him all day long. Returning from the symposium to the hotel, we stopped by at the construction site of his latest work, Uffici IMM a Carrara, by chance. When he explained the building, in his finely chiselled face I discovered a persona filled with a deep melancholy that might have been felt by architects of the Renaissance era. For Mangiarotti, I suspect that «Form is a reduction of ethics to a question of aesthetics».

イタリアの建築家達の間で何回か文化交流を行う機会を得た。その最後のシンポジウムがイタリアのカラーラの近くで行われた。その際マンジャロッティがイタリア側から参加し、一日親しく行動を共にする機会を得た。シンポジウムからホテルへの帰路、たまたま彼の最新作『IMM社オフィス』の工事現場に立ち寄ることが出来た。その建物を説明する彼の彫りの深い横顔に、私はふとルネッサンスの時代の建築家達がもっていたであろうあの深い憂愁に満ちたペルソナを発見したのである。

　マンジャロッティにとって、かたちとは美を追求するプロセスから生まれる彼自身の倫理の姿への帰結に他ならなかったのではないだろうか。

鈴木敏彦

Toshihiko Suzuki

はじめに

Preface

　本書はスイスの展覧会「Angelo Mangiarotti / La tettonica dell'assembraggio」に合わせて出版された同名のカタログ書籍（Silvana出版、2015年）の日本語版となる。「アンジェロ・マンジャロッティ／構築のリアリティ」と題した東京での展覧会の開催と合わせて、オリジナルの本にイタリア語と英語で掲載された内容を日本語に訳した。原文に加えて新たに建築家の槇文彦氏が書き下ろした巻頭言、鈴木敏彦の序文、マンジャロッティ・アソシエイツ・ジャパンの河合俊和氏、諸角敬氏、堀川絹江氏が執筆したプロダクト製品に関するコラム、そして川上元美氏のあとがきを日本語と英語のバイリンガルで掲載した。

　本展は、2006年にスイス・イタリア語圏大学メンドリシオ建築アカデミーが実施したマンジャロッティの建築に関する研究成果を、同大学のグラフ教授とアルバーニ教授のキュレーションと、ミラノのアンジェロ・マンジャロッティ・アーカイブ（AAM）の協力によって紹介する。ティチーノにある同大学での展示（2015年9月17日〜10月25日）を皮切りに、ヴィンタートゥールのスイス応用科学大学（2016年10月4日〜10月20日）、チューリッヒの建築フォーラム（2017年6月1日〜7月14日）、ジュネーブのシクリ・パヴィリオン（2018年8月31日〜9月16日）の順にスイスを巡り、イタリアのノヴァラ城（2019年5月10日〜6月2日）を経て、最終巡回地として東京・九段下のイタリア文化会館（2019年9月13日〜9月29日）にて6回目の展示を開催する。

　私はマンジャロッティ本人にはお目にかかることは叶わなかったが、かねがね建築からプロダクトまでデザイ

This book is the Japanese version planned in accordance with the exhibition in Switzerland, "Angelo Mangiarotti. La tettonica dell' assemblaggio / the Tectonics of Assembly," and the catalog book under the same name (Mendrisio Academy Press and Silvana Editoriale, 2015). In association with the exhibition in Tokyo, we translated the contents of the original book in Italian and English into Japanese. The book consists of an original part and a new part, preface specially written for the book by architect Fumihiko Maki; an introduction by Toshihiko Suzuki; columns about products written by Mangiarotti Assosiates Japan Toshikazu Kawai, Kei Moroumi, and Kinue Horikawa; and a postscript by Kawakami Motomi in bilingual text, Japanese and English.

The exhibition is based on a research on Mangiarotti's tectonics of assemmly conducted at the Mendrisio Academy of Architecture-Università della Svizzera italiana by Professor Graf and Professor Albani, and is curated by the two Professors in cooperation with the Angelo Mangiarotti Archive in Milan (AAM). The Swiss exhibition tour started from the exhibition at the same university in Ticino (September 17–October 25, 2015), at the ZHAW Zurich University of Applied Sciences in Winterthur (October 4–20, 2016), at the Architekturforum in Zurich (June 1–July 14, 2017), at Pavillion Sicli in Geneva (August 31–September 20, 2018), and at Novara Castle in Italy (May 10–June 2, 2019). Finally, the sixth exhibition will be held at the Istituto Italiano di Cultura in Tokyo, Japan (September 13–29, 2019).

Although I did not have an opportunity to meet Mangiarotti, I regarded him as an architect who crosses the borders of design, from buildings to products. In my book "Architectural Product Design: Design Ideas for Things and Spaces that Dramatically Change Life" (Kodansha Publishing, 2013), I wrote about Angelo

ンの領域を横断する建築家として注目していた。2013年に上梓した『建築プロダクトデザイン――暮らしを劇的に変えるモノと空間の設計思想』（講談社）では、バックミンスター・フラー、ジャン・プルーヴェ、アルネ・ヤコブセン、レンゾ・ピアノ、ジョエ・コロンボ、ヴェルナール・パントンと並んでアンジェロ・マンジャロッティを取り上げた。基本的なシステムを家具から建築にまで応用する仕組みは21世紀を代表する巨匠ならではの発想だと思う。

その出会いは2011年にさかのぼる。ミラノ工科大学との国際交流のプログラムで、工学院大学の学生13人とミラノのアンジェロ・マンジャロッティ事務所を訪れた。突然の訪問にもかかわらず、マンジャロッティの娘であり、ミラノ工科大学の建築・建築環境・建設工学学部の博士課程主任教授でもあった、アンナ・マンジャロッティ教授が私達を歓迎して事務所の建物の一階のバールでプロセッコを振舞ってくれたのが今でも記憶に新しい。まるで女優のような風情のアンナ先生に向かって、私の学生が「君、可愛いね」と覚えたてのイタリア語で話しかけたのには唖然としたが、アンナ先生は「ありがとう」と笑顔で答えてくれた。後で堀川氏に聞いたところ、「恐れ多くてそんな風に話しかけるミラノ工科大学の学生はいないから、かえって嬉しかったのだろう」とのことだった。

2012年にアンナ先生と堀川氏が来日した。工学院大学に水野明哲学長を訪ねた後、学生も交えた懇親会で再会を祝った。東京で開催した展覧会「アンジェロ・マンジャロッティの哲学とデザイン：マエストロと日本人スタッフとの協働の記録」（イタリア文化会館、2012年6

Mangiarotti, as well as Buckminster Fuller, Jean Prouvé, Arne Jacobsen, Renzo Piano, Joe Colombo, and Bernard Panton. I think that the basic mechanism that he used from furniture to architecture is one of the great ideas representing construction methods in the 21st century.

I valued my encounter in 2011. I visited the Studio Mangiarotti in Milan under the international exchange program of Politecnico di Milano with 13 students of Kogakuin University. Despite our sudden visit, Professor Anna Mangiarotti, who was the daughter of Angelo and the head of Faculty board of PhD programme of ABC Department at the Politecnico di Milano, welcomed us and opened prosecco bottles in a bar located on the first floor of the building. I was dumbfounded that one of my students spoke in his beginners' Italian to Anna, who looked like an actress. «You are cute». She replied with a smile, «Thank you». Later, Horikawa told us, «There is no student at Politecnico di Milano that talks to her like that because of hesitation, so she was glad». Anna and Horikawa came to Japan in 2012. After meeting with Akira Mizuno, the president of Kogakuin University, we celebrated a reunion with our students. Then we helped them at the exhibition at the Istituto Italiano di Cultura in Tokyo (June 14–30, 2012). An architect, Kei Morozumi, who was a lecturer in the Department of Architecture, taught us that «A Japanese architect can show his or her ability in making models in Italy because of skillfulness with own fingers» from his experience working in Milan as a Mangiarotti associate. It was an episode that inspired students to find jobs abroad. On the last day of the exhibition, Angelo Mangiarotti passed away at the age of 91 in Milan. Then when I saw his products, such as lighting and tables in the Milan Salone, I felt sympathy. After a while, Horikawa told of Anna's

月14日〜6月30日）では微力ながら学生と共に展覧会を手伝った。建築学科の講師を務めていた諸角敬氏はかつてマンジャロッティ・アソシエイツとしてミラノで働いた経験から、「手先が器用な日本人はイタリアでの模型制作で力を発揮する」と教えてくれた。学生にとっても海外での就職が急に身近に感じられるようになるエピソードだった。その展覧会の最終日に、アンジェロ・マンジャロッティがミラノで亡くなった。91歳だった。その後のミラノ・サローネでマンジャロッティの照明やテーブルなどプロダクト作品を目にしても、心にぽっかりと穴が空いたような気がした。しばらくして、2016年1月30日にアンナ先生が急逝した。堀川氏を通じて、いずれ3ヶ月間ほど日本の建築を見て回りたいと聞いていたので、連絡を心待ちしていた時期だった。2018年になり、堀川氏から「アンナの希望を叶えるためにも日本への巡回展を実施したい」との連絡があった。目頭が熱くなるのを感じながら、できる限りの協力をすると即答した。

　スカイプでグラフ教授たちと挨拶した後に、東京展の実現に向けた準備がはじまった。日本を代表するプロダクトデザイナーである川上元美氏を筆頭に、今はそれぞれ建築家として活躍する竹居正武氏、濱口オサミ氏、三井一成氏、奥田宗幸氏、諸角敬氏、豊島夕起夫氏、元良信彦氏、宮川格氏、河合俊和氏、堀川絹江氏らマンジャロッティ・アソシエイツ・ジャパンのメンバーに私が加わる形で、『アンジェロ・マンジャロッティ／構築のリアリティ』展実行委員会が組織された。交互にマンジャロッティの下で学んだアソシエイツの連体感は素晴らしく、彼のために協力を惜しまない人々が結集したと実感

wish to look around Japanese architecture for about three months, so I was looking forward to seeing them, but she passed away suddenly on January 30, 2016. In 2018, Horikawa informed me that she would like to carry out a Mangiarotti's exhibition also in Japan to make Anna's wish come true. I immediately swore with her to do my best.

After meeting with Professor Graf and Professor Albani on Skype, we began preparing for the realization of the exhibition in Tokyo. The committee was organized by Mr. Motomi Kawakami, who is the leading product designer in Japan; the members of Mangiarotti Associates Japan, who are active architects in their individual companies; Masatake Takei; Osami Hamaguchi; Kazushige Mitsui; Muneyuki Okuda; Kei Morozmi; Yukio Toyoshima; Nobuhiko Motora; Ital Miyakawa; Toshikazu Kawai; and Kinue Horikawa. Then I joined the group. I felt that strong bond of associates who are willing to cooperate for Mangiarotti.

Now, inspired by the activities of Professor Graf and Professor Albani, I assigned the original book to students in the master's course in my class at Kogakuin University in the first term of 2019. Ten students read each description about 10 architectural works made of prefabricated concrete to understand and analyze Mangiarotti's design philosophy, and they worked on redesigning them at the end of the seminar. Regarding the mechanism of trilithon that appeared many times in the book as a basic concept of his design, Emiliano Cappellini of Atelier OPA, who participated in the class as a guest, drew a picture with two stones and a stone on it on a whiteboard. He explained that this basic module (called Trilite in Italy) is the foundation of European architecture and classical orders. Even though we knew it had a simple composition like Stonehenge, when it came to architecture, the Japanese

した。

　さて、グラフ教授とアルバーニ教授の活動に刺激を受けて、工学院大学大学院の2019年度前期の授業でマンジャロッティのオリジナルの本を読み解いた。プレハブ工法のコンクリートで作られた10の建築作品の章を10人の学生が順番に担当しマンジャロッティの設計思想の理解に努め、最後の演習では一人ずつそのリデザインに取り組んだ。マンジャロッティの設計の基本概念として繰り返し記述に出てくる三石塔式の仕組みについては、折しも授業に参加していたアトリエOPAのエミリアーノ・カッペリーニがホワイトボードに直立する二つの石の上に一石を載せた絵を描き、イタリア語ではトリリテと言ってヨーロッパの古典建築の基本を成す構造だと説明してくれた。ストーンヘンジの写真にその単純な仕組みを目にしてはいても、建築と言えば木造軸組工法を基本に習う日本人には新鮮な概念で、まさに構築のリアリティを継承したひと時だった。

　こうして展覧会の準備と本書の翻訳と出版を通して、マンジャロッティの設計の思想に改めて出会うことができた。イタリアのモダンデザインの巨匠の設計の思想に定期的に触れられるのは、一重に日本とイタリアの架け橋を築いてきたマンジャロッティ・アソシエイツ・ジャパンのおかげである。そして、イタリア文化会館をはじめ、尽力を惜しまなかった関係各社の皆様に心よりお礼を申し上げる。東京での展覧会をアンジェロとアンナ・マンジャロッティに捧げたい。そして読者が本書を通じ、スイスとイタリアから薫陶を授かり、新たな建築のチャレンジへと踏み出す一助になれば幸いである。

basically learned a wooden frame structure, so it sounded like a fresh idea to us. It was the moment that we inherited the reality of construction in Europe.

Thus, through the preparation of the exhibition and the translation and publication of the book, we could touch the design philosophy of Mangiarotti. Besides, thanks to Mangiarotti Associates Japan who built a bridge between Japan and Italy, we can touch the design of a master of Italian modern design from various angles. We are grateful for the Italian Culture Center and all the other companies and contributors. I would like to dedicate the exhibition in Tokyo to Angelo and Anna Mangiarotti. Finally, I hope that the readers of this book will be led by excellent guidance from Switzerland and Italy and will take a step into new architectural challenges.

目 次
Contents

4　槇 文彦
　　マンジャロッティと私
Fumihiko Maki
Mangiarotti and I

8　鈴木敏彦
　　はじめに
Toshihiko Suzuki
Preface

15　アンナ・マンジャロッティ
　　建築に捧げた人生
Anna Mangiarotti
A Life Given to Architecture

23　フランツ・グラフ
　　プレハブ工法の倫理 古風な技法と普遍性
Franz Graf
**The Ethics of Prefabrication:
Archaism and Universality**

43　フランチェスカ・アルバーニ
　　忘れられたアイコン 工業建築の緑青
Francesca Albani
**Forgotten Icons.
The Patina of Industrialized Architecture**

63　堀川絹江
　　巨匠の軌跡
Kinue Horikawa
The Traces of the Master

72　フランツ・グラフ、フランチェスカ・アルバーニ
　　建築の組み立て方 10のバリエーション
Franz Graf, Francesca Albani
Assembling to Build: Ten Variations on a Theme

EXPERIMENTATION

82　**1**　スプリューゲン・ブロイ社倉庫およびオフィスビル
　　　　メストレ（ベネチア）
　　　　1961–1964
Splügen Bräu warehouse and office building
Mestre (Venezia), 1961–1964

98　**2**　海の見本市展示館
　　　　ジェノヴァ
　　　　1962–1963
Exposition pavilion at the Fiera del Mare
Genova, 1962–1963

112　Column　河合俊和
　　　　　　その素材で何ができるのであろうか？
Kawai Toshikazu
What will be completed with that material?

Gravity

116 **3** エルマグ社工場
リッソーネ（モンツァ・エ・ブリアンツァ）
1963–1966
Elmag factory
Lissone (Monza e Brianza), 1963–1966

132 **4** レマ社工場
アルツァーテ・ブリアンツァ（コモ）
1969–1979
Lema factory
Alzate Brianza (Como), 1969–1979

146 **5** フェグ社エントランス棟
ジュッサーノ（モンツァ・エ・ブリアンツァ）
1976–1979
Feg entrance pavilion
Giussano (Monza e Brianza), 1976–1979

160 **6** フィアット代理店
ブッソレンゴ（ヴェローナ）
1976–1979
Fiat dealership
Bussolengo (Verona), 1976–1979

174 Column 諸角 敬
重さがデザインになる
Morozumi Kei
Weight is the design

Module

178 **7** アルミタリア社の工場及びオフィス
チニゼッロ・バルサモ（ミラノ）
1968–1971
Armitalia offices and factory
Cinisello Balsamo (Milano), 1968–1971

192 **8** スナイデロ社のオフィス、展示場とサービス施設
マイアーノ（ウディネ）
1971–1978
Snaidero offices, showroom and services
Majano (Udine), 1971–1978

208 **9** 集合住宅
モンツァ
1968–1975
Residential building
Monza, 1968–1975

216 **10** 集合住宅
アロジオ（コモ）
1974–1978
Residential building
Arosio (Como), 1974–1978

230 Column 堀川絹江
タイムレスなデザイン
Kinue Horikawa
Timeless design

233 アンジェロ・マンジャロッティ
プロフィール
Biography

242 **Bibliography**

248 著者プロフィール
Authors

250 川上元美
あとがき
Motomi Kawakami
Postscript

1950年代前半のアンジェロ・マンジャロッティ
Angelo Mangiarotti in the early fifties. (Angelo Mangiarotti Archive, AAM, Milano).

アンナ・マンジャロッティ

Anna Mangiarotti

建築に捧げた人生

A Life Given to Architecture

　私たちはスイス・イタリア語圏大学メンドリシオ建築アカデミーに感謝の意を表したい。特にフランツ・グラフ教授は同大学の展覧会にてミラノのアンジェロ・マンジャロッティ信託財団のアーカイブから最も重要な設計図を選び、大いなる関心を示してくれた。また展覧会と同時に、内容と編集の模範となる書籍を大学の出版局で制作し出版してくれたことに敬意を表したい。この本はマンジャロッティの作品を再考する機会を作り出し、さらに、令名高いメンドリシオ建築アカデミーに通う若い学生たちに指標となるモデルを示している。

　同じ職種を選び、プロジェクトは異なるものの同じスタジオで働き、生涯私の傍にいた父について記すのは、不可能ではないにしろ非常に難しい。彼と自分の能力の比較、あるいは設計の知識を比較する道筋は、まるでフィルターをかけるように日々の建築を理解する上で役立った。私は彼の傍で建築の進化と起こりゆく変化を学習したので、他の情報はろ過され、純化され、清められた。彼の教えはかけがえのないものだった。特に押し付けられることもなく、私はその行程を観察した。

　細心の技術と言語学的情報に基づいた道筋から、細かな技術、方法、建築とデザインの成果を定義する要素が生まれる。熟考から分析的で学際的なデザインの仮説の定義が導き出されるので、常に新しい問題が起きても修正は可能である。アンジェロ・マンジャロッティは建築とデザインに人生を捧げた。薄紙や菓子店の包装紙を前に製図台に座り、鉛筆やマーカーやクレヨンを手に持ち、一日も休むことなく毎日12時間考え、毎晩頭の中で駆けめぐるイメージや形や構造のアイデアをノートやあち

We have to acknowledge the commitment shown by the Academy of Architecture of the Università della Svizzera italiana and, in particular, my colleague, Professor Franz Graf, not just for the great interest shown in exhibiting in Mendrisio some of Angelo Mangiarotti's most significant drawings, selected from the archive of the Trust Fondazione Angelo Mangiarotti in Milan, but also in producing this volume, published at the same time as the exhibition in the Academy series, which is exemplary in terms of its contents and editorial layout. This book offers the opportunity for a critical re-reading of Angelo's works and, most importantly, it represents a possible reference model for the young people who attend this prestigious Academy.

It is very difficult for me, if not impossible, to write about a person who was beside me all my life, having chosen the same profession and worked in the same firm, albeit often dealing with different projects. This pathway, this likening of my ability to his, or perhaps, better still, to his ability to design, helped me understand architecture day after day as if through a filter. Being close to Angelo, my way of learning about the evolution of architecture and the changes underway were filtered, rarefied, cleansed of all other information. His teaching was invaluable to me, and it was never forced upon me: I was the spectator of a pathway.

A pathway mindful of the techniques and linguistic sources that make up the parameters for the definition of a meticulous technique, a method, a product of either architecture or design. The considerations that were developed have led to the definition of a design hypothesis based on an analytical and interdisciplinary method, one that is capable of being modified when it comes into contact with new issues that are constantly being developed. Angelo Mangiarotti devoted his entire life to architecture, to design-

パレルモ大学にてアンジェロ・マンジャロッティ1984年
Angelo Mangiarotti at the University of Palermo in 1984. (AAM, Milano).

こちの紙の上にすぐに書き留める必要があった。この作業はミラノのスタジオ、ガルダ湖のムルロンゴのスタジオ兼住宅、彼が「瞑想の場」として用いたヴィチェンツァのヴァルマラーナ・アイ・ナーニ邸の厩舎から改築したスタジオ、さらにはヴォルテッラのアラバスターの職人の工房、またはアンジェロが頻繁に訪れた日本人建築家のスタジオの中でも行われた。

アンジェロの特徴を理解するには、様々な大学で開催された会議や授業、セミナーで表現した考えを示すのが最善の方法だと思う。特に興味深いのは、1982–1985年にパレルモ大学の開催で著名な教授として招かれたセミナー、2002年にミラノ工科大学でインダストリアルデザイン学部の名誉学位を授与された時の講演、そして2004年の東京のギャラリー間で開催された自分の作品の展覧会の講演である。アンジェロは、学生を指導する年寄りと話すよりも、建築やデザインに興味がある学生と直接話すほうが良い成果を生むと考えていた。アンジェロは、いつどこでデザインを始めたのだろうか。第二次世界大戦中、彼はスイスで拘留され数ヶ月間を過ごした。そこで幸運にもエルネスト・ロジャース、マックス・ビルや他の建築家と出会った。その後、ビルの紹介で1953年にシカゴのイリノイ工科大学に客員教授として招待された。そこで彼はミース・ファン・デル・ローエ、ヴァルター・グロピウス、フランク・ロイド・ライト、

ing, seated at his drafting table with sheets of tissue paper of the kind used by confectioners back then, or tracing paper, with his pencils, felt-tip markers and pastels, twelve hours a day every day of the week, and every night during which thoughts, images, ideas for shapes and structures sprang into his mind and had to be immediately jotted down in notebooks or on pieces of paper scattered here and there. This took place in the offices in Milan, or in our studio-home in Murlongo on Lake Garda, or in Vicenza, in the stables of Villa Valmarana ("Villa dei Nani"), which Angelo used as a studio as well as a thinking room. Or else in Volterra, in the workshops of the artisans who worked the alabaster, or in the offices of the Japanese architects whom Angelo would frequently visit.

I think that the best way to understand some of Angelo's distinctive qualities is to present some of the ideas he expressed in the meetings, lessons and seminars he took part in in various universities. Of particular interest are the seminars that were organized by the University of Palermo in 1982-1985, where he was invited as a "distinguished professor", the talk he delivered at Milan Polytechnic in 2002 on the occasion of his honorary degree in Industrial Design, and the one he gave in Tokyo in 2004 on the occasion of an exhibition of his work at the Gallery MA. Angelo believed it was more fruitful to speak directly to students who were interested in architecture and design, rather than to those who were older and whose job was to train those students. When and where did Angelo begin to deal with design? During World

ギャラリー間でのマンジャロッティの展覧会2004年
Exhibition devoted to Mangiarotti at Gallery MA in Tokyo, 2004.
(Mitsumasa Fujitsuka, AAM, Milano).

コンラッド・ワックスマンと知遇を得た。都市や地方で建物の一部または全体に標準規格の木材を使った架構式構造に興味を持ち、その意味と重要性を理解したのはその頃だった。

このユニークな状況にあったアメリカに留まるよう勧められたが、アンジェロはイタリアに戻り働くことを望んだ。後に、マックス・ビルがウルム造形大学を設立した時に、教員陣の一員になるように依頼したが、アンジェロはイタリアにいることを選んだ。それは間違った選択だったかもしれない、と彼は時折口にした。アメリカからイタリアに戻り、ミラノのランツォーネ通りに最初のスタジオを開設した。その後、何年にもわたり、大勢の日本人スタッフが出入りするようになって、現在も日本人が残るに至った。同時期に日本国際交流基金から、彼が最も興味を抱いていた日本に滞在し実際に見て学ぶ機会が与えられた。日本での経験は重要だったと彼はしばしば言っていた。利用可能な道具にはいろいろな種類や質があり、本質的な形のデザインを探求し、そこにユーザが参加することを観察した。そして興味深い結実がもたらされた。その後のアンジェロが創造した建築、デザイン、彫刻の作品の多くにその経験が反映されている。

民家が並ぶ京都の住宅街を友人と散策した時のことを彼は良く思い出した。若い女性が灰色の木製の建具を自宅の入り口から取り外しているのに気が付いた。幼い息

War II he spent several months interned in Switzerland, where he had the good fortune to meet Ernesto N. Rogers, Max Bill and other architects. And it was in 1953, thanks to Max Bill, that Angelo was called to the Illinois Institute of Technology in Chicago as a visiting professor. This gave him the chance to meet Ludwig Mies van der Rohe, Walter Gropius, Frank Lloyd Wright and Konrad Wachsmann. It was then that he became interested in and began understanding the meaning and importance of the balloon-frame system, which involves the use of a series of standard solid wood members used for building both in the city and the countryside, for parts of buildings or whole ones, one example being the corn cribs used in agriculture.

Despite this unique situation and the offer to stay in the United States, Angelo chose to return to Italy and work there. Later, when Max Bill founded the Ulm School of Design, he asked him to be part of the teaching staff. Again, Angelo preferred not to leave Italy. Perhaps it was a mistake, as he himself said on many occasions. When he returned to Italy, he opened his first firm in Milan, in Via Lanzone. Over the years, many Japanese collaborators passed through the office and some of them are still there. During that same period, the Japan Foundation offered him the chance to visit Japan, so that he could view and grow familiar with what interested him most. He often said that his Japanese experience was important because in that country the type and quality of the means available, the design and the search for an essential form, as well as the participation of the end-users them-

シカゴのイリノイ工科大学にてアンジェロ・マンジャロッティと学生たち1953-1954年
Angelo Mangiarotti in Chicago with some students from the IIT, 1953-1954 (AAM, Milano).

子が乱暴に壊したのだ。どうするのか興味に駆られて彼女の後を追うと、近くの建材店に入って行って、よく似た格子の建具を買うと、家に戻って手間なく古いものと取り替えた。アンジェロは何年経っても、おそらく40年以上このエピソードを忘れなかった。彼が目にした「機能と方法の自然な適合」に現代建築の本質的なメッセージが含まれていると信じていた。

若者と彼の職業について話すときはいつも、基本的な概念を強調した。

- 50年以上も絶えずユーザのニーズを模索し、職人との作業と工業的な活動の両方で本物の関係を追求した。
- あらゆる素材（石、コンクリート、ガラス、ブロンズ、鋼鉄、アルミニウム、雪花石膏〈アラバスター〉）の性質を学び、その素材の本質を理解しようと努めた。
- 建築でもデザインでも常にユーザを巻き込み、完成時に参加できる手段を提供した。
- 同じ道を選んだ若者たちに、祖先の文化を超えて行くように勧めた。
- 仕事を通じ重要な目的に寄与することが必要だと信じていた。
- 誠実さが疑われるえせ文化的な立場を拒否した。
- 他者と協力して製品の品質と量を追求した。
- 人間の貢献に常に不足があるとすれば（現在、かつてないほど不足している）、全ての製品は人間の所

selves, had achieved extremely interesting results, which were often echoed in many of the works of architecture, design and sculpture made by Angelo himself.

He often recalled the time when, in the company of a friend, while strolling through a residential area of *minka* houses in Kyoto, he had noticed a young woman removing a grey wooden panel from the entrance to her house; it had been broken by her rambunctious little boy. Curious to see what she was up to, they followed her to a store not far away where building materials were sold. The woman entered, bought a grey panel similar to hers, went home, and in no time at all she had replaced the old one. Even after many years had passed, more than forty, I believe, Angelo never forgot that episode. He believed that it contained an essential message for contemporary architecture, which he saw as being «naturally appropriate in its means and its functions».

Whenever he spoke to young people about his profession he would emphasize several basic concepts:

– in over fifty years' experience he sought genuine relationships and a continuous contact with the needs of the users, as well as with the productive side, both artisanal and industrial;

– he always tried to learn about and understand all that the material itself could offer, whatever that material may be (stone, concrete, glass, bronze, steel, aluminium, alabast

– in both design and architecture, he always tried to involve the end-user, offering instruments suited to the completion of the work;

アメリカの架構式構造の建物1954年
Model of an American balloon- frame building, 1954. (AAM, Milano).

産であるとして芸術を支持した。

マンジャロッティは2004年に東京で講演会を開催し、グローバリゼーションの時代に地球上で起こっている事を建築の分野においても理解するのは私たちの務めである、と口火を切った。言語のグローバリゼーションは建築にも影響を及ぼし、その場所のリアルな文化や材料とはかけ離れた新しい様式を生み出す危険性がある、と理由を述べた。よって建築学校が担う責任と機能とは、全学生のそれぞれの能力を養い、磨き、伸ばすことであって、特定の時期の様式や教師が信じるものを学生に強制することではない、とアンジェロは信じていた。そして彼は言った。「寛大で機敏な人間がもっと参加できるように、新世代には建築、デザイン、芸術の新しい方法を提唱する義務がある」

そしてこの参加を促すため、もっと尽力すべきだと彼はつづけた。

「現在こうした分野で学生の参加が減っているのは、ある意味で、ビックネームが作品に署名することの裏返しである。教師とは学生の技能を最大かつ最適に伸ばすことを好む人々であり、教師個人の思想に従わせる人々ではない。これに関して日本の教員は手本になる。逆説的に言えば、真の教師の役割とは独学者を養成することだ」

彼の専門であるデザイン開発は分析と検証で構成されていた。アイデアと洞察力とデバイスの発明と同様に、原理と、構造的、生産的、技術的制約を歓迎した。この現実と状況を踏まえてプロジェクトの特性を決定した。具体的には、建築又はデザイン作品のアイデアから初期

– he advised the young people who had chosen the same path as his to go beyond the culture of their forebears;

– he believed it was always necessary to endow his work with significant content;

– he rejected pseudo-cultural stances of dubious honesty;

– he invited others to seek quality as the product of quantity;

– if it is true that a human contribution is always lacking (today this is so more than ever), then he supported art, in that every product is a human artefact.

In 2004 he held a conference in Tokyo where he began by saying that in an age of globalization it is our duty, also in the field of architecture, to understand what is happening on our planet. The reason for this is that the globalization of languages, which affects more than just architecture, risks creating new styles that are far removed from the cultural reality and material of places. On this is based the responsibility and function of architecture schools, whose task, Angelo believed, is to cultivate, hone, and enhance the skills of each and every student, and not to force him or her to surrender to what is in style at that particular time, or to what the teacher believes. Hence, he said, «the new generations have a duty to put forward in architecture, design and art new instruments for a more generous and incisive human participation».

It is precisely to this *participation*, Angelo continued, that we must devote many of our energies: «The current reduction in participation on the part of students is, in a certain sense, the counterpart of the works signed by the big names. The masters – and to this regard the Japanese example is fundamental – are those who favour the best and most appropriate development of their students' skills, not their compliance with their teachers' personal

の設計までの構想段階と、最終的な計画から実施までの開発段階で、全体の複雑な軸を構成する部品や要素を検討した。計画と最終的な成果の両方を読み解き理解する上で、組織の全体像と細部の分析は両輪を成す。このすべての工程をアンジェロはホモ・ファベル（ラテン語の『工作人』。アルベルト・スポジト著「美学と科学技術」『デメトラ誌』1992年2号pp. 8-17）として指揮した。

メンドリシオ建築アカデミーの学生たちに、アンジェロについて、そして今日もなお尊敬を集める彼の教育原則について話したいと思った。客観的にはなれないので、彼のおびただしい多様な芸術作品について私が意見を表明することはできない。しかし確かなことが一つある。複数の表現（建築、工業製品、芸術の実践としての彫刻）を横断する彼の作品の複雑性は未だ研究されていない。しかし、この本がアンジェロの未だ知られざる作品の多くの側面に批評の光を当てることを私は確信している。

ideas. Paradoxically, the role of a real master is to train autodidacts».

In his professional practice, developments in designs were structured as fields of analysis and verification, which welcomed ideas, insights, and inventive devices, on the one hand, and laws, structural, productive and technical restraints, on the other. This link with both the reality and the context was what determined the characteristics of the project. Specifically, the conception (from the idea to the preliminary project) and the development of the project (from the definitive plan to its execution) made it possible to come to terms with a work of architecture or design and its component parts or elements within the complexity of their holistic dimension, where the overall vision of the organism and the analysis of the detail constitute two inseparable phases in the reading and understanding of both the project and the final product. All this took place in a *processo formante* (training process) conducted by Angelo as *homo faber* (A. Sposito, *Estetica e Tecnologia*, in "Demetra", 1992, no. 2, pp. 8-17).

I wanted to talk about Angelo to the students of the Mendrisio Academy of Architecture, and to tell them about some of his teaching principles that, I hope, are still respected today. I am not able to express an opinion on Angelo's copious and multifarious artistic production because I cannot be objective. But one thing is certain: that the complexity of his work is yet to be studied in its multiple expressions (works of architecture, industrial products, sculptures as a field of artistic practice). I am certain, however, that this publication will cast critical light on many of the aspects of his work that are still little known.

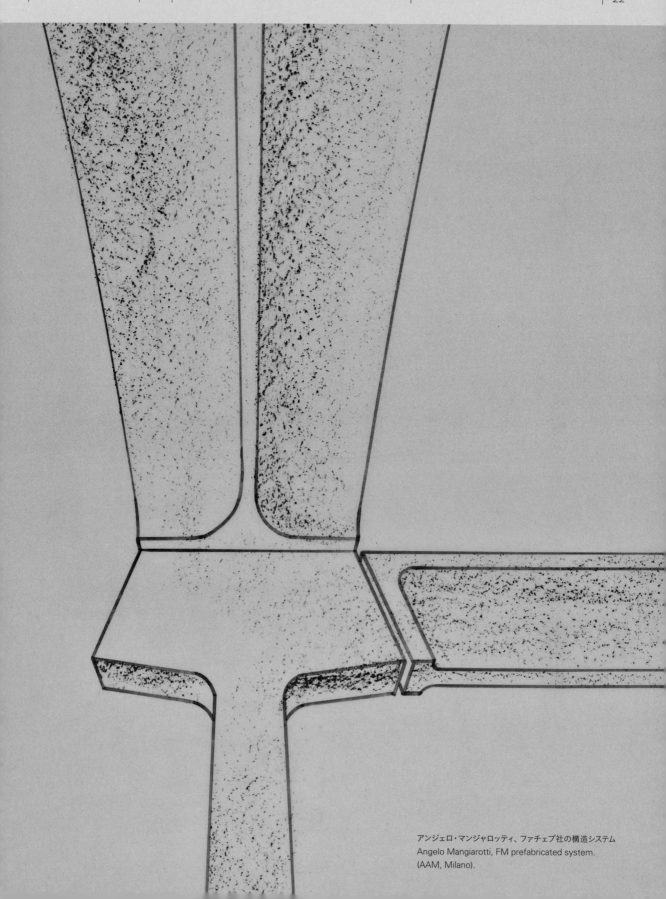

アンジェロ・マンジャロッティ、ファチェブ社の構造システム
Angelo Mangiarotti, FM prefabricated system.
(AAM, Milano).

フランツ・グラフ

プレハブ工法の倫理
古風な技法と普遍性

「現代の建築の概念は『部材』、つまり複雑な構成部材で出来ている。設置には『建設』方式と『建物』の組成という要件があり、必要な条件が既に揃っていることが重要かつ象徴的だろう。もし、全体およびすべての部品が同じ論理的な建設のコンセプトに基づいており、設計や建設に同じアプローチを適用すれば、建物の実現性と正確性と一貫性を決定する助けとなる」[1]

70年代後半からプレハブ工法は建築的な議論や建設過程から消えゆく傾向にあったが、アンジェロ・マンジャロッティが21世紀初頭においても構成部品による設計を思想でも実践したという事実[2]は、技術的な論点を凌駕している。マンジャロッティは生涯を通して建築家であり、工業デザイナーであり芸術家だった。[3] その倫理的な姿勢から設計に厳密な規律が生じた。「もし建築の工業化が創造活動に危機をもたらすか、と尋ねられたら、実用的な工法が出現する以前であっても、結果的に変化している現在の建設過程においても、新たな形成の原理として理解する必要があると強調したい」[4] マンジャロッティは、コンラッド・ワックスマン、マックス・ビル、バックミンスター・フラー、ジャン・プルーヴェといった有名な建築家、芸術家、発明家の思想や行動のいくつかの例を挙げて、自身を関連付けた。

そこでは自分の作品と距離を置いて問題を批判的に眺め、辛抱強く、注意深く考えることが出来た。他の利害関係者（顧客、建築業者、製造業者、職人、ユーザなど）を異なるレベルに連れていくため、一方では工業的な製造工程によって優れた品質レベルを達成することを期待し、他方では「結果として真実を実践する」[5]と言って自身

Franz Graf

The Ethics of Prefabrication:
Archaism and Universality

«The contemporary conception of architecture "by parts", namely by complex components, in which both the requirements of the [construction] system and the [building] organism they constitute are already present and already possess the essential requirements for their installation, may be significant and emblematic. And adopting such an approach to design and construction helps to determine the reality, correctness and coherence of the building, if the whole and all the parts are based on the same logical-constructive concept».[1]

The fact that Angelo Mangiarotti continued to offer an ideational and executive praxis inherent in design by components still at the beginning of the 21st century, when prefabrication had been tending to disappear from the architectural debate and construction process since the late seventies,[2] is a point that goes far beyond the technical issue. It was an ethical attitude with which Mangiarotti engaged throughout his life as an architect, industrial designer and artist,[3] making it a strict discipline of design. «If I am asked whether the industrialisation of building might lead to a crisis in creative activity, I would stress that, even before being a

– 1. A. Mangiarotti, *Pratica alla via analitica in architettura*, in A. Dal Lago (ed.), *Progettare e costruire nel XXI secolo*, Abitare Segesta Cataloghi, Milano 2000, p. 111.
– 2. During the eighties prefabrication would be used in Italy only partially and for components, as a simple technical operation that had only a tangential relationship with architectural design.
– 3. Throughout this volume, analysis of Angelo Mangiarotti's architectural work is mainly directed towards manufactured and prefabricated works, focusing on the theme of assembly. For a more general interpretation of Mangiarotti's architectural production, see my essay *The architecture of Angelo Mangiarotti: a journey through his works*, in F. Burkhardt (ed.), *Angelo Mangiarotti. Complete works*, Motta Architettura, Milano 2010, pp. 20-37.

ミース・ファン・デル・ローエ、イリノイ工科大学同窓会館の角
シカゴ1945
Ludwig Mies van der Rohe, corner of the IIT Alumni Memorial Hall.
(Navy Building) in Chicago, 1945 (Hedrich-Blessing).

– 4. *Sei domande a otto designer, Angelo Mangiarotti*, in "Edilizia Moderna", 1965, no. 85, p. 16.
– 5. A. Mangiarotti, *Architettura oggi*, in E.D. Bona, *Mangiarotti*, Sagep Editrice, Genova 1988, p. 10.
– 6. Angelo Mangiarotti sought refuge in Switzerland during the last years of World War II. He stayed on the campus for students at the Italian University of Lausanne, whose director was Gustavo Colonnetti. With him there were also Ernesto Nathan Rogers, Aldo Favini, Silvano Zorzi, Vico Magistretti and many others. He made contact with Swiss architects such as Max Bill and Alfred Roth. The experience was to have a profound significance for Mangiarotti, who on his return to Italy developed its themes and contents encountered as well as the collaborations. An example is the work he did with Aldo Favini.
– 7. See Angelo Mangiarotti's observations on "memory rarefied", establishing links between Shaker interiors and those of the Unity Temple at Oak Park, in A. Mangiarotti, M. Luchi, L. Bonesio, L. Magnani, *In nome dell'architettura*, Jaca Book, Milano 1987, pp. 86-87.
– 8. Mangiarotti firmly endorses the words of Mies van der Rohe: «Now as then I believe that the building art has little or nothing to do with the invention of interesting forms or personal predispositions. True building is always objective and expresses the inner structure of the epoch out of which it arises», in L. Mies van der Rohe, *The Artless World. Building Art of My Time (My Professional Career)*, Massachusetts Institute of Technology, Cambridge, Mass. 1996, p. 336.
– 9. «My choice was then ... to find my own way, fleeing almost from that of the master, whose emulation would not have allowed me to develop a different position», in A. Mangiarotti, M. Luchi, L. Bonesio, L. Magnani, *In nome dell'architettura*, cit., p. 18.

の言語と建築を結び付け、素材と伝統的演習を利用した。20世紀のプレハブ工法は工業で描き出したユートピアだ。建築と技術の多様な関係を作り出し、時にはエンジニアが用いる概念や用途を美的および象徴的な次元で超越する、単なる構成部品でもある。1950年代から60年代の世界中の建設状況と同様に、厳密に経済的な手法とその合理性は戦後復興の時代に重要だった。1945年にスイスから戻り、6 1953年にアメリカへ出発するまでマンジャロッティが過ごしたイタリアでは、際立ったテーマとして工業化とプレハブ工法が文化的に成熟した。1945年の建築研究運動、1948年の具体芸術運動、1945年の建築研究運動、1945年の「メトロン」発刊、1946年の「カンティエーリ」発刊、1949年にベルガモで開催された第7回近代建築国際会議（CIAM）で広く議論が行われた。1953年と1954年にアンジェロ・マンジャロッティはイリノイ工科大学で生活し、教鞭を執った。マンジャロッティの人生でアメリカでの経験が果たした役割を理解するためには1950年代のシカゴを想像する必要がある。工業文化の強さ、力、即時性を表す高層ビルや跳ね橋が、穀物倉庫と隣り合う架構式構造の低層住宅と調和していた。シカゴ滞在中にマンジャロッティはヴァルター・グロピウスやコンラッド・ワックスマンに会い、フランク・

practical system and the most consequent transformation of the building process of our time, it has to be understood as a new principle of figuration».[4] In this respect he associated himself with the thoughts and actions of illustrious architects, artists, inventors and builders, such as Konrad Wachsmann, Max Bill, Richard Buckminster Fuller and Jean Prouvé, to name only a few.

This position enabled him to distance himself from his own production and look critically at the issues, exploring them patiently and attentively, so as to bring other stakeholders (clients, building contractors, manufacturers, craftsmen, users, etc.) into the process on different levels, expecting on the one hand to attain excellent quality levels thanks to the industrial manufacturing process and on the other to exploit materials and traditional practices while also articulating his vocabulary and architecture as the «implementation of the truth as an event».[5]

Prefabrication in the 20th century is a utopia that is described as industrial and that exploits the multiplicity of relations between architecture and technology, sometimes through an aesthetic and symbolic dimension that goes largely beyond the conception and use that the engineer makes of it and is concentrated solely on the structural component. Strict economy of means and their rationalization, essential factors in the postwar period, were hallmarks of reconstruction as well as global construction in the fifties and sixties. On returning to Italy from Switzerland[6] in 1945 until his

バックミンスター・フラー、建設中のダイマキシオンハウス1945
Richard Buckminster Fuller, the Dymaxion House under construction, 1945.

ロイド・ライトの建築を観察し考えた。[7] ミース・ファン・デル・ローエの作品にも魅了されてその精神と重要性を解読して吸収した。しかしそのイメージを機械的に反復することはなく、[8] また、過剰な影響を受けずに自分の道を進むことに成功した。[9] イリノイ工科大学同窓会館には伝説の角がある。柱の端は2回突出し間にわずかな凹みを作り出す。角に集中する張力を強調しながら隠れた構造を即座に理解させる構造から、ミースの建築作品におけるあらゆるセンスが解釈できる。

マンジャロッティはバトラー社が製造した農業用建築にも魅了された。簡素で平凡で実用的、言い換えれば原始的で古風な建物だった。アメリカ平原にはガルバリウム鋼板で出来た穀物エレベーターが点在していた。1940年から1941年に、バックミンスター・フラーはそれを軍隊の兵舎やダイマキシオン居住装置に変え、1944年から1945年にバトラー社を巻き込んでダイマキシオンハウスの大量生産を試みた。ジオデシック・ドームのプロジェクトに先駆けて科学技術を搭載したウィグワム（アメリカインディアンのテント型ドーム）[10]としては、1967年のモントリオール万国博覧会のアメリカ館が有名だ。グローバルな表現と技術を超越した構成の外観では軽さと普遍性が重要だった。ミラノの建築家は

departure for the United States in 1953, Angelo Mangiarotti lived through a period of cultural ferment in which industrialization and prefabrication were prominent themes, widely discussed by various parties, including the Movement for the Study of the Architecture (1945), the Concrete Art Movement (1948), the reviews "Metron" (1945) and "Cantieri" (1946) and the CIAM VII held in Bergamo (1949). To understand the role played in Angelo Mangiarotti's life by the American experience – in 1953 and 1954 he lived and taught at the Illinois Institute of Technology – we have to immerse ourselves in Chicago in the fifties, where the strength, power and immediacy of the industrial culture of skyscrapers and movable bridges matched that of the low-rise balloon-frame houses flanked by ordinary grain elevators. During his stay Mangiarotti met Walter Gropius and Konrad Wachsmann, and observed and reflected on Frank Lloyd Wright's architecture.[7] He was also fascinated by the work of Mies van der Rohe, decoding and absorbing its spirit and significance without mechanically reproducing its image,[8] at the same time as he avoided being overly influenced by it and succeeded in following a path of his own.[9] The lesson of the legendary corner detail of the Alumni Memorial Hall at the IIT, where the doubling of the external profile forms a slight indentation with the covered edge of the pillar, accentuating the tension concentrated at this point and making even its hidden structure immediately comprehensible, was to be rein-

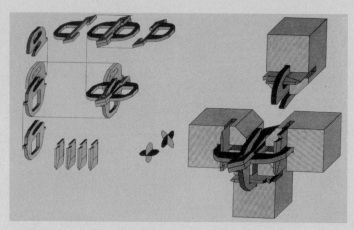

– 10. A *wigwam* is a domed dwelling, resting on a frame, used by some of the peoples of North America in the past and sometimes still today for ceremonial purposes [ed.].
– 11. K. Wachsmann, *Holzbau*, Editions Ernst Wasmuth, Berlin 1930.

ヴァルター・グロピウスとコンラッド・ワックスマン
一般パネルシステム1943-1945
Walter Gropius and Konrad Wachsmann,
General Panel System, 1943-1945.

この空想的にも単純にも見える構想を決して共有しなかった。1975年に四角いグリッドに基づくプレストレストコンクリートのプロジェクトがあったが、大規模なプロジェクトであっても、マンジャロッティは設計から建設まで工業のルールに従った建設を好んだ。マンジャロッティの作品にもう一つの痕跡を記したのは一般パネルシステム（GPS）というプレハブ工法の木材を構成する工法である。1943年から1945年にかけて、以前から工業化に向けてモジュラーを設計していたヴァルター・グロピウスと、クリストフ＆アンマック木構造会社のディレクターにして建設技術の理論家だったコンラッド・ワックスマン[11]が研究の論理的かつ完全な成果として設計した。木材は「変形」させてから設置する材料であり、黎明期から利用可能な資源でもある。19世紀後半のシカゴは、木材の組み立てが簡易化し、架構式構造での大量使用が普及する重要な時期にあった。GPSは、取り外し可能で外からは見えない優れた金属製コネクタを用いて、パネルを中心から四方に組み立てるモジュラー式システムだった。マンジャロッティはこの構成から四方に繋げるプレハブ工法の着想を得た。機能と構造的表現を集約した「Cub8」や「In/Out」システムがその例である。組み立ての理論化には次の概念を下敷きにした。「組み立てには芸術文明のあらゆる形態と建設の可能性がある。ゆえに、初めから歴史上の経験と批評を通じて導き出された建築物であり、実際にすべての建築の現象学でもあ

terpreted in every sense in his architectural work.

Mangiarotti was also fascinated by the agricultural structures manufactured by the Butler Company. These were plain and mundane practical buildings that might even be described as elementary and archaic. There were grain elevators made of welded galvanized sheet steel that studded the great American plain. Between 1940 and 1941, Buckminster Fuller would turn them into military barracks, Dymaxion Deployment Units, and in 1944-1945 would involve Butler itself in an attempt at large-scale production of the Dymaxion House, a technological *wigwam*[10] that preceded his projects for geodesic domes – a well-known example being the one made for Expo 67 in Montreal – in the expression of a globalizing and hyper-technological constructional outlook in which lightness and universality were the key issues. This utopian vision, at times rather naive, was never shared by the Milanese architect, who favoured the production of a new architecture guided by the rules of industry, from design to construction, even on large-scale projects, as in the case of the 1975 mega-structure based on a square grid in prestressed concrete.

Another work that would leave a trace in Mangiarotti's work was the General Panel System (GPS), a building system consisting of prefabricated timber elements. It was designed between 1943 and 1945 by Walter Gropius, in perfect harmony and as a logical consequence of his previous research into industrialization and modular design, and Konrad Wachsmann, director of the Christoph & Unmack timber construction company and a theorist of architectural technology.[11] Timber is a material that is installed after

アンジェロ・マンジャロッティ、押し出しPVCによる"In-Out"システム1968年
Angelo Mangiarotti, In-Out interwall system made by extruded PVC, 1968. (Giorgio Casali, AAM, Milano).

– 12. G.C. Argan, *Modulo-misura e modulo oggetto*, in "La Casa", no. 4, 1957 (special issue on industrialized construction). The text states that «the great discovery of modern architecture is the replacement of the measurement module with the object module».
– 13. Elementary does not mean simple. A work without composition is simple, whereas what is elementary is formed through the composition of given elements according to definite rules.
– 14. A. Mangiarotti, M. Luchi, L. Bonesio, L. Magnani, *op. cit.* at note 7, p. 67, caption to illustration 18.

る」[12]

マンジャロッティは機能を定義せず、倉庫、工場、教会、展示パヴィリオン等の機能を建築の基本[13]に組み込んだ。建築は素材とサイズと敷地という特質で決まる。この点で彼は有名な例に従った。ジャン・プルーヴェの建物には「柱廊型、船型、金庫室型、松葉杖型、スツール型」という「建設」の種類がある。ミース・ファン・デル・ローエは劇場や美術館等を「公共建築物」という一種類に類型化し、ペレ兄弟は「国王のシェルター」というコンセプトを用いた。

本質の表現とは「少ない要素はあいまいさを排除し明解な解釈をもたらす」[14]
メストレのスプリューゲン・ブロイ社倉庫とジェノヴァの海の見本市展示館

「建築の設計とは、仕様を特定し建物の性質を決定することを意味する」というマンジャロッティの言葉を思い出す。[15]メストレにあるスプリューゲン・ブロイ社倉庫（1961－1963年）のテーマは突き出した屋根だ。プレハブ工法の部品で構成したリブ屋根は片方に8メートル、もう片方に半分の4メートル突出し、それを4本の

being "transformed" as well as being a resource available since the dawn of time. The late 19th-century in Chicago was a key period which facilitated its assembly and promoted its mass use in the form of balloon-frame houses. The GPS was a modular system made up of panels that could be assembled isotropically using refined removable and virtually invisible metal connectors. These elements were the inspiration for the multiform nodes of all Mangiarotti's prefabricated systems, in which the function and constructional expression were concentrated: these included the Cub8 and In-Out wall systems. The theorization of the module-object involved the concept that «the object-module contained in a nutshell all the formal and constructive possibilities of a given artistic civilization and was therefore, from the very start, an architectural object, derived through experience and criticism from history, indeed the whole phenomenology of architecture».[12]

Maintaining independence from the defined function, Mangiarotti combined the functions of storage, factory, church, exhibition pavilion etc. in an elementary – we might say concrete – architecture[13] determined by the characteristics of the material, the scale and even the place. In this he followed illustrious examples: Jean Prouvé building by "constructional" types («*les portiques, les coques, les voûtes, les béquilles et les tabourets*»), Mies van der Rohe bringing together theatres, museums etc. in a single typology, that of the "public building", or the Perret brothers with their concept of *l'abri souverain*.

The representation of essentiality in which «a few elements allow for a clear reading with absolutely no ambiguity».[14]
Splügen Bräu warehouse in Mestre and Pavilion

アンジェロ・マンジャロッティ、スプリューゲン・ブロイ社倉庫、メストレ1963
海の見本市展示館、ジェノヴァ1963
Angelo Mangiarotti, models of the structure of the Splügen Bräu warehouse in Mestre, 1963, and the exhibition pavilion in Genoa, 1962-1963. (Giorgio Casali, AAM, Milano).

– 15. Angelo Mangiarotti expressed this idea during a conversation with me in Geneva on 8 February 2001.
– 16. «I believe that technical development, the refinement of calculation and the use of the resources of our time are elements that help ensure greater historical relevance in the work. There is no doubt, however, that the structure is a means to architecture and never the converse», A.M., *Angelo Mangiarotti, 1955-1964*, Seidoh-Sya publishing, Tokyo 1964.
– 17. A. Mangiarotti, *Pratica alla via analitica in architettura*, in A. Dal Lago (ed.), op. cit. at note 1, p. 112.

円錐形の柱が支える。アーチの内側にかかる一種の「空間的スリル」はここでは見られない。代わりにエンジニアのアルド・ファヴィーニはフレシネー工法に着想を得てポストテンション方式を開発した。技術と形態の複雑な関係は、静的計算の「形」に満足できなかった建築家とエンジニアの協働から生まれた。戦後のイタリアの技術的状況と密接に結びついたピエール・ルイージ・ネルヴィの作品を注意深く読み解き、そこから学んだことすべてをこの作品で具現化した。最新の建設機器を使わずに、熟練した職人が建物の敷地に木製型枠を設置したところに、経済的な材料を用いてプレハブ工法の建物を伝統的な石積で設営した。

ジェノヴァ港に竣工した展示パヴィリオン「鋼から船へ」（1962－1963年）の建設のテーマは凸面形状の屋根だった。ここでも鉄筋コンクリート製の4本の円錐形の柱が湾曲したスチール製の屋根を支えた。来場者は凸面状の屋根の下で海を水平線まで眺める。鋼板の膜を船形に張って造船の芸術というテーマを表現した。しかしその形状はレンズ型構造ではない。梁の端を囲むように屋根が架かっている。[16]

for the Fiera del Mare in Genoa

«Designing a building means identifying the constructional specifics that determine its character,» as Mangiarotti reminds us.[15] In the Splügen Bräu warehouse in Mestre (1961-1963), the theme is that of the overhang. Four truncated-conical columns support a ribbed plate comprising prefabricated elements with an overhang of 8 m on one side, while on the other side the overhang is about half as much at 4 m. A sort of "spatial thrill", that the reading of the intrados does not make fully explicit, as does the post-tensioning system developed by the engineer Aldo Favini, inspired by the Freyssinet system. The complexity of the relation between technical and formal expression was the basis of the collaboration between the engineer and the architect, who was not content with the "package" of static calculations. This work embodied all the lessons learned from a careful reading of the work of Pier Luigi Nervi, closely bound up with the technological situation in postwar Italy: the tradition of masonry built with economy of materials, prefabrication on the building site with the use of wooden formwork installed by skilled workers, and the absence of sophisticated construction equipment.

 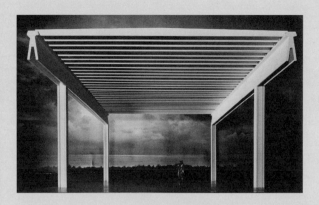

アンジェロ・マンジャロッティ、ファチェップ社のシステム模型
Angelo Mangiarotti, models of the Facep systems.
(Giorgio Casali, AAM, Milano).

「プレハブ工法の構成部品を見れば、建設の本質と工法の明快さがわかる。それは単純な形態と明解な機能の表現である」[17]

リッソーネ、ブッソレンゴ、アルツァーテ・ブリアンツァ、ジュッサーノの工業施設の建設方式

ジャン・プルーヴェは「建築の工業化」というテーマを大事にして、常に実現可能な「建設の発想」を具体化し製品化した。マンジャロッティもこのテーマを据えて、ガラス製の花瓶のシリーズであれプレストレスト鉄筋コンクリート製のプレハブ工法の工場であれ、生産の原則に従った。後者の建物には力強く古風な三石塔式の設計原則を適用した。柱と梁と屋根という最小の部品で、最小限の形状とコストと調和と再現性と無限の拡張性を実現した。部材の接続や組み立ては次の一点に集約された。「思想的および方法論的な観点から、個々の部材を一体化する組み立て構造の最終段階として、また真のデザイン手法として設計を熟考した」[18] これこそ、マンジャロッティの作品において私たちが「構築のリアリティ」と呼ぶものだ。[19] ここでは組み立てを、間近で観察すると本質的に自己を投影する教訓的な真髄として捉えた。この建築家に関する一般的な著述において抜け落ちているのはまさにこの視点である。[20]

マンジャロッティは自分が開発した建設方式を用いた。図面や、構成部材とその組み立てを解説する模型写真や、組み立ての過程に焦点を当てた敷地のスケッチにおいても自分のシステムを用いた。各システムは個別の建設テーマに発展した。リッソーネにある三石塔式システムを適

In the exhibition pavilion "From Steel to Ship" built in the port of Genoa (1962-1963), the construction theme was the roof with a convex intrados. Once again the four truncated-conical columns made of reinforced concrete support a curved steel roof. The convex form projects the gaze across the sea towards the horizon, while the form of a ship's hull in steel plate with the membranes in tension is a theme that belongs to naval art. But the form that is seen is not that of the lenticular structure, since the roof is raised so as to encompass the edge beams.[16]

«The constructional essentiality and compositional clarity of the system, observable in the connection between prefabricated elements, is expressed with simplicity of form and clarity of function».[17]

Construction systems for industrial buildings
at Lissone, Bussolengo, Alzate Brianza and Giussano

Very close to the idea of "architecture for industry", a theme dear to Jean Prouvé, who embodied his production in "constructive ideas" that were always absolutely feasible, Angelo Mangiarotti addressed this theme in accordance with the production principles themselves, whether it involved a family of glass vases or prefabricated factories in prestressed reinforced concrete. For the building of the latter he adopted the archaic and powerful trilithic design principle, since the pillar/beam/roofing segment offered regularity, repetitiveness and scope for unlimited expansion, a minimum number of elements, formal and financial economy. Within the connection between the elements, within the assemblage, were concentrated the «ideational and methodological aspects of the design, so that they can be considered as a veritable design technique and not only as the final stage of assembly of a

アンジェロ・マンジャロッティ、U70イゾチェルとブリオナ72のシステム模型
Angelo Mangiarotti, models of the U70 Isocell and Briona 72 systems.
(Giorgio Casali, AAM, Milano).

– 18. *Ibidem*, p. 111.
– 19. See F. Graf, *op. cit.* at note 3, p. 26. The term "tectonics" has been so abused by critics of architecture in the last twenty years that it has lost its meaning. It has also sometimes been used improperly, but in this case it is essential to speak of the work of Mangiarotti.
– 20. On the one hand Angelo Mangiarotti's oeuvre has been the subject of refined analyses and comprehensive studies like those by Enrico Bona, Guido Nardi or François Burkhardt, while on the other many have let themselves be enchanted by the beauty of his sketches, the elegance of his objects of industrial design and the refinement of his works of art.
– 21. Mangiarotti worked with various manufacturers of prefabricated building materials. Facep, Fabbrica Cementi Precompressi in the case of building in Lissone, V. Precompressi for the Isocell system series U-70 used in Alzate Brianza, Sacie prefabricated elements for the studies of the Briona 72 system used for example at Giussano. The clients of the "prototype factories" were entrepreneurs in the furniture, mechanical or automobile sector in northern Italy. It is not uncommon to come across an industrial plant with one of these construction systems, but it is surprising to see that only their creator is able to express their potential by reaching levels of excellence.
– 22. S. Sabatto, *Des clavetages aux coins: l'optimisation de l'ouvrabilité des systèmes constructifs conçus pas Konrad Wachsmann durant la guerre froide sous la supervision des agences gouvernementales américaines*, in F. Graf, Y. Delemontey (ed.), *Architecture industrialisée et préfabriquée: connaissance et sauvegarde*, Presses polytechniques et universitaires romandes, Lausanne 2012, pp. 169-196.

用したエルマグ社工場では、ハンマー型の柱頭で主梁の安定感と短さを実現した。ブッソレンゴにあるフィアットの販売店（1976－1979年）では柱の先を細くして梁のくぼみにはめ込んだ。非常に強い安定感が得られたので、突き出した屋根を支えることができた。マンジャロッティはこのように単純な支えで部材を組み立てる建設方式を次から次へと設計し、優れた安定性という視点と、大きく突き出た屋根の可能性を追求した。しかし、アルツァーテ・ブリアンツァのレマの工場（1969－1979年）においては、システムの積載量とスパンの関係から従来のサイズを逆転した。H字型断面の柱の台形の柱頭で逆U字型の梁を支え、大きな屋根を架けた。そして、ジュッサーノにあるフェグ社エントランス棟では前後左右に拡張する可能性を探った。ブリオナ72システムで梁は柱の四方に接続できる。梁と屋根材の耐荷重部材は同じ厚さで融合した。

　他の著名な建築家と同様に、マンジャロッティは高度な技術と革新性を証明する特許を取って建設した。彼は特許を開発する前に実寸大の試作品を作るように製造業者に要求した。[21] マンジャロッティが自身の独創性を最大に発揮したのは構成部材を組み立てる段階だった。一般パネル住宅（GPH）において、コンラッド・ワック

structure, in which the individual parts are united».[18] This is what, in the case of Mangiarotti's work, we have called "the tectonics of assembly",[19] in which the assembly was conceived as the didactic and quintessence of an essentially self-reflective architecture observed closely. It is precisely this aspect that is missing from the more general literature on the architect.[20]

Mangiarotti himself staged the construction systems adopted. He did so in drawings, in photographs of models which illustrated the components and their arrangement or in images of the construction site, where he focused on the process of assembly. Each system developed a specific constructive theme. In the trilithic system adopted in the Elmag factory at Lissone (1963-1966), the pillar is hammer-headed, a form whose purpose was to support and stabilize the main beam, while enabling it to be shortened. In the Fiat dealership at Bussolengo (1976-1979), the head of the column was tapered and fitted into the hollow of the beam, stabilized so strongly that it could even be extended into a cantilever. Within the same constructional family, in which the elements are assembled so they are simply supported, Mangiarotti passed from one system to the other, developing its aspects and potential (greater stability and additional roofing areas without supports). In the Lema factory at Alzate Brianza (1969-1979), however, he reversed the traditional dimensional relation between carrying capacity and span in a system in which the H-shaped head of the

アンジェロ・マンジャロッティ、ブリオナ72のシステムで建設したサーチェのデモ用パヴィリオン
Angelo Mangiarotti, Sacie demonstration pavilion built with the Briona 72 system. (AAM, Milano).

スマンは木の柱の外からは見えない内部にのこぎり状の再生鋼製コネクタを挿入した。そして1944年から1945年の合衆国空軍の鋼管構造の格納庫[22]にて、幾何学を極めた「ばね風の締め付け装置」を研究した。また、ジャン・プルーヴェは金属曲げ機の可能性を研究し、折曲げ薄鋼板とアルミニウム板を使用して建設した。プルーヴェは柔軟性と変形性の論理からオープンジョイント工法や鋼板側面の塗装、インフィルの部材を実験したが、[23]形態は開発しなかった。[24] バックミンスター・フラーはステンレス鋼ケーブルでダイマキシオンハウスの張力構造を作り、二重に湾曲したアルミニウム製のシートメタルで覆った。モントリオール万国博覧会（1967年）のジオデシック・ドームの三次元鋼管構造ではアクリルを用いた。どちらの場合も細部まで科学技術でアプローチした。[25] 対照的にマックス・ビルはこの方法を拒否した。1964年にローザンヌで開催したスイス国立展覧

pillar with a trapezoidal profile supports an inverted U-beam on which rest the roofing segments of larger dimensions. In the Feg entrance pavilion in Giussano (1976-1979) he investigated the potential for a two-way extension: in the Briona 72 system, the beams connect the columns in two perpendicular directions and in the same thickness is fused the head of the vertical load-bearing element, the beam and the roofing segment.

Like other eminent architects Mangiarotti worked with the construction industry on the basis of patents that attest to a high level of technique and innovation. Before exploiting the patent he required the manufacturers to build full-scale prototypes.[21] The phase in which the design of Mangiarotti expressed all his originality was the assembly of the components. In the General Panel House (GPH) system, Konrad Wachsmann inserted toothed recycled steel connectors inside the wooden posts, where they remained invisible, or in 1944-1945, for the tubular steel structures of the hangars of the USAF,[22] he studied the "spring-like clamp-

– 23. F. Graf, *Jean Prouvé par le détail*, in id., *Histoire matérielle et projet de sauvegarde,* Presses polytechniques et universitaires romandes, Lausanne 2014, pp. 115-136.
– 24. Jean Prouvé stated: «I will be categorical. It is not the form that makes something beautiful. It is the way it is built», excerpted from the film *Jean Prouvé, constructeur* by Guy Olivier and Nadine Descendre, 1982.
– 25. E.R. Ford, *The Details of Modern Architecture*, vol. 2 , *1928 to 1988*, The MIT Press, Cambridge, Mass. 1996.
– 26. F. Graf, *Le pavillon "Eduquer et créer" de Max Bill à l'Expo 64 Lausanne: construction et survie d'une structure éphémère*, in *op. cit.* at note 23, pp. 273-290.
– 27. «In my work as a designer, where architectural design and the design of the industrial product have always been present in a symbiotic relationship, the research carried out into the design of a building component has played a leading role. The design of the component makes it possible to work on the language of architecture from its primary elements: the constructive details. It is only through careful control of the details that you can control the architecture as a whole», in F. Cocucci, *Angelo Mangiarotti. Tecnologia e cultura del progetto*, in "Proporzione A", no. 4, June 1994, p. 6.

会のパヴィリオン「教育と創造」において、ビルは印象の薄い装置に普通の素材を使用した。垂直の柱とガルバリウム鋼管をボルトで固定した構造で中立的な美学の姿勢と極端な客観性を示した。[26] もし、工業化の過程でこのような優れた建築家たちが生まれたのだとしたら、マンジャロッティの作品との類似点を見つけるのは簡単だ。しかしマンジャロッティには独自の特徴がある。まず、原寸大での設計を通し形態を完全に管理している。[27] 機能、静応力、生産性、輸送性、そして組み立てと構造の敷設までを総合的に手掛け、これらを再定義して丸みを帯びた形状で張力の境界を表現し、ニーズを概念の手段に読み替えた。プルーヴェは家具の構造と家の構造を区別しなかった。マンジャロッティもテーブルや照明を設計するのと同じ感覚で、プレキャスト鉄筋コンクリートの組み立て部材を設計し、材料が内包する論理の表現と理解に励んだ。ジュッサーノフェグ社エントランス棟では四角い柱頭に丸い柱を合わせた。

これには多くの理由がある。型枠から簡単に取り外し、運搬中に端部が破損する可能性と、施工に携わった人が怪我をする可能性を減らすためである。また、梁と屋根材の組み立てを改良し、経年のずれを吸収し、水分を排水し、最終的には建設の初期段階からわかりやすいように、そして柱にかかるプレートの重量を表現し、まるで柱が柔らかい材料にわずかにのめりこんだように見せた。

マンジャロッティの建物の二つ目の特徴は、重力を考

ing device" with an obsessive geometry. Jean Prouvé built using folded sheet steel and aluminium, starting from the potential offered by the metal-bending machine. He experimented with open joints, the coatings of the steel profiles or the infill elements in a logic of flexibility and deformability,[23] distancing himself from any formal purpose.[24] Buckminster Fuller used double-curved aluminium sheet metal to cover the tensile structure made of stainless steel cables in the Dymaxion House, and an acrylic material for the three-dimensional tubular structure of the geodesic dome in Montreal (1967), in both cases with a scientific-technical approach to detail.[25] By contrast, Max Bill rejected this approach: in the pavilion "Educate and Create" at the 1964 Swiss National Exhibition in Lausanne he instead used natural materials through an inexpressive installation that reflected a neutral aesthetic attitude and extreme objectivity, as evidenced by the structure of galvanized steel tubes bolted to the vertical columns.[26]

If the industrial process strongly conditioned the designs by these outstanding builders, it is easy to find similarities with Mangiarotti's work, which yet has some distinctive features of its own. The first was his absolute formal control through design[27] up to a scale of 1:1, in which he not only integrated the functions, static stresses, production, transportation and laying, including assembly and the systems networks, but redefined them within a perimeter in tension that was expressed in rounded forms, turning needs into instruments of conception. Prouvé did not differentiate the construction of a piece of furniture from that of a house and Mangiarotti designed the assembly of elements in precast rein-

マックス・ビル、スイス国立展覧会のパヴィリオン
「教育と創造」の金属製構造、ローザンヌ1964年
Max Bill, metallic structure of the
"Educate and Create" Pavilion
at the Swiss National Exhibition in Lausanne, 1964.

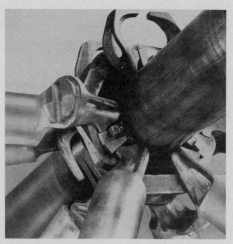

コンラッド・ワックスマン、ジオデシック・ドームの
3次元鋼管構造の継ぎ手、モントリオール万国博覧会1951
Konrad Wachsmann, joint of
the three-dimensional tubular structure
of the geodesic dome in Montreal, 1951.

ジャン・プルーヴェ、クリシー人民の家の
ファサードのパネル1938
Jean Prouvé, façade panels of
the Maison du Peuple in Clichy, 1938.

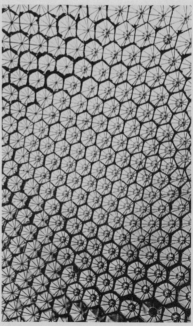

バックミンスター・フラー、
ジオデシック・ドームのアクリル製の外皮、
モントリオール万国博覧会1967
Richard Buckminster Fuller,
acrylic envelope of the geodesic dome
in Montreal, 1967.

アンジェロ・マンジャロッティ、モンツァの集合住宅の
プレキャスト鉄筋コンクリートのパネル 1968-1975
Angelo Mangiarotti, precast reinforced concrete panels.
on the residential building in Monza, 1968-1975. (AAM, Milano).

– 28. Heavy prefabrication will never produce architecture known for its quality with the exception of a few buildings, for example, some Gordon Bunshaft's structures or façades by Marcel Breuer. We must emphasize that the «confusion between production technique and assembly technique has led to the reasons of production to predominate over the reasons of design», in A. Mangiarotti, *op. cit.* at note 17, p. 114.

慮し鉄筋コンクリートの部材の重さに取り組んだことだ。彼はこの一般的で古風かつ普遍的な素材を経済的に実り多い原材料として受け入れた。プレストレスによってコンクリートを鋼よりも有利な材料に変え、静電性と形態の両方においてコンクリートの実力を大いに引き出した。これまでに述べたプレハブ工法では、木、鋼、アルミニウムという軽量の材料が20世紀の建築の基礎を成した。[28] この場合、部材の接合点を減らして機械的に組み立てて固定した。対照的に、マンジャロッティは鉄筋コンクリートの性質に合わせて組み立て方を開発した。人工的な石材の部材を交互に重ねると圧縮と摩擦が生じ重力で組み立てられる。マンジャロッティは支持体の基部を広げ、荷重を軽減し、分割し、端部を隠す代わりにむき出しにした。彼の作品には端を覆う材料、リベット、ボルト、接着剤、金具は一切使われていないが、接合点で互いに摩擦が働く。つまり、組み立てる材料に空気を使ったのだ。この観点はマンジャロッティの研究が導いた逆説の一部で、むしろ矛盾語法と言おうか。そこに真空があれば、そこには見えずともガラスの材料がある。二つのV字型フックから成る照明用のモジュール（ジョーガリ）を次々にぶらさげて組み立てれば、意外にも静止摩擦が働き、ガラス製の小さな滝ができ上がる。ガラス

forced concrete with the same care as he took in designing his tables or lamps, in which he sought to express and understand the inner logic of materials. Even the square capital of the building in Giussano had a rounded form with bevelled corners.

There were many reasons for this, starting from greater ease in removal of the formwork and passing through the reduction of the possibility of breakage of the edges during transport or possible injury for anyone involved in the laying, for better assembly between the beam and the roofing segment, greater capability of absorbing movements over time, the arrangement of the guttering for the disposal of water and ultimately the greater legibility of the elementary assembly of the construction and the expression of the weight of the plate on the column, seeming to sink slightly as if into a still soft material.

The second feature of his buildings was the way he worked with gravity, with the weight of the elements in reinforced concrete. Angelo Mangiarotti embraced this common material, archaic and universal at the same time, as an imposition of the economic-productive system, as a raw material: pre-compression made it a more advantageous material than steel but also offered the possibility of its substantial redefinition in both static and formal terms. All the cornerstones of prefabrication in 20th-century architecture that we have mentioned above involved lightweight materials: wood, steel and aluminium.[28] They were assembled

アンジェロ・マンジャロッティ、アロジオの集合住宅の
ファサードの不透明と透明なモジュール1974-1978
Angelo Mangiarotti, opaque and transparent façade modules
on the residential building in Arosio, 1974-1978.
(Giorgio Casali, AAM, Milano).

– 29. *Orientamenti moderni nell'edilizia*, Over, Milano n.d.

加工ではすべて手作業で一対のトングを用いて同じ形に引き伸ばして成型する。

「ユーザの参加を広義につのり、設置場所の自由度を高めた建築用部材を生産する」²⁹
モンツァとアロジオの住宅建築

マンジャロッティの逆説的なプレハブ工法の建築からもう一つの住宅建築の観点が見えた。木製の窓の金具に不透明または透明なパネルを重ね合わせた構造は、垂直（ファサード面）にも水平（窓側）にも動かすことができる。物体の重力を意に介さず、建物の輪郭や形状を自由に変えてみせた。モンツァの集合住宅は32×32 cm最少限のグリッドに基づき、各操作によってシステムが完成するように意図していた。一方、アロジオの住宅建築ではパネルの種類を減らした。各戸で異なる内装や間取りから、建物の外観にバリエーションが生じた。さまざまな暮らしが「予測不可能」でランダムな設計を可能にする。ニュートラルで組み合わせ自由な部材から、ファサードの連続性や角を凹ませた納まりなど、建物を幾何学的に構成できるようになった。こうして平面的にも空間的にも構成が異なる階層を水平方向に配置した。マン

mechanically by reducing the points of contact and optimizing the material in relation to its static capacities. On the contrary, Mangiarotti developed assemblies that were in accordance with the nature of reinforced concrete, an artificial stone whose elements are superimposed on each other and assembled by gravity, working by compression and friction. He broadened the base of the support, reduced the forces and divided them, and worked with open corners instead of closed elements. His works had no closures, rivets, bolts, glues or metal connecting elements, but only continuity and friction against one another: he used air as his assembly material. This aspect is part of the paradox, or rather oxymoron, that guided Angelo Mangiarotti's research. On the one hand there is a vacuum, on the other only an almost invisible material: glass. As in the modular V+V hooks for luminaires, pure assemblages in which one element is hung from another, turned into a cascade of glass, the material most unexpected to work by traction, made viscous and stretched with the common technique of all: hand-forming with a pair of tongs.

«Continue the search for participation by the users, in the broadest sense, and putting into production the architectural components with a high degree of freedom of positioning».²⁹
Residential buildings at Monza and Arosio

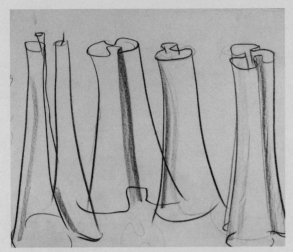

アンジェロ・マンジャロッティ、陶器の花器シリーズ1964
Angelo Mangiarotti, set of ceramic vases, 1964.
(AAM, Milano).

– 30. This theme deals with the first phase of his activity as an architect. See the "infinite construction", a movable wall that becomes "a minimum machine with maximum effects" of Angelo Mangiarotti with paintings by W. Klein, 1952, Milan, published in "Domus", no. 268, March 1952. Fascinated by the variety of what he photographed, from this collaboration Klein gave up painting and took to photography.

Another point of view that was shot through with paradox in the prefabricated architectures of Angelo Mangiarotti's were the residential buildings. In their construction, opaque or transparent panels were superimposed on wooden window fittings, staggered in both the vertical plane (the façade) and the horizontal plane (the plan), and making a mockery of the gravity of the mass, he defined the perimeter/fractal of a volume "stretched" in height. The buildings were based on a rigid modular coordination – the module was 32 x 32 cm – in the name of a minimum composition in which each operation was intended to perfect the system, in particular by reducing the typologies of the panels, fewer in number at Arosio than in Monza. The combinations and variations of the envelopes of the buildings are the consequences of the definition of internal distribution and a different interior design for every apartment. The different ways of living therefore made it possible to produce the "unpredictable", the random. The neutral and configurable components included all possible geometrical combinations – continuity, corner solutions recessed or protruding – and were arranged in horizontal bands with different configurations both in the plane and in space. This was Mangiarotti's way of introducing variation by starting from a rigid grid[30] and of interpreting industrialization and prefabrication as a new principle of figuration that not only did not limit creative activity, but rather enabled architecture to be considered as a liberatory instrument.

Simple comparison between these residential buildings and European prefabricated production provides the opportunity to ob-

ジャロッティは厳密なグリッド[30]から始めてバリエーションを構成し、工業化とプレハブ工法を解釈してみせた。創造的な活動を制限するどころか、むしろ建築を解放する手段として新しい形態の原理を考案した。

このような住宅建築とヨーロッパのプレハブ工法を単純に比較すると、二つの世界の間に横たわる大きな溝が見える。マックス・ビルが最初の学長を務めたウルム造形大学ではマンジャロッティの考えに深い示唆を得て、建築家、芸術家、デザイナーを区別せず、戦後のヨーロッパの人々の創造性を鍛えるための授業を組んだ。彼らに課された仕事は高度に工業化した社会で進化した需要から生じた問題を解決することだった。この目的を達成するための教育方法は科学的な知識や、合理的な方法の実践や、研究テーマに関係する分析に基づいていた。創造性という概念が詳細に吟味され、あらゆる形態の芸術は「世俗化」のプロセスを通過した。「客観性」を通じたプロジェクトの見事なコントロール、マトリックスを用いたアプローチ、ダイアグラムの使用、普遍的な性質を併せ持つサイバネティクスなどの新しい手段、そして特に繰り返しとバリエーションに関することが建築家の活動に影響を与えた。[31]

さらに、プレハブ工法の提唱者が倫理的な観点から夢中になった連続性と繰り返しというテーマは、匿名的、中立的、「古風」かつその土地に根差した建築を見出した。幾つか例を挙げれば、ジャン・プルーヴェが喚起する従

アンジェロ・マンジャロッティ、アルミタリア社の工場
及びオフィスの基本計画と断面図、チニゼッロ・バルサモ
Angelo Mangiarotti, general plan and sections
of the Armitalia industrial complex
in Cinisello Balsamo. (AAM, Milano).

アンジェロ・マンジャロッティ、建設中のアルミタリア社の工場
Angelo Mangiarotti, the Armitalia factory under construction.
(Giorgio Casali, AAM, Milano).

– 31. «What I have wanted to say by introducing a concept of repetition that triggers invention and difference is that the transition to mass production is a continuation of that horizontality of architectural thinking that, opposing the monumentality and verticality of the work, falls into a logic of rejection that, instead of unrealistic subjectivism, has chosen the problematic immanence of meanings in the elementary unity», Angelo Mangiarotti in E.D. Bona, *op. cit.* at note 5, p. 72.
– 32. A. Mangiarotti, *La tradizione quale "lezione di metodo"*, in "Domus", no. 405, 1963, pp. 47-50.

serve the wide gap that existed between these two worlds. Angelo Mangiarotti's thinking was deeply marked by the adventure of the School of Ulm, with Max Bill as its first director and with its programmed objective of training the European creatives after the war, without distinction of category between architects, artists and designers. Their task was to solve the problems created by the evolution in the needs of a highly industrialized society. The teaching methods to achieve this aim were based on scientific knowledge, the application of rational working methods and the analytical relevance of the research themes. The concept of creativity was dissected and art in all its forms was subjected to a process of "secularization". The masterful control of the project through *Sachlichkeit*, the matrix approach and the use of diagrams, together with new instruments such as cybernetics, with its universal nature, inspired the architect's activities, in particular as regards repetition and variations.[31]

Moreover, the theme of series and repetition, which obsessed the protagonists of prefabrication seen in ethical terms, found a privileged place in anonymous, neutral, "archaic", vernacular architecture, some examples of which could be the technical honesty of traditional architecture evoked by Prouvé or the 18th-century houses in the Val Divedro studied by Angelo Mangiarotti;[32] or certain industrial elements such as the bicycle frames and wheels mentioned by Konrad Wachsmann in the introduction to *Wendepunkt im Bauen*; or even ordinary buildings like the various versions of the Durisol system reported in Max Bill's book *Wiederbauen* in 1945.

Even the typology of the farmhouse in the territory of Fer-rara represented common, local, rational, functional architecture, which adapted to changes and was repeated in thousands of ex-

来の建築の技術的な率直さや、マンジャロッティが研究したヴァルディヴェドロにある18世紀の家、[32]『建物の転換点』の序章でコンラッド・ワックスマンが言及した自転車のフレームや車輪など特定の工業用パーツ、あるいは1945年にマックス・ビルが著書『再構築』で報告した多様なバリエーションのドゥリゾルシステムのような平凡な建物が挙げられる。

フェラーラ地方の典型的な農家でさえ、その土地で共通の合理的かつ機能的な建築を表現したもので、変化に合わせて何千回も作り換えた模範であった。マンジャロッティはパッラーディオ設計の邸宅「ラ・ロトンダ」に直面した。記念碑的な建築は複製することができない。彼の目には建築の需要に合わせてつまらない演習は刷新する必要があるように映った。「よみがえった記憶とは感覚のコピーではなく、現在と結びついた感覚だ。プロジェクトとは過去と現在の類似点の再現ではなく隠喩である」[33]

「主題についての知識、すなわちその振る舞い、製造技術、応用の可能性が、客観的に比較し表現する主な言葉となる」[34]

チニゼッロ・バルサモとマイアーノの工業施設

軽さに絶対的な価値があると考えられていた時、例えばバックミンスター・フラーは建物を重さとの関係で判断した。もしマンジャロッティが重力をプラス要因として考えていたら、繊細な感覚で一般的な素材を使っただろう。前述の鉄筋コンクリートに加え、スチールやアルミニウムといった工業用材料、PVCおよびポリスチレ

– 33. Angelo Mangiarotti, in E.D. Bona, *op. cit.* at note 5, p. 71. These words were spoken at a conference held in June 1983. In 1980, with the edition of the Venice Biennale entitled *The Presence of the Past*, academic research retreated to instrumentalised history and speculative interests prevailed over architectural reflection. In this way Angelo Mangiarotti continued his solitary research.
– 34. A. Mangiarotti, *Pratica alla via analitica in architettura*, in A. Dal Lago (ed.), *op. cit.* at note 1 p. 111.
– 35. L. Mies van der Rohe, *op. cit.* at note 8, p. XIV.

ンフォームなど工業的研究から得られた合成材料、石、大理石、テラコッタ、木材のような手で扱える天然材料がある。もしマンジャロッティがマックス・ビルやコンラッド・ワックスマンとどこかで工業化に関して対話していたら、といってもマンジャロッティの材料はほぼイタリア製で、作品は特に北イタリアで建てられたが、耐荷重構造の鉄筋コンクリートにヴィチェンツァの人造大理石を組み合わせ、巧みに空間を構成してムラノのシャンデリアで照らしただろう。「建築とは現実に形を与えることを意味する」³⁵ そして建築家はその多様性、立派な質を備えた伝統的技術、最高の仕様をかなえる先進技術を利用した。時折マンジャロッティはそれらを組み合わせた。チニゼッロ・バルサモにあるアルミタリア社工場では、耐荷重を視覚的に演出するプレハブ工法パネルを用いた。強引に車両のイメージを作りだし、モルタルを混ぜた明るい赤で塗装して、遊び心にわずかな反語をこめて電車の動きを不動の石造建築で表した。

同じ調子で、しかし将来を見越して、マイアーノにあるスナイデロ社工業施設（1971-1978年）ではボリュームのあるオフィスを構成した。ファイバーグラス製の湾曲したパネルで外皮を構成し、楕円形の舷窓を外に向かって並べた。地元の石を乱石積み（オプス・インケルトゥム）にして、壁をつり下げ、水の塊のイメージを表現した。マンジャロッティはこの工業施設でサスペンション構造の鉄筋コンクリートを用いた。4本の大きな柱に屋根を架け、そこに組んだ梁から実際にオフィスの床版を吊り下げた。1976年の地震で耐荷重構造の鉄筋コンクリート建築の建設を中断した後に、マンジャロッティは

emplars. Mangiarotti confronted Palladio's Rotunda, a monumental architecture that could not be duplicated, in his eyes a sterile exercise in relation to the needs of architecture, which has to renew itself: «What memory restores to us is never a copy but the sense of relationship with the present; the project does not restore the analogy between past and present, but its metaphor».[33]

«The knowledge of the subject, ... its behaviour, its production technologies and its potential for application is the main term of confrontation and objective expression».[34]

Industrial complexes in Cinisello Balsamo and Majano

If Mangiarotti considered gravity a positive factor at a time when lightness was considered an absolute value – for example Buckminster Fuller judged a building in relation to its weight – his sensibility to the matter led him to use common materials such as reinforced concrete in the manner described above, industrial materials such as steel profiles or aluminium, synthetic materials derived from industrial research, such as PVC and polystyrene foam, but also natural materials such as stone, marble, terracotta, wood, laid by hand. If his dialogues on industrialization with Max Bill and Konrad Wachsmann occurred elsewhere, in his almost exclusively Italian production – built especially in the northern regions – he combined the load-bearing structures in reinforced concrete with the *terrazzo of* Vicenza and composed spaces skilfully, lit by a Murano chandelier. «Building means giving form to reality»,[35] and the architect exploited its diversity, traditional techniques with their nobler qualities as well as more advanced ones offering the best specifications. Sometimes Angelo Mangiarotti combined them, as in the case of the perimetric load-bearing prefabricated panels in the Armitalia factory in Cinisello Balsamo

アンジェロ・マンジャロッティ、スナイデロ工業施設のオフィスの三角形の支柱
Angelo Mangiarotti, steel portals with triangular section of the services building of the Snaidero industrial complex in Majano. (AAM, Milano).

アンジェロ・マンジャロッティ、スナイデロ工業施設のオフィスの格子の正面図
Angelo Mangiarotti, front view of a bay of the Snaidero services building. (AAM, Milano).

二種類の鉄骨構造を設計し製造した。1つは柱と三角トラスがある食堂用で、もう一つは6つの網状の入り口が約2500平米のオープンスペースを作り出すショールーム用だった。まさにプルーヴェが鋼板、金属チューブ、木材、鉄筋コンクリートでポルチコ構造を造ったように、マンジャロッティは鉄筋コンクリートを組み立てた時と同じ優雅さで、鋼鉄部品の組み立てというテーマを扱った。ほぼパイオニアとして定義される二人の建設家は、自分たちの研究に基づき特定の材料と工法を好んだが、同時に他の実験的な材料や建築方式でも同様に能力を発揮した。

(1968-1971), forcibly modelled to create the image of a passenger carriage and coloured light red with a mixture of aggregates of *cocciopesto*, playing with subtle irony on the movement of the train and the immobility of masonry.

In the same vein of thought, but with a more visionary language, he composed the volume of the office building of the Snaidero industrial complex at Majano (1971-1978). The envelope with its curved panels was made of fiberglass and the oval portholes were extroflected. Suspended over walls of local stone in *opus incertum*, it reflects its hypertechnological image in a body of water. In this industrial complex Mangiarotti used a suspended reinforced concrete structure. The floor slabs of the offices were actually suspended from a network of roof beams resting on four large columns. After the 1976 earthquake, which interrupted construction work on buildings with load-bearing reinforced concrete structures, two steel structures were designed and produced, the first for the works' canteen with pillars and triangular trusses, and the second for the showroom where six reticular portals make it possible to create an open floor space covering some 2500 sqm. Mangiarotti dealt with the theme of the assembly of steel elements with the same elegance as he designed those in reinforced concrete, just as Prouvé built his portico structure out of sheet steel, metal tubing, timber and reinforced concrete. These builders, who could almost be termed pioneers, in their research favoured a specific material and system, but at the same time they also displayed the same skill in their experiments with other materials and construction systems.

アンジェロ・マンジャロッティ、スナイデロ工業施設の眺め
Angelo Mangiarotti, view of the
Snaidero industrial complex. (AAM, Milano).

– 36. A. Mangiarotti, *Sull'oggettività del progetto di architettura*, in G. Nardi, *Aspettando il progetto*, Franco Angeli, Milano 1997, p. 178.

最後に

20世紀の終わりまで、職業上の倫理から実践したプレハブ工法や、建物本体の製造工程を工業化するユートピアは関心を集めなかった。「情報」の概念が「構造」の概念に取って代わり、ソフトウェアから地盤のネットワークまであらゆるスケールがかけ合わさり、構造と使用する材料との間に混乱が生じ、20世紀の分析機器で判読することは不可能だった。ごく最近のデジタル技術の普及とともに、プレハブ工法という課題が前線に返り咲いた。マンジャロッティはこのことを明らかに理解し、90年代にはCNC加工装置を用いてカラーラの大理石の塊に取り組んでいた。

マックス・ビル、コンラッド・ワックスマン、バックミンスター・フラー、ジャン・プルーヴェが先見性から自分たちを認めていたように、建築家の仕事を明確に定義すると、材料と環境の通訳者[36]となる。現代の製造事例を古風な母数の概念に基づいて理解するには、20世紀のプレハブ工法の歴史を新たな視点から分析することが肝要だ。アンジェロ・マンジャロッティは懸命なまでの厳密さと、限りない反語法と自由によって最大の貢献を成し遂げた。

To conclude

By the end of the 20th century, the practice of using prefabrication as professional ethic and the utopia of the industrialization of the production process of the architectural organism were emptied of interest. The concept of "information" replaced that of "structure" and, by multiplying on all scales, from software to territorial networks, it created confusion between the structure and the materials used, rendering it illegible with the 20th-century's instruments of analysis. Only recently, with the spread of digital technology, has the subject of prefabrication returned to the fore: this was something that Mangiarotti had clearly understood, working in the nineties with blocks of Carrara marble and CNC machines.

The architect as an interpreter of materials and the environment[36] is a fine definition of a profession in which figures such as Max Bill, Konrad Wachsmann, Buckminster Fuller and Jean Prouvé could recognise themselves, with their advanced vision.

To understand the contemporary instances of a production that was based on archaic and parametric concepts, it is essential to analyse with new eyes the history of prefabrication in the 20th century, to which Angelo Mangiarotti, with his great rigour – even his hardness, but also with a limitless irony and freedom – made a fundamental contribution.

海の見本市展示館、ジェノヴァ1962-1963、解体
The Exhibition pavilion at the Fiera del Mare in Genoa, 1962-1963, demolished. (AAM, Milano).

フランチェスカ・アルバーニ

Francesca Albani

忘れられたアイコン
工業建築の緑青

Forgotten Icons.
The Patina of
Industrialized Architecture

今日まで多くの学者がアンジェロ・マンジャロッティの建築と工業製品と彫刻を研究、分析して、その作品の特徴と特質と意味を弱点も含めて述べようとしてきた。しかし、彼が設計し、建設した住宅建築、工場、オフィスや倉庫が、時の試練にどのように耐えてきたかを探求しようとする人はいなかった。建物が存在するのか、またどのような状態にあるかを調べた人はおそらく皆無である。本稿の目的はこの溝を埋め、あるいは少なくとも答えの概要を示し、異なる未来に至った理由を観察し順序だてることである。ミラノのアンジェロ・マンジャロッティ・アーカイブ[1]に保管されたアーカイブ資料に基づき、マンジャロッティがブルーノ・モラスッティとの事務所から独立してから手掛けた最も興味深い10軒の建物の現状を調査し比較した研究を以下に示す。これらの建物は数十年にわたり不具合が生じ劣化して無秩序な状態にある。[2] 21世紀の建築の経年劣化は細部まで非常に複雑だ。物理的な観点から見ると、現在の材料で劣化が進行するのは伝統的な材料に備わっていた耐久性を欠いていることに思い当たる。上手に作られた鉄筋コンクリートが良い状態を保てるのは50年、長くとも70年だ。エジプトのピラミッドの花崗岩や初期のキリスト教聖堂のレンガ積みの耐久性とはとても比較にならない。鋼鉄は特に海辺にある場合定期的なメンテナンスが必要だ。プラスチック建材の外皮はファサード南面で不可避の熱影響に耐えることができないし、ゴム製ジョイントは弾性が劣化するため定期的に交換する必要がある。

しかし材料の退化だけが問題ではない。経年によって建築が獲得する（失う）重要性と価値もまた問題なのだ。

To date many scholars have sought to describe the characteristics, qualities and meanings, but also the frailty of Angelo Mangiarotti's work, studying and analysing his architecture, industrially produced objects and sculptures. No one, however, has so sought to explore how the residential buildings, factories, offices and warehouses which he designed and built have stood the test of time. Perhaps, even more simply, no one, or hardly anyone, has asked whether they still exist and what state they are now in. The object of this essay is to bridge the gap, or at least to present the outlines of an answer and give order to a number of observations on the reasons for such different futures. The research presented below is based on a comparison of the information obtained from archival sources kept in the Angelo Mangiarotti Archive in Milan[1] and the existing state of ten of the most interesting buildings that he built after splitting from Bruno Morassutti, with a survey of the alterations and conversions they have been subjected to over the years as well as the pathologies and disorders of deterioration.[2] The subject of how twentieth-century architecture ages is highly complex and detailed. This is the case from the physical point of view, if one thinks of the progressive deterioration of materials that lack the durability of traditional ones. Reinforced concrete, even when well made, will remain in good health for fifty, or at most seventy, years. It is in no way comparable with the

---

– 1. See the essay *Assembling to build: ten variations on a theme* by Franz Graf and Francesca Albani in the present volume.

– 2. In surveying pathologies of deterioration reference has been made to standard UNI Normal 11182:2006 "Materiali lapidei naturali ed artificiali. Descrizione della forma di alterazione – Termini e definizioni". This standard was developed after the work of the Normal (Normativa Manufatti Lapidei) committee, which in 1988 proposed standard methods for the definition of pathologies of stone materials. A large number of these recommendations have been adopted in UNI document, so rendering their use obligatory.

海の見本市展示館。曲線を描く屋根の下に設置された基壇と展示台
Detail of the pavilion with display cases set on a "podium" protected by the curvilinear roofing. (AAM, Milano).

– 3. A. Mangiarotti, M. Luchi, L. Bonesio, L. Magnani, *In nome dell'architettura*, Jaca Book, Milano 1987, p. 16.

durability of the granite of the Egyptian pyramids or the brick masonry of the early Christian basilicas. Steel, especially in maritime areas, requires regular maintenance, while the plastic envelopes of buildings cannot withstand the inevitable thermal excursions on a south-facing façade, and neoprene joints have to be replaced periodically because they lose elasticity.

But the problem is not only decay: it is also a question of the significance and values that the architectural work acquires (or loses) over time. It is evident, for example, that in the collective imagination there is nothing that so much suggests featureless and blighted suburbs as the concept of "prefabricated architecture". Drabness, seriality, reinforced concrete produced cheaply, architectural structures that are the fruit of chance or speculation create a series of preconceptions which disturb, and sometimes distort, our reading and understanding of works that draw their strength from experimentation, variation in repetition, construction techniques and modular coordination. An essential operation to decode much of Mangiarotti's architecture is to reconstruct «its ties with the technical and building culture that produced it. Only then do we realize the value of what we may have considered of secondary importance»,[3] as he himself observed in 1987 in a little book by various authors titled *In nome dell'architettura*.

Another key point that often determines the fate of buildings is their intended uses and the way they change over time. Mangiarotti built primarily for private clients, in genres such as workplaces and dwellings, whose dynamics are obviously dated, being related to the time when they were built. But ways of working and living are constantly changing. The complex dynamics established in this respect necessarily lead to alterations, which, if not controlled, entail choices that in the light of more careful consideration may appear at best inappropriate, if not frequently mistaken.

その証拠に例えば「プレハブ建築」という概念は何の特徴もない廃れた郊外の集合住宅を連想させる。くすんだ連続的な鉄筋コンクリートは安っぽい建築構造を生み出した。偶然または推測から生じた一連の先入観が、実験や繰り返しによるバリエーションや、構造技術とモジュラー構成から強さを獲得したコンクリート作品についての理解を妨げ、時には歪んだ理解をもたらす。マンジャロッティの建築の大半を解読するためには「建築を生む建築技術と建築文化の結びつき」を再構築する作業が不可欠だ。「私たちが熟考してきた重要な二次的な価値をそこから初めて実現する」[3]と、様々な著者による『建築の名において』と題した1987年の本の中でマンジャロッティは自身を観察した。

建築の運命を握るもう一つのカギは、当初の用途とは常に変わる使用方法だ。マンジャロッティの建物の依頼主の大半は個人だった。竣工した時期に比べて仕事場や住居の使い勝手は明らかに時代遅れとなった。働き方や生き方は絶えず変化する。複雑なダイナミクスには必ず変化が生じるので、もし管理が無ければ、慎重に熟考した挙句に良くて不適切な、悪くて頻繁に間違った選択をするだろう。

— 4. www.mentelocale.it/2465.
— 5. The Trust Fondazione Angelo Mangiarotti in Milan preserves graphic and photographic materials, prototypes and sketches of almost all Angelo Mangiarotti's works. In particular, reference is made to the photographic collection of the Pavilion for exhibitions at the Fiera del Mare.

海の見本市展示館の夜景
Night view of the pavilion. (Giorgio Casali, AAM, Milano).

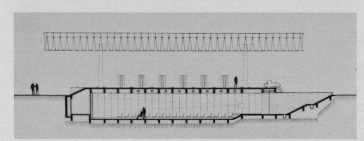

海の見本市展示館の縦断面図、トレーシングペーパーの写し。
ミュンヘン工科大学建築博物館が原本を所蔵
Longitudinal section of the pavilion,
copy on tracing paper of the original in
the Architecture Museum at the
Technische Universität in Munich. (AAM, Milano).

真夏の犯罪

「ジェノヴァ港でマンジャロッティがIRIの展示場として建てた『海の見本市展示館』(1963年)は沈黙のうちに破壊されて消え去った。忘れてはなるまい」[4] オンライン新聞はマンジャロッティの優れた作品の一つが解体されたことをこのように非難した。決定と解体は完全に水面下で進行した。海の見本市展示館のように類まれなる美しい建築の解体に、一体誰が駆けつけられるだろうか？ひどい建物の状況や展示場拡張のニーズを理由にして破壊を正当化する軽率な対応は鵜呑みにできない。まず始めに指摘したい。所有者は確信に足る理由もなく経済的価値のある貴重な建築をあきらめるべきではなかった。また、見本市の活動からたまたま生じたニーズで、こんな重大な行動を始めるべきではかった。

考慮すべき点ははるかに複雑だ。私たちがここで扱っているのは、建築作品が次第に変化し重要性を失う経緯である。ミラノのアンジェロ・マンジャロッティ・アーカイブ[5]のアーカイブに保管された写真がはっきりとこの経緯を示している。絵的かつ詩的な展示館の形状は、多くの人の手による建築的成果であり、様々な目的を果たし、非常に象徴的な価値を統合した建築作品として認

A midsummer crime

«Demolished in silence, Mangiarotti's IRI Pavilion for the Fiera del Mare in Genoa (1963) is gone. Lest we forget».[4] With these words an online newspaper denounced the dismantling of one of Angelo Mangiarotti's finest works, a decision taken and carried out in complete silence. How can one go so far as to demolish an object of rare beauty like the Exhibition Pavilion for the Fiera del Mare? The instinctive response, justifying demolition by the building's poor condition and the need to expand the exhibition space, is only partially credible. First we should consider that no owner would give up a prized object with an economic value without a convincing reason. Hence an act of this magnitude cannot stem solely from the contingent needs bound up with the activity of the trade fair.

A considered response is much more complex. Here we are dealing with a process in which the architectural product progressively undergoes changes and loses its significance. A series of photographs preserved in the archives of the AAM[5] clearly reflects this process. The pavilion, with its graphic and poetic forms, was the result of architectural research conducted by many hands, working with different objectives, and which received their synthesis in an architectural work with a highly symbolic value. The interests

– 6. *Storia dell'IRI*, in particular volume 2, F. Amatori (ed.), *Il miracolo economico e il ruolo dell'IRI, 1949-1972*, Laterza, Roma-Bari 2013, and volume 6, P. Ciocca, *L'IRI nella economia italiana*, Laterza, Roma-Bari 2014.
– 7. G. Veronesi, B. Alfieri, *Padiglione IRI alla Fiera del Mare, Genova, Angelo Mangiarotti*, in "Lotus Architectural annual 1964-1965", Bruno Alfieri, Milano 1964, pp. 124-129.
– 8. A study of the relation between architecture and the land is contained in E.D. Bona, *Angelo Mangiarotti, il processo del costruire*, Electa, Milano 1980, pp. 80-81.

運河に映るスプリューゲン・ブロイ社倉庫とオフィスビル、メストレ1963
View from the canal of the Splügen Bräu warehouse and office building in Mestre, 1963. (Giorgio Casali, AAM, Milano).

められた。その興味と用途は多岐にわたった。まず、施主の目的である。IRI（産業復興協会）は1930年代に設立されたイタリアの国有持株会社で、1990年代に民営化され2002年に解散した。[6] 並外れて経済が上り調子の時期には、協会は自社が管理した活動や、国内経済で果たそうとした役割を世間に開示したかった。次に、マンジャロッティの目的は、構造的、造形的、構築的、理論的な研究を指揮し、構造計算を担当したフィンサイダー社のエンジニアと共に、協会が主導的な役割を果たしていた鉄鋼部門を象徴する、洗練されたミニマルな構造の姿を探求することだった。最後に、ジェノヴァの「見本市展示館」の役割がある。見本市会場を魅力的に魅せる何らかの重要な建築で、その存在を区域から広げたかった。よって、これらをすべてつなぐゴールは「演出」であった。

「港の入り口からの眺めは日夜壮観である」[7] この展示館の建物で、マンジャロッティは自身を含め全員の望みに応えることに成功した。来場者は眼下から水平線まで延びる風光明媚な景色を眺め、海上に繰り広げられたIRIの活動から、より良い未来の希望の象徴や、戦後の第一歩を実感した。アーチ推力を必要としない、素晴らしい曲線を描く屋根と、形態と素材の限界に関する研究が、「基壇」[8] の上に実現した。このような床面はマンジャロッティの作品で初めてではない。バランザーテの教会や、メストレにあるスプリューゲン・ブロイ社倉庫で用

and objectives were manifold. Firstly, in the role of the client, there was the IRI (Institute for Industrial Reconstruction), an Italian public holding company set up in the thirties, privatized in the nineties and wound up in 2002,[6] which at a time of extraordinary economic development wished to present to the public the activities of the companies it controlled and the key role it intended to play in the national economy. Then there was Angelo Mangiarotti, whose purpose was to conduct his compositional, formal, constructive and theoretical research, and the engineer at Finsider, who with his calculations sought to define a refined and minimalist structure, emblematic of the steel sector in which the company was a leading player. Finally there was the Fiera del Mare in Genoa, which with this artefact enhanced its precinct with another significant object, making it even more attractive as a trade fair venue. What united all these goals was therefore the "mise en scène".

In building this pavilion «at the entrance to a port, hence having a grand, continuous spectacle by day and night»,[7] Mangiarotti succeeded in giving an answer to everyone, including himself. The scenic route presented to visitors embraced the activities of IRI from below ground up to the horizon of the sea, a symbol of hope in a better future, a fundamental feeling in the postwar period. The great curvilinear roof in the form of a non-thrusting arch and the research into the relations between the form and the limits of the material were staged with determination by means of a "podium".[8] This element was not new in Mangiarotti's work: he had used it at Baranzate for the Church of Mater Misericordi-

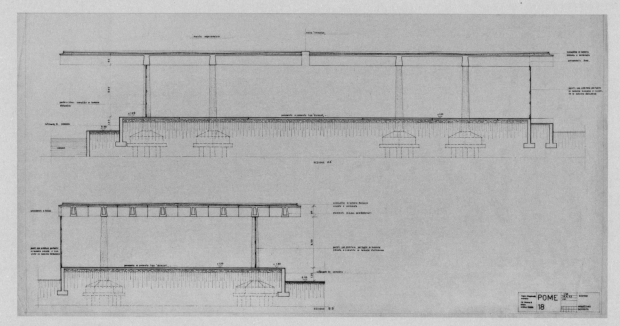

基壇の上に設置したスプリューゲン・ブロイ社倉庫の断面図
マンジャロッティ事務所のエンリコ・マッリによる設計図1962年4月14日
Sections of the Splügen Bräu warehouse
set on a sort of stylobate, scale 1:50,
drawing by Enrico Malli, Studio Mangiarotti,
14 April 1962. (AAM, Milano).

– 9. R. Grassi, *Gli edifici liguri del '900 andati perduti*, in "Il Secolo XIX", 26 April 2001. The article recounts a project for archiving and reconstructing twentieth-century buildings that have been lost, which took the form of the Virtual Museum of Twentieth-Century Architecture in Liguria promoted by the School of Architecture of the University of Genoa within the scope of the course on Exhibit Design and Museology held by Professor Enrico Pinna.

いられて来た。これはギリシャ神殿で一種の基壇の上に建物を配置する祝祭的な方法だ。しかしジェノヴァで来場者は基壇に立ち、信じがたいほど詩的な屋根の下で海の水平線を眺める。

　すべてかみ合っていた要素がもはや見えなくなると、目まぐるしい下降が始まり資産の損失につながった。[9] パヴィリオンに展示場としての機能が無くなると、凹面状の展示台も解体されて、象徴的な意味が失われた、単なる「片流れの屋根の小屋」と化した。物体を保護する機能があっても、簡単に交換できる物であればさして注意は払われない。基壇を展示物の「ステージ」として使う重要性が失われて、建物は囲われた。結局そこでメンテナンスは止まったのだ。海辺にそびえ立つスチール屋根に、この決断は素材面や視覚面で重大な結果をもたらした。それゆえ解体の段階に進むのは早かった。風化しさびついた金属製の小さな小屋を壊したところで、特に深刻には見えなかった。

　メストレでも同じような経緯が異なる方法で既に始まっていた。試験的な管理という名目で、運河を行く船

ae and at Mestre in the Splügen Bräu warehouse. But while in these cases the gesture of placing the architecture on a sort of stylobate, like a Greek temple, is a way of celebrating it, in Genoa the podium from which the visitor looks at the horizon of the sea is protected by an incredible, poetic roof.

When all these contributory factors were no longer present, then began the vertiginous descent leading to the loss of the asset.[9] When the Pavilion no longer had a function as an exhibition venue, following the dismantling of the concave display cases, it lost its symbolic value, becoming simply a "shed roof". An element that affords protection against the elements is only a functional object, which can be easily replaced and which does not receive special care or attention. The possibility of "staging" something on a podium is no longer important and so it is enclosed, but above all maintenance is no longer kept up. In the case of a steel roof on the seafront this decision leads to serious consequences in terms of materials and visual perception. The step leading to demolition is therefore short, since it does not appear particularly serious to knock down a small metal shed, weathered and rust-stained.

– 10. I wish to thank Enrico Venuda for showing me the location of the warehouse and enabling me to contact its present owner.
– 11. *Struttura per un capannone*, in "Domus", no. 392, 1962, pp. 5-6, where the project was published, while the articles *La nuova copertura del deposito della società Poretti a Mestre*, in "L'industria italiana del cemento", January 1966, pp. 25-34, and *Deposito a Mestre*, in "Domus", no. 451, June 1967, pp. 2-5, deal with construction of the complex.

スプリューゲン・ブロイ社倉庫、メストレ1964
View of the Splügen Bräu office building in Mestre, 1964.
(AAM, Milano).

からより効率的に積み込みや荷卸しを行うため、マンジャロッティの建物に屋根と板金など増築が加えられた。これで事実上マンジャロッティの建築を認識することが出来なくなった。メストレの産業地帯に隠れた、あるいはほぼ埋もれたスプリューゲン・ブロイ社倉庫は、現在、他の会社が所有している。その痕跡は失われてしまった。建築作品の所有者と連絡を取り様々な状況を監視するマンジャロッティ事務所ですら、もはや何のニュースも得られなかった。メストレの若い建築家の[10] 忍耐強い研究によって調査が可能となった。いろいろな試みの後に、ぶざまに建てられた小さなオフィスビルと、波状の鉄と木で出来た建物の間に一辺22mの正方形のモジュールから成る2つの倉庫が見つかった。[11] この倉庫の最も重要な側面は、形態と新技術の関係を研究して生まれた。ポストテンション方式で運河に8メートル張り出した、プレキャストコンクリートの洗練されたデザインは驚くべき結果を生み出した。倉庫の床面積を増やすため張りだした屋根の周りが囲われると、建物は並外れた実験作品から、コンクリートの炭酸化と鉄筋の腐食がなすがままに単なる倉庫に変わった。建物はまだ使えるので存在しているが、すぐに機能を失って海の見本市展示館と変わらない運命をたどるだろう。

The same process, though in a different way, has already started in Mestre. Roofing, sheet metal, equipment added in the years to enable materials to be loaded and unloaded more efficiently from boats passing through the canal, are making one of the most significant objects, in terms of its experimental charge, of Mangiarotti's whole oeuvre virtually unrecognizable. The Splügen Bräu warehouse, now owned by another company, appears hidden, almost buried, in the industrial area of Mestre. Its traces had been lost, so that even the Studio Mangiarotti, which keeps up contact with the owners of works and monitors their various situations, no longer had any news of it. It was possible to inspect it only through the patient research of a young architect in Mestre[10] who, after various attempts, recognized the small office building, clumsily elevated, and the warehouse consisting of two square modules measuring 22 m per side[11] submerged in corrugated iron and wooden structures. The most significant aspect of this complex is the warehouse, where research into the relationship between the form and use of new techniques, in this case post-tensioning, produced stunning results, such as the 8-m overhang towards the canal or the refined design of the precast concrete element. Once this overhang had been enclosed, so as to increase the floor space for storage, the building was transformed from an extraordinary experimental prototype into a simple storehouse, at the mercy of carbonatation of the concrete and corrosion of the reinforcing

拡張、変更、増築されたスプリューゲン・ブロイ社倉庫
Extensions, alterations and elevation of
the Splügen Bräu office building. (Francesca Albani, 2014).

– 12. D. Duva, M. Invitti, E. Miliam, M. Pirola (ed.), *Maestri del design: Castiglioni, Magistretti, Mangiarotti, Mendini, Sottsass*, Bruno Mondadori, Milano 2005, pp. 91-92.
– 13. Article 9 of the Italian Constitution of 1948 states: «The Republic fosters the development of culture and scientific and technical research. It protects the landscape and the nation's historical and artistic heritage».
– 14. A. Mangiarotti, B. Morassutti, G. Morassutti, *Un capannone industriale prefabbricato*, in "Casabella continuità", no. 218, 1958, pp. 84-89.
– 15. D. Duva, M. Invitti, E. Miliam, M. Pirola, *op. cit.* at note 12, p. 91.

4人の若手建築家の2001年のインタビューが2005年に出版された。自分の建築が解体される知らせについての対応を尋ねられたマンジャロッティはこう答えた。「ジェノヴァの海の見本市展示館が取り壊された時、理由は忘れたが私はそこに居合わせた。解体というよりペンキを塗っているように見えた。彼らは展示場にはもっと場所が必要だから、こうすれば展示館を再利用できると言った……。もし予め教えてくれていたら、私は写真を撮りに行っただろう」[12]

制度による保護と著作権

イタリア憲法第9条13項が定める文化の促進、歴史的、芸術的、環境的遺産の保護と保存の基本原則を信じる人々は制度による保護に信頼を寄せる傾向にある。[13] マンジャロッティ自身がこの原則を信じていた。彼はモラスッティ家の会社が所有する1958年竣工のパドヴァの鉄鋼倉庫[14]について2001年のインタビューでこう話した。「リストの掲載に必要な50年が経過していなかったので、彼らはショッピングセンターを建てられるという理由から倉庫を取り壊した。解体工事が始まり、夜になって権限を持つ判事が止めたが、時既に遅く湾は破壊されていた」[15] 判事による効果的かつ決定的な介入は難しいように思えるが、マンジャロッティが遺憾に思う言葉の背景には、リストに載れば本当に解体を防げたのかという問題がある。リストに掲載された建物は解体できないのは明らかだが、掲載の事実が保存やメンテナンスを保証するものではない。これについては沢山の事例がある。ミラノで最も重要な例は、国際的に重要な作品でもある

bars. It is still useful and so it still exists, but as soon as it loses its function its fate will be no different from that of the exhibition pavilion in Genoa.

In an interview he gave in 2001 to four young architects, published in 2005, when asked how he reacted to the news of the destruction of some of its buildings, Mangiarotti replied: «When the pavilion in Genoa was demolished, I happened to be there, I forget for what reason, and it seemed that they were painting it. Instead they knocked it down. They said the trade fair needed more space, and on the whole they could reuse that pavilion... If they had warned me, I would have gone there and taken some photographs».[12]

Institutional protection and authorship of the work

There is a tendency repose great confidence in institutional protection, seen through the eyes of those who believe in the fundamental principles set out in Article 9 of the Italian Constitution,[13] which speaks of fostering culture and protecting and preserving the historical, artistic and environmental heritage. Angelo Mangiarotti himself believed in these principles. In the 2001 interview he talked about the ferrous metals Warehouse in Padua, a building owned by the company of the Morassutti family[14] completed in 1958. He commented: «They demolished it because fifty years had not yet gone by to be able to list it, so they were able to build a shopping centre. When they started demolishing it, at night, the magistrate, a person of some ability, halted the work but they had already demolished a bay and it was too late».[15] Although effective and decisive intervention by the magistrate seems difficult, the question that emerges in the background of Mangiarotti's regretful words is real-

レマ社工場の屋上の眺め、アルツァーテ・ブリアンツァ 1969-1979
View of the roofing of the Lema factory in Alzate Brianza, 1969-1979. (AAM, Milano).

– 16. F. Graf, L. Tedeschi (ed.), *L'Istituto Marchiondi Spagliardi*, Mendrisio Academy Press, Mendrisio 2008.
– 17. A. Artioli, G.C. Borellini, *Conservazione del paesaggio architettonico e strumenti di legge: l'Istituto Marchiondi, un caso applicativo*, in A. Piva, E. Cao (ed.), *Vittoriano Viganò. A come asimmetria*, Gangemi, Roma 2008, pp. 115-117.
– 18. Regulation of copyright, Law no. 633 of 1941.

ヴィットリアーノ・ヴィガノ設計のマルキオンディ・スパリアルディ研究所[16] だろう。法的証書[17] がその後の展開を避けるために用いられ、未だ適用され、建物は放棄されている。90年代初めに早すぎる死を迎える直前に、ヴィガノは現代建築の保存にとりわけ積極的だった行政官に連絡した。既に、ジュゼッペ・テラーニ設計のカサ・デル・ファッショとノボコムとカサ・ルスティチ、ジョバンニ・ムツィオ設計のパラッツォ・ダルテ（ミラノ・トリエンナーレ）、ジャーナリストの村にあるルイジ・フィジーニの家、BBPR設計の日光療法施設は、通知により解体が制約されていた。研究所を設計したヴィガノはまだ生きており建物は50年を経過していなかったが、彼の提出に基づき監督官のルチア・グレモは著作権の法的証書[18]によって研究所に制約を適用した。多くの課題をともなう複雑で段階的な文化的プロセスに続き、高度な検査を実施し、50年が経過した2008年4月23日[19] に、遺産文化省と、ジーノ・ファミリエッティが監督するロンバルディア州の文化遺産と景観ランドスケープ局は、この研究所を「記念碑的」作品[20] として解体を制約する建

ly whether listing it could have prevented its demolition. Clearly a listed building cannot be knocked down, but the fact of being listed in itself is no guarantee of its conservation and maintenance.

There are numerous examples of this. Perhaps the most significant in the Milan area is the Instituto Marchiondi Spagliardi, a work of international importance by Vittoriano Viganò.[16] Here all the instruments provided by law[17] were used to try to avoid what happened then and is still in progress: its dereliction. In the early nineties, shortly before his untimely death, Viganò had contacted the Superintendency, which had been particularly active in protecting contemporary architecture. Notification had already been made of the constraints applied to the Casa del Fascio, the Novocomum and the Casa Rustici by Terragni, the Palazzo della Triennale by Muzio, the Villa al Quartiere dei Giornalisti by Figini and the Heliotherapic Facility by BBPR. On the basis of the submission by Viganò the superintendent Lucia Gremmo applied the constraint by invoking the instrument of copyright,[18] since the complex was not yet fifty years old and its author was still alive. Following an involved and highly articulated cultural process, which entailed a number of subjects and ensured the building re-

レマ社工場の北側立面
Detail of the north elevation of the Lema factory.
(Francesca Albani, 2014).

– 19. Between the late nineties and 2010 there were numerous national and international conferences, publications and projects dealing at different levels of complexity with the question of the Istituto Marchiondi Spagliardi. Among the many other initiatives, a widespread appeal was made by Do.co.mo.mo International, *SOS per l'Istituto Marchiondi di Viganò* in "Do.co.mo.mo Italia giornale", no. 22, 2008, p. 12.
– 20. The building was declared of historic and artistic interest in accordance with Article 10, paragraph 1, of Legislative Decree no. 22 January 2004 no. 42, as amended.

物のリストに加えた。その次に何が起こったか。特筆すべきことはない。多くの建物について多くの議論が行われた。その間ずっと放置されていた建物の老朽化が進んだ。事実、過去8年間で指数関数的に物理的、社会的に解体する数が増した。これは建築資産の修復と再利用に至るプロセスがはるかに複雑であることを示している。この場合は少なくとも考慮すべき優先事項が他にあった。特定の教育プログラムに応じて市内の主要周辺部に建てられた、かなり部屋数の多い建物を他の用途に転用するのは難しかった。不動産市場が縮小しており、複雑な構造物を修復する費用を確保する難しさを抜きにしても、偶像的かつ象徴的な建物は公共の利用には向かなかった。

リストに載っても、該当する建築に明るい未来が保証されることもなければ、建築資産の破壊を防ぐ緊急手段として保護制度が頻繁に適用されるわけでもなかった。マリオ・プッチ（1949-1953）[21]が設計したモデナのバス停では2008年8月6日に起こった。この資産を有する[22]モデナ市が受け取った「文化的興味の宣言」は、ミラノの「歴史的芸術的権利」[23]や、コルベッタの過去の地域農業を証明する[24]旧農業共同体に影響した。[25]

それでは、マンジャロッティの作品を未来へ確実に伝えるための最善策とは何か。もちろん、70年未満の建

ceived a high level of scrutiny,[19] on 23 April 2008, fifty years having passed, the Ministry of the Heritage and Culture, in particular the Regional Directorate for the Cultural Heritage and Landscape of Lombardy, directed by Gino Famiglietti, listed the Institute as a "monumental" work[20] in addition to the previous constraint. What happened next? Nothing significant: many projects, much talk, discussions. Meanwhile the building lies in the same state as before, aggravated by the fact that physical and social decay over the last eight years has increased exponentially. This shows that the process leading to the restoration and reuse of an architectural asset is much more complex. Evidently, at least in this case, other factors and considerations prevail. The principal ones are the difficulty of finding an intended use compatible with a building possessing highly articulated spatial qualities, created to respond to a specific educational program and peripheral to the city's main centres. The result is that this iconic and symbolic complex is unattractive for public activities, without considering the difficulty of finding the substantial financial resources to restore such a complex structure when the real-estate market is shrinking.

Clearly listing is no guarantee of a positive future for the architecture in question, nor is the fact that often the processes of institutional protection are interpreted solely as emergency procedures necessary to prevent the demolition of an asset. This is what hap-

エルマグ社工場、定期修理の対象になった部分。リッソーネ 1963-1966
Detail of the Elmag factory in Lissone, 1963-1966,
subject to regular maintenance. (Francesca Albani, 2013).

– 21. I. Bastiglia, C. De Cunto *Conservazione e riuso di un edificio del dopoguerra: la stazione delle autocorriere di Mario Pucci a Modena (1949-1953)*, degree thesis, Politecnico di Milano, Scuola di Architettura e Società, supervisor F. Albani, a.y. 2011-2012.
– 22. The Ministry of the Heritage and Cultural Activities, in particular the Regional Directorate for Cultural the Heritage and Landscape of Emilia-Romagna with its director Carla Di Francesco, by Decree D.R. of 7 July 2008 issued under Articles 10 to 12 of the Decree D. R. 42/2004, made a notification of the «statement of interest» under Article 15, paragraph 1, of Legislative Decree 42/2004, since the bus station is a public asset.
– 23. According to Article 10, paragraph 1 and 12, of the D. Lgs. 42/2004.
– 24. C. Di Francesco, *La tutela del patrimonio architettonico minore del Novecento. Strumenti e casi studio tra Emilia Romagna e Lombardia*, in F. Albani and C. Di Biase (ed.), *Architettura minore del XX secolo: strategie di tutela e intervento*, Maggioli, Santarcangelo di Romagna, 2013, pp. 155-161.
– 25. Protected under Article 10 of Legislative Decree no. 42/2004 (Decree of Constraint-Regional Direction of Cultural Heritage and Landscape of Lombardy, prot. 11429).
– 26. The law for protection of copyright is no. 633 of July 16, 1941, with amendments of the Legislative Decree of 21 February 2014, no. 22, and the Legislative Decree of 10 November 2014, no.163. Among the amendments is the change of the threshold period, increased from fifty to seventy years.
– 27. G. Barazzetta, *Il restauro di un involucro degli anni Cinquanta*, in "Archi", no. 5, 2014, pp. 96-103.

物や生存中の作者に適用する「著作権の制約」過程はもはや適用できない。[26] それは自分の権利を保護したいと望む個人が率先して行うプロセスだ。制約を受けた建物には、あらゆる観点から保護されるのではなく、単に作者が設計を変更する権利が認められる。公的機関は介入できないし、作者以外、相続人でさえ介入を命じることができない。芸術家の創造性と結びついた個人的権利は譲渡不可能だ。こうして作者の死後にすべての作品は自動的に対象外になる。これが2012年に亡くなったマンジャロッティの作品に起った経緯である。制約が唯一適用されたのは、ブルーノ・モラスッティとアルド・ファヴィーニと共に建てたバランザーテの教会で、2003年1月13日改正の法令の対象となった。[27]

マンジャロッティが遺した建築のほとんどは私有財産であったから、2011年に文化的権利の資産を宣言する歴史的判断が50年から70年に引き上げられ、この規則が公的財産、または非営利の私的法人が所有する財産を扱おうとも、適用されない。[28] しかし、彼のすべての作品を「重要な歴史的、芸術的権利」宣言で解決しようという考えは余り意味をなさない。[29] 一方、権利の拡大によってマンジャロッティの建てた建築に加えて戦後の一般の建造物に「歴史的関係の制約」[30] が適用される。建

pened at the Modena bus station by Mario Pucci (1949-1953)[21] on 6 August 2008, after notification of the «declaration of cultural interest» to the City of Modena, the owner of the asset,[22] which is to all effects of "historical-artistic interest",[23] or the former agricultural consortium of Corbetta,[24] in the province of Milan, which bears testimony to the area's agricultural past.[25]

So what would be the best way to ensure the transmission of Angelo Mangiarotti's works to the future? Certainly the process of the «constraint of copyright», which currently applies to buildings less than seventy years old and whose author is still alive, is no longer viable.[26] It is a process based on the initiative of a private individual who wishes to protect his or her own rights. Rather than protecting the work in all its aspects and meanings it simply recognizes the right of the author to design any alterations when the asset is subject to a constraint. The public authority is not able to act intervene officially and it cannot be summoned to act by any other person apart from the author, not even an heir. It is a personal right and is non-transferable, since it is bound up with the artist's creativity. In this way all those works whose author is no longer alive are automatically excluded. This is the case of Mangiarotti, who died in 2012. His only work subject to constraint in this way is the Church of Mater Misericordiae at Baranzate, built with Bruno Morassutti and Aldo Favini and subject to a decree of 13 January 2003, recently renewed.[27]

レマ社工場の塗装室の天井。安全上の理由から近年改修完了
Interior view of the roof of the painting room at the Lema factory, recently replaced for safety reasons. (AAM, Milano).

– 28. D.L. 70, 13 May 2011.
– 29. Article 10 of the D. Lgs. 42/2004
– 30. The "historical relational constraint" was already envisaged under Article 2 of Law 1089 of 1939, then expanded and revised in Article 10, paragraph 3d, of Legislative Decree 42/2004 and Legislative Decree. no. 62 of 2008, and concerns, «All things movable or immovable, belonging to anyone which are of particular importance because of their reference to political, military, literary, artistic, scientific, technological, industrial and cultural history in general, namely as evidence of the identity and history of collective public or religious institutions».
– 31. D. Lgs. 42/2004, art. 2.
– 32. A. Mangiarotti, M. Luchi, L. Bonesio, L. Magnani, *op. cit.* at note 3, p. 17.

物の50年の経過や設計者の死と関係なく、技術、産業、文化全般に関する私有財産も含めた建築に適用できる。この制約はマンジャロッティが設計した工業建築や住居などの建物にふさわしい。複雑な一連の要因から意味と価値が増した建物は文化的資産、つまり「文化的価値を有する歴史的に重要な作品」として定義される。[31]

この建築の制約は次に挙げる直接的な制約と似ている。外部または内部のあらゆる変更について大臣の承認を得る必要性、州または地方自治体の先買権によって売却し管轄外になった建物と税金および寄付金を得る可能性を報告する義務である。マンジャロッティの言葉に応えれば、彼の建築の未来を確保できる法的証書がたくさん存在することに気付く。自他ともに建築の保存で重要なことがある。「私たち全員が目指すべきはその時代の知識や、自身と来たる時代の知識に基づき行動することだ」[32]

In the case of Mangiarotti's legacy, consisting mainly of privately owned assets, the fact that in 2011 the threshold of historicity for declaring an asset of cultural interest was raised from fifty to seventy years is irrelevant,[28] because this rule applies only to property publicly owned or owned by non-profit private legal entities. Still, it does not have much sense to think of solving the problem by applying the declaration of "important historical and artistic interest" to all his works.[29] Of greater interest, not only to the projects built by Mangiarotti but more generally the built heritage of the postwar period, is the «historical relational constraint»,[30] applicable to property, including privately owned buildings, which is of particular interest by its reference to technique, industry and culture in general, without requiring the building to be more than fifty years old or the designer to have died. This constraint is perfectly suited to industrial architecture or dwellings like those designed by Mangiarotti, which only within a more complex set of factors acquire those meanings and values that define these buildings as cultural assets, meaning «works of historic importance possessing a cultural value».[31]

The consequences of this constraint on architecture are similar to those of direct constraint, such as the need to receive ministerial approval for any type of external or internal alteration, the obligation to report its alienation by sale with the faculty of pre-emption by the state or local authorities, the possibility of applying for tax and contribution facilitations. Echoing the words of Mangiarotti, and well aware that there are many possible instruments to ensure a future for his architecture, starting with those of conservation, it is important to remind ourselves, as well as others, that «what we should all aspire to is to act with the knowledge of the time, of ours and of that to come».[32]

モンツァの集合住宅のファサードの詳細 1968-1975
Detail of a façade at the Residential building in Monza, 1968-1975.
(Giorgio Casali, AAM, Milano).

アロジオの集合住宅の詳細、
プレハブ工法の部材が厚くなり耐久性が向上 1974-1978
Detail of the Residential building in Arosio, 1974-1978,
with thicker prefabricated elements for greater durability. (AAM, Milano).

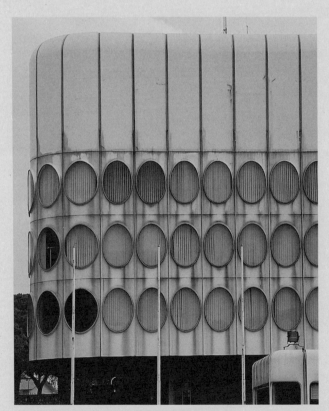

スナイデロ社のオフィス棟のファサード、マイアーノ 1971-1978
Main façade of the office building
at the Snaidero industrial complex in Majano, 1971-1978.
(Francesca Albani, 2014).

スナイデロ社のオフィスビルのファイバーグラスとポリウレタン発泡材
Detail of façade panels in fiberglass
and polyurethane foam at the Snaidero office building.
(Giorgio Casali, AAM, Milano).

– 33. A. Mangiarotti, in E.D. Bona, *Mangiarotti*, Sagep editrice, Genova 1988, p. 109.
– 34. The Snaidero company is now headed by the son and daughter-in-law of the Cavalier Rino Snaidero, the client of Angelo Mangiarotti. I wish to thank them for their generous hospitality.
– 35. I had several conversations with Enrico Malli concerning these buildings, the principal ones being those between October and December 2014.
– 36. *Alloggi su misura*, in "Domus Prefab", supplement to the review "Domus", no. 610, no. 4, 1980, pp. 46-47.
– 37. *Angelo Mangiarotti: Prefabrication/Participation, gli utenti partecipano al progetto*, in "Domus", no. 567, February 1977, pp. 5-8.

素材の経年と壊れやすさ

「建築とは本質的に知識である。設計者と施工者とその真実から恩恵を受ける人たちが共有する経験である」[33] この観点はマンジャロッティの工場や住居において正しく真実である。そこで働き暮らす人々は建築から喜びを得て建築を愛している。モンツァとアロジオの住宅建築から、フリウリのマイアーノにあるスナイデロ工業団地[34]、リッソーネにあるエルマグ社工場、メローニ家が所有するアルツァーテ・ブリアンツァにあるレマ社工場まで沢山の事例がある。マンジャロッティの同僚のエンリコ・マッリが良く言っていたように、「マンジャロッティの本物のファン」が構成している建物だ。[35] みんなが愛する活気ある住居や職場という単純な理由から、すべて丁寧に維持管理されている。1960年代から1970年代に建てたプレハブ鉄筋コンクリート製の建物すべてにある種の劣化の兆候が見られる。表面付着物、漏水、苔など付着物塩水によるエフロレッセンス、そして稀にコンクリート表面に剥離が生じる。

マンジャロッティが設計で熟考した耐久性の問題の存在が良くわかる。アロジオの住宅建築の鉄筋コンクリート[36]では数年早く竣工したモンツァの住宅建築を元に改善が見られ、特にファサードのプレキャストパネルが改良された。[37] モジュラーの構成に基づき厳密にパネルを

Aging of the materials and fragility

«Architecture is essentially knowledge. It is experience shared between those that design it, that build it and that benefit from its truth».[33] In the case of Angelo Mangiarotti's factories and homes, this aspect is particularly acute and real. Those who work and live in them take pleasure in the architecture and love it. There are many possible examples of this: from the residential buildings in Monza and Arosio, to the Snaidero industrial complex at Majano in Friuli,[34] the Elmag factory at Lissone and the Lema factory at Alzate Brianza owned by the Meroni family, which, as Enrico Malli, a colleaue of Angelo Mangiarotti, used to say, is made up of "true Mangiarotti fans".[35] These buildings are all subject to careful maintenance for the simple reason that they are much-loved and vital dwellings and workplaces. The signs of deterioration are of the kind found on all buildings made of prefabricated reinforced concrete built in the sixties and seventies: surface deposits, seepage, biological patinas, saline efflorescence, and some rare instances of spalling in the concrete cover.

It is easy to see that the issue of durability was very much present in Mangiarotti's design considerations. This is shown, in the case of reinforced concrete, by the residential building at Arosio.[36] Here the improvements made compared to the building in Monza,[37] completed only a few years earlier, included, among other things, the precast panels in the façade. In this case they were elements strictly organized on the basis of a modular coordination,

スナイデロ社のオフィスビルのファサード、アルカリ骨材反応と錆汚れによる老朽化
Mineral deposits and rust stains are the main forms of decay on the façades of the Snaidero office building.
(Francesca Albani, 2014).

– 38. A. Pica, *Nel Friuli uffici in campagna*, in "Domus", no. 591, February 1979, p. 10.
– 39. There are only some small fissures in the summit area corresponding to the main edge beam on the façade facing south.

設計し、それ以前の建物よりも枚数を少なく、一連のパネルに比べて厚くした。モンツァの建物は外皮の薄さから内在的な脆さがあることにマンジャロッティは気が付いていた。施工後すぐに鉄筋の腐食によって劣化の最初の兆候が現れたからだ。

しかしスナイデロ社オフィス棟はマンジャロッティの設計がうまくいった例である。すべての部材に詳細な管理が行き届いたので、建物は優雅に年を重ねている。よって、30年以上が過ぎて、アニョルドメニコ・ピカが竣工の数か月後に記した言葉は間違っていたことが証明された。1979年にピカは述べた。「この種の工業建築では不確実性を正当化する必要がある。家具、電車、ボート、飛行機など乗り物の典型と同じく、耐久性の限界を予測する」[38] 実際にファイバーグラスとポリウレタンフォームの外皮は、表面付着物や雨水の浸透による湿気は別として、その弾性と軽さのおかげで年数を経ても良い状態で立っている。パネルと支持構造の間の接続方法の重要性が証明された。温度変化により連続的に生じた機械的張力は、この大きさのファサードでは広範囲で連続して消失した可能性がある。[39]

もしマンジャロッティが、経年によって起こりうる問題を予想していてもうまくいかなかっただろう。例えば、三石塔式の鉄筋コンクリートで建てた工場のように、単

lower in number than in the previous building and thicker in the area of the string courses. Mangiarotti had noticed that the slenderness of the profiles of the Monza building had resulted in an intrinsic fragility of the façade, which after a short time started to display the first signs of deterioration due to the corrosion of the reinforcing bars.

The Snaidero office building, however, is a further example of how Mangiarotti built well, lavishing care on all those elements that are capable of ensuring his building aged gracefully. Hence, more than thirty years later, the words written by Agnoldomenico Pica a few months after the building was completed proved to be incorrect. In 1979 Pica observed: «The necessary precariousness of an industrial building of this kind justifies its overt formal relationship with the type of furniture, even the vehicle – car, train, boat, plane – with which it shares its foreseeable limited durability».[38] In reality, the fibreglass and polyurethane foam envelope, apart from the presence of normal surface deposits and various instances of damp due to the seepage of rainwater, has stood up very well to the passing of time thanks to its elasticity and lightness. One point that might have proved critical is the system of connection between the panels and the supporting structure, where continuous mechanical tensions due to temperature changes present in a façade of this size might well have caused widespread loss of continuity.[39]

If Mangiarotti sought to anticipate some of the problems that

– 40. See the analysis on p. 122 of this volume.
– 41. After the creation of the Crema Campus by the University of Milan, in particular the Faculty of Computer Science, which following a collapse commissioned the engineer Ezio Giuriani to consolidate its structure.
– 42. In the analysis of this theme I wish to thank Professor Mario Monotti for his kindness and generosity.

might arise in his buildings over time, with regard to others he was unsuccessful. An example is safety in the presence of seismic stresses, which are particularly critical in buildings composed of elements simply supported on each other, like the factories built with trilithic systems in precast reinforced concrete. Although the zones of Brianza straddling the provinces of Milan, Monza and Como are at low seismic risk – as was Modena itself before the 2012 earthquake – questions about the behaviour of these structures when subjected to the horizontal actions of earthquakes are absolutely justified because they are busy workplaces. Since these buildings draw their identity from the fact that the space is determined by the juxtaposition of the elements, to prevent the component parts from reacting to the earthquake by slipping apart and so collapsing,[40] it is essential to carefully assess methods of intervention, which will have to be delicate and complex, though not new. The same issues have already been raised in a number of buildings, especially in the south of Italy, where the seismic risk is higher, but also in the north. An example is the Olivetti factory in Crema designed by Marco Zanuso in the seventies and subject to structural consolidation in 2010-2011[41] following a collapse. During this work, preceded by a broad and comprehensive diagnosis, the most prevalent attitude in relation to these prefabricated buildings in areas with a low seismic risk, whose elements are simply supported on one another, was to avoid dealing with the problem. In this case, the reasons were primarily due to with financial factors rather than the desire to retain the static functioning of the building as an element that defines its identity. The central question, in fact, is that to improve the behaviour of the building in case of earthquake the static system would have to become "monolithic" with a behaviour attributable, in principle, to that of a box structure.[42] Finding a suitable compromise between the different needs, regulatory and cultural, is a complex matter that requires great sophistication on the part of everyone involved, in the first place the structural engineer.

純に互いに支え合う要素で構成した建物において地震応力に含まれる安全性は特に重要である。2012年の地震が起きる前のモデナと同様に、ミラノ、モンツァ、コモをまたぐブリアンツァ地域では地震のリスクは低いが、構造の揺れが問題である。地震で水平方向に揺れても忙しい仕事場では構造の問題を完全に正当化できる。地震で構成部材が滑り落ちて崩壊することを防ぐため、[40] このような建物では部材を並置して空間を決定して形を維持する。古来の繊細かつ複雑な補強方法を慎重に評価する必要がある。既にイタリア北部でも、そして特に地震の危険性が高いイタリア南部でも多くの建物で同様の問題が発生した。クレマにある1970年代にマルコ・ザヌーゾが設計したオリベッティの工場がその一例だ。崩壊後、2010年から2011年[41]にかけて構造改革の対象となった。

広範囲にわたる包括的な診断が行われる前に、この地震の危険性が低い地域では、部品を単純に組み合わせたプレハブ建築は問題とみなさず対処を先延ばしにしていた。それは建物の外観保つため建物の静的機能を維持したいと考えたからではなく、主に経済的な理由からだった。実際に問われたのは、建物の地震の際の挙動を改善するため、静止システムが箱型構造の原則の「一枚岩になる」ことだった。[42] 調整と文化の異なるニーズに適切な妥協点を見つけることは複雑で難しい。関係者、特に構造エンジニアに高度な解答が求められた。

急激に変更が加えられる前のアルミタリア社施設 1971
View of the Armitalia industrial complex in 1971,
before being progressively alterated.
(Giorgio Casali, AAM, Milano).

未来への戦略

　マンジャロッティの作品が置かれた状況を観察して様々な展望が見えた。それは解体から最も丁寧で愛に満ちた維持管理まで多岐に渡った。そのような異なる未来が生じた理由は多様で複雑だ。意図した建物の用途や建築の結果に起因するものではない。ある建物は最も興味深く象徴的で、常に機能的論理性を優先し、丁寧に維持管理が施された仕事場だったが取り壊された。制度的な保護を欠いたことも理由にはならない。多くの出版物で建築批評家がくり返し建物を称賛したから、設計者が無名であったわけでもない。どの建物も保全にあたり技術的に複雑でも出費をともなう状況でもなかったから、維持管理の問題として理由を探ることもできない。建物の未来を確保するためにもっと多くのことができるはずだ。どんな形の保護でも少なくとも資産の損失を防ぐことができる。一方、より広範なコミュニケーション戦略が、これらの場所の将来を戦略的に決定する関係者の意識を高めるだろう。少なくとも個人で所有する作品の場合、建築を施工した所有者が建築資産の質と重要性を認識し、建築と絆を深めることが重要だ。所有者が設計と施工の段階から参加し、そこに住み、その空間的形態的価値を称賛し、マンジャロッティ個人を讃え、その場所が保有する文化的価値を理解するまでの数々の幅広い活動から評価が生じるかもしれない。

　この点でチニゼッロ・バルサモにあるアルミタリア工場とオフィスが重要だ。使用者と建築の直接的なつながりがほころび、もはや感情が働かなくなると、建物の将来は危険にさらされる。数年前から小さな改造が始まり、

Strategies for the future

Observation of the current state of the body of works by Angelo Mangiarotti presents a very varied panorama. It ranges from demolition to the most careful and affectionate maintenance. The reasons for such different futures are many and complex. They are not attributable to the intended use of the buildings or the architectural outcome, since one of the most interesting and symbolic buildings has been demolished while the workplaces, in which a purely functional logic is usually the overriding concern, are subjected to careful maintenance. Nor are the reasons a lack of institutional protection, and even less the fact that their author is unknown, since they have been repeatedly celebrated by critics of architecture in many publications. The reasons cannot even be sought in issues related to the conservation of artefacts, since none of the cases entails situations so technically complex or expensive as to make conservation problematic.

It is clear that much can be done to secure the future of these works. Some form of protection, of whatever kind, would at least prevent the loss of the assets, while more extensive communication strategies would lead to greater awareness of the actors involved in the strategic decisions for the definition of the future of these places. One critical point, at least in the case of privately owned works, is the bond that their owners establish with the architecture and that leads them to recognize quality and significance in the architectural asset. Such dynamics may be of many kinds and range from the owners' participation in the design phase and construction, to a life lived in those places whose spatial and formal values are prized, personal appreciation of Angelo Mangiarotti or an understanding of the cultural values that these places possess.

– 43. Confining our view only to the external works, in the first phase the enlargement of the factory windows, which were square but were made rectangular, then the conversion of the roof of the office building into a refreshment area with the addition of wooden balustrades. Later, between 2012 and 2013, windows were inserted on the top floor of the highest building in a point where perforated panels were present, and the concrete panels were painted with a *cocciopesto* finish.
– 44. A. Mangiarotti, M. Luchi, L. Bonesio, L. Magnani, *op. cit.* at note 3, p. 15.

取るに足らない変更だったが、複合施設の使い方に妥協が生まれた。[43] ブッソレンゴのフィアットの代理店でも同じ事が起きた。所有権の変更と多国籍企業による買収の後、その会社の基準に沿って改造され、建物は単に倉庫として認識されるようになった。

どの状況も、どの建物にも変更や転換や劣化を招いたそれぞれの経緯がある。唯一の解決策は無いが、様々な解決策がある。確かにマンジャロッティの建築の未来を確保した法的証書の文言は、制度的な保護から保全や維持管理の必要性を十分に認識した設計の実施まで多岐にわたった。基本となる事実は複数の視点から考え建築物の知識を得るプロセスだ。学習と分析と研究は、この問題に対する新しい建築家の訓練と同様に確実に意識の向上に役立つが、このような建築作品を理解し広く共有することがもっと役立つだろう。この研究を通じ、これらの建物の強化と保全を目的とした過程への貢献を目指す。マンジャロッティ自身の言葉である「ある立場、知識を得る瞬間、思考する場所」[44] から建築の存続を確保したい。

An example of the importance of this point is the Armitalia factory and offices in Cinisello Balsamo. When the direct link between user and architecture is broken and the feelings no longer play a leading role, the building's future is jeopardised. In this case several years ago there began a trickle of small alterations, apparently of no great importance, but they have actually compromised the legibility of the complex.[43] Something similar has happened to the Fiat Agency at Bussolengo. Following a change of ownership and its acquisition by a multinational, the application of corporate standards prevailed and alterations were made, as a result of which the building was perceived solely as a container.

Each case is different and each building has its own history leading to alterations, conversions and deterioration. There is no single solution, but many possible solutions. Certainly in terms of instruments for ensuring a future for Mangiarotti's architecture, ranging from institutional protection to a cultivated design fully aware of the need for conservation or maintenance practices, a fundamental factor is the process of knowledge of the architectural artefacts, read in a plurality of dimensions. Study, analysis and research, as well as the training of new architects in these matters, can certainly help promote a greater awareness, but above all a more widely shared understanding of such architectural works. The most ambitious goal of this study is to contribute to a process aimed at the enhancement and conservation of these buildings, to ensure that they continue to represent, in Mangiarotti own words, «a position, a moment of knowledge, a stage of thought».[44]

ミラノ地下鉄ヴェネツィア駅
アンジェロ・マンジャロッティによるスケッチ1982年
Venezia underground station of the Passante ferroviario (cross-rail system),
Milan, sketch by Angelo Mangiarotti, 1982. (AAM, Milano).

堀川絹江

Kinue Horikawa

巨匠の軌跡

The Traces of the Master

アンジェロ・マンジャロッティのスケッチには常に驚かされる。彼の建築、デザイン、彫刻作品のスケッチのほとんどは、プロジェクトを始める際の作品に対する思い入れや、完成予想をイメージして描かれたものだが、実際に出来上がった作品は、始めの絵やスケッチそのものなのだ。時には、建物の竣工写真やプロダクトの完成写真よりも、彼のスケッチの方が出来上がった作品の様相や雰囲気を忠実に表現するほど完成度が高い。

通常、プロジェクトの実現にあたって、経済的な要因や施工上の問題、クライアントの要望まど、何かしら変えざるを得ない事象が起こる。当然、マンジャロッティの多くの作品でも施工製作段階で多種多様な変更があった。それにもかかわらず、最初のイメージをそのまま完成に結びつけられたのは彼の特筆すべき才能であろう。毎回あらゆる状況において、このプロジェクトではここまでできるに違いない、というリミットを的確に予測しながらスケッチを描いたのである。

マンジャロッティは建築作品のスケッチで、意匠のみならず構造的な配慮や、設備、施工方法の提案を視野に入れて、それぞれの作品に込める考え方を一本一本の線で表現している。デザインや彫刻作品のスケッチに見られる何気なく引かれた曲線は、それぞれを創造するための技術的な可能性や、理にかなった人間工学的な形状を勘案しつつ、選択した素材の特質をいかに引き出せるか、そして、独自のアイデンティティをいかに作品にこめられるかを、瞬時に計算して描いたものである。

マンジャロッティにとってスケッチとは作品を実現するための重要なコミュニケーションツールでもあった。

Angelo Mangiarotti's sketches have always been a source of surprise. At the origin of every project – whether for architecture, design, or sculpture – they left on paper the early trace of his first impressions, a prerequisite for any sort of realization. And the finished works are indeed perfectly congruent with these first sketches; at times even more so than the photographs taken of the work, the sketches themselves faithfully reproduce the original inspiration, the creative climate that sparked the very idea of the work.

Regrettably, over the course of its realization, a project can undergo a series of changes attributed to the requests of the client, economic factors, or problems inherent in the design itself. Needless to say, many of Angelo Mangiarotti's works were no exception, and underwent changes while they were being elaborated as well. And yet, despite everything, the proximity between the works realized and the first insights sketched out in the drawings is a fact that can only be ascribed to the author's outstanding talent. Each time, in every situation, Mangiarotti made his sketches while clearly foreseeing an overall design to be taken into account so as not to distort the original plan.

The sketches of Mangiarotti's architectural plans include not just drawings, but also reveal his special concern for structural analyses and the modes of the construction of the building and design of its interiors. Mangiarotti devoted his undivided attention to every occasion, and to every subject in order to consolidate as precisely as possible the idea that he had in mind so that he could bring it to fruition. That same curved line, apparently traced with nonchalance, which characterized all the sketches of his design objects and sculptures, was actually what made their realization technically possible, and when they finally came time to put it into practice, they proved to have been made with all the care needed

母の肖像画、1930年代　アンジェロ・マンジャロッティ
Angelo Mangiarotti, Portrait of his mother, thirties. (AAM, Milano).

毎朝事務所に着いたスタッフは、前晩または早朝にマンジャロッティが用意したスケッチをそれぞれのテーブルの上に見つけて1日を始めた。この光景は事務所に在籍したスタッフなら誰もが経験したであろう。私自身、今日はどんなスケッチが待っているのだろう、とワクワクする気持ちで毎朝事務所に向かったのを今でも覚えている。マンジャロッティは建築、デザイン、彫刻という広範囲に渡るデザイン活動を続けたが、創作の進め方は一貫していた。スケッチをベースに模型を作り、その後図面を作成するという作業の流れが全ての創作活動の基本であった。模型や図面の修正にも、マンジャロッティがその都度新たなスケッチを詳細に描き、それに沿ってスタッフが手直しや変更を繰り返し、最終の模型と図面を仕上げていった。クライアントとの打ち合わせの時に、相手の話を聞きながら絶えずマンジャロッティの手はスケッチを続けていたことも記憶に新しい。プロジェクトの提案や、新しいプロジェクトでしばしば発生した難しい施工方法の問題解決にも、言葉や文章で対応するよりマンジャロッティの明確なスケッチの方がクライアント

to enhance the potential of the materials used. It is a curved line whose rationale can be explained in ergonomic terms as well, which tells us that Mangiarotti sketched out his schemes with instantaneous insight and calculation, so that he could bestow a unique identity on each of his works.

For Angelo Mangiarotti those sketches were also a means of communication aimed at the realization of each project. Every day, when he arrived at the office, those of us on his staff would begin by gathering the preparatory sketches he had made the evening before or even early that same morning. Anyone who was ever a part of Studio Mangiarotti will say they had the same experience. I remember going to the office each morning excited at the thought of finding some new sketch by the Master. Mangiarotti's activity ranged from architecture, to design, to sculpture, but the creative technique he employed was always coherently the same. On the basis of his sketches, a model would be made, which then became a full-fledged project. And even when he needed to make changes to a model or a design, he would make a detailed sketch of what was new; the staff would then apply the changes and improvements to the model or design so as to make the final realiza-

ミラノ地下鉄レプブリカ駅 アンジェロ・マンジャロッティによるスケッチ1982年
Repubblica underground station of the Passante ferroviario (cross-rail system), Milan, sketch by Angelo Mangiarotti, 1982. (AAM, Milano).

に納得してもらえることが多かった。事務所にはマンジャロッティが受けたプロジェクトごとに、未完成で終わったものも含めて、何百枚ものスケッチが存在する。このアーカイブを目にするたびに、2012年に逝去する直前まで連日精力的にスケッチを続けていたマンジャロッティの姿が目に浮かび、彼のモノづくりに対する真摯な姿勢に改めて敬服せずにはいられない。

マンジャロッティのスケッチは、繊細でありながらスピード感のある斬新な線で描かれているのが特徴で、建築家のスケッチというよりも、画家、とりわけ水彩画家の作品に近いように思う。これは、マンジャロッティが幼少の頃から独自でデッサンを嗜んでいたことと、ミラノ工科大学に入る前に国立ブレラ美術学院へ2年間通い、本格的に美術やデッサンの勉強をしたことに起因する。

ここに、マンジャロッティが少年時代に描いたスケッチがある。彼の母親を描いたもので、60年近く大切に事務所に飾られていた。ずいぶん前になるが、マンジャロッティに幼少時代の思い出や、モノを創造しはじめる手がかりになる個人的な原風景について尋ねたところ、

tion of the work as easy as possible. I can clearly recall that during his meetings with the firm's clients, even while the client was talking to him about what had to be done, his hand continued making marks on the sheet of paper before him. With each proposed new work, just as with each hypothetical solution to the problems that occasionally arose during the difficult development of a new project, we always managed to come to an agreement with the client thanks to Mangiarotti's precious drawings, which freed us from having to use words or written reports to explain things.

Studio Mangiarotti still has many of the sketches Angelo Mangiarotti made, divided into individual projects, whether or not they were ever actually produced.

Each time I see those sketches, my mind goes to the memory of the Master, who continued each day and with great vigour, until shortly before his passing, to cover his work sheets with drawings. I cannot but feel great admiration for that unfailing attitude of genuine loyalty to his own special way of conceiving his creations.

Mangiarotti drew with a light, quick hand. His drawings can be

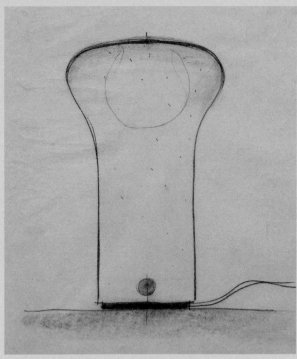

吹きガラス照明「サッフォ」
アンジェロ・マンジャロッティによるスケッチ 1966年
"Saffo" blown glass lamp, sketch by Angelo Mangiarotti, 1966.
(AAM, Milano).

次のように語った。

「少年時代に水彩画にいそしんだことを覚えている。私の家では正午に家族全員がテーブルについて昼食をとった。私はいつも母の隣の席に座っていたものだ。両親はベーカリーを営んでいた。母は毎朝早くに起き、家事に追われ、常に家庭と仕事で忙しくしていた。今でも良く覚えているのは、昼食が終わるとすぐテーブルで疲れてうつらうつら居眠りをする母の姿をデッサンしたことだ。デッサンは私にとっていつも身近な楽しみだった。このデッサンは70年以上も前（2004年のインタビュー時点）に描いた。その頃からずっと自分が見たものを描き留めておきたいという強い気持があった」

マンジャロッティは、1950年代からの80年代の前期にはアメリカ製のフロマスターのマーカーペンを好んで使用した。後半の1980年代以降にはスイスのカランダッシュのホルダーに日本の三菱ユニ6Bの太い芯を入れて描き、クレヨンで色を付けた。当時、イタリアではこの6Bの太い芯は存在せず、事務所の日本人スタッフや日本人の友人がこの三菱ユニ6Bの芯を日本から何ダース

compared to those of a painter, especially a watercolourist, rather than an architect. This probably stems from the fact that ever since he was a child Mangiarotti enjoyed drawing, to such an extent that before attending Milan Polytechnic he spent two years at Brera Fine Arts Academy, taking courses on art history and drawing.

The portrait of his mother reproduced here is the work of the Master himself: he made it when he was still very young, and for sixty years it hung on one of the office walls. Many years ago, when I asked him what he remembered about his childhood, and which spiritual landscape he perceived to be at the roots of his creative drive, he answered me with these words: «When I was a boy, I remember that I often worked hard on watercolour painting. At the time, at home, the whole family would gather for the noon meal, and I would sit next to my mother. My parents were running a bakery. My mother was always very busy, she would get up early in the morning, and was constantly bustling about doing the housework. I clearly remember that, after lunch, I would make a drawing of her as she dozed off while still seated at the table. Drawing was an inexhaustible pleasure for me. I made this

ペデルツォーリ邸、バルドリーノ、ヴェローナ
アンジェロ・マンジャロッティによるスケッチ1971年
Villa Pederzoli in Bardolino, Verona,
sketch by Angelo Mangiarotti, 1971. (AAM, Milano).

も土産に買って帰ることが定番であった。スケッチに使用する紙は時代ごとに変わらざるを得なかったが、マンジャロッティが特に好んで使用したのは、一昔前までミラノのほとんどの菓子屋で包装に使用していた砂色（または薄いベージュ色）の非常に薄い紙であった。マンジャロッティはこの紙がいずれ無くなることを危惧し、大量に購入したため、事務所にはいつもこの紙があった。予想通り、現在ではこの種の紙を使う菓子屋をミラノで見つけるのは不可能となってしまった。

新しいプロジェクトが始まる際の、白紙を前にしたマンジャロッティのいきいきとした表情が今でも忘れられない。マンジャロッティにとって「スケッチを描く」こととはどのような意味があったのだろうか。私のこの問いに、彼はこう答えている。

「自分のためだ。後に残すために素敵なスケッチを描こうと思ったことはない。自分の考えをはっきりさせるため、描いては捨て、描いては捨ての繰り返しだ。スケッチは気分が良い時、悪い時、元気な時、疲れている時など、その時の状況を反映する身体に直結した道具だ。最

drawing more than seventy years ago [my meeting with the Master took place in 2004]; that was when I began to harbour a strong desire to draw what I saw with my own eyes». During the early period of his activity, Mangiarotti preferred to use American Flo-Master felt-tip markers for his sketches. Later, he would move on to Swiss Caran d'Ache coloured pencils with a Mitsubishi Uni 6B tip, and after that he began to use pastels. At the time, you couldn't find those thick-tipped B6 pencils in Italy, so his collaborators and Japanese friends ended up having to get boxes and boxes of Mitsubishi Uni 6B tips for him as a sort of souvenir from the Land of the Rising Sun. The reams of paper used for the sketches had to be replaced frequently, but the Master continued to show his preference for sand-coloured (or light beige) paper, that in those days was used in confectioners' shops for wrapping sweets. He was afraid that type of paper would one day be unavailable, so he would buy up great quantities of it. We always used this type of paper in the Studio. And Mangiarotti was right: nowadays you can't find a single bakery in Milan where they still use that kind of paper.

I will never forget the excitement you could see in his face when,

近は一般的にスケッチよりもコンピュータのグラフィックソフトが使われているが、私は使ったことがないし、これからも使うことはない。もちろん、コンピュータの可能性は無限にあるが、身体との関係を断った手段は私には限度があるように思う」

確かに、マンジャロッティが常々提唱してきた「モノづくりはデザイナーの手によるスタディ、職人との協働、そして新しい技術の融合がなければ成り立たない」という手法はもはや主流では無くなりつつある。今や、建築およびプロダクトデザインを制作する技術は細分化され、コンピュータの進歩によって短期間での完成が可能となった。しかし、機械のみを介して制作した完成品が容易に受け入れられるわけではない。

何百枚ものスケッチからマンジャロッティは数々の作品を創り上げた。時代を超え世界中の人々がマンジャロッティの作品に魅了されているのは、マンジャロッティの思いが出来上がった作品に忠実に反映されている証であろう。作品に対する強い情熱や希望を一本一本の線に込めたスケッチ、躊躇することなく新しい挑戦を描いた躍動感あふれるマンジャロッティのスケッチを見るたびに、建築家、デザイナーとして心から敬意を表するとともに、「モノを創造すること」と「デザインすること」の意義を再考せずにはいられない。

as a new project was about to get off the ground, he would find himself sitting in front of a blank sheet of paper. What did it mean, for Angelo Mangiarotti, to "make sketches"? He once answered this question as follows: «I make sketches for myself. I have never even considered making nice sketches to be left to posterity. These sketches help me to straighten out my thoughts; I draw something, then I throw it out, I draw something else, and throw that out too, that's why I have to keep on doing it. After all, I don't consider it to be anything more than a means that is capable of coming to my aid at that very moment. The sketch is a means that is in close contact with one's physical self, it reflects the conditions of that specific moment. When I feel well or when I don't, when I feel particularly energetic as well as when I'm feeling tired, and so on. Nowadays, generally, people use graphic design software rather than sketches, but I have never used anything of the sort, nor do I expect to do so in the future. Naturally, the computer's potential is endless, but on my part I think there's a limit to using this technique, as it has interrupted all relations with our physical side».

Undoubtedly, what Mangiarotti always said, i.e. that «creation is successful when there is a perfect fusion between the study made by the designer, the craftsmanship, and the means of the new technologies», runs the risk of becoming increasingly marginalized. Today, contemporary architecture and the technologies whose purpose is to create product designs are becoming increasingly disarticulated. Thanks to the progress made in computer science, projects can be completed in a very short amount of time. However, the final object made by using these new methods is not always accepted willingly.

Mangiarotti succeeded in completing many works starting from hundreds and hundreds of sketches. In spite of the fact that so much time has gone by, the Master's works continue to interest people from all around the world, and this is proof that his creations are a faithful reflection of their conceiver. Each time I see one of his sketches – marks made spontaneously, each line a concentrate of energy and self-confidence – I think of the meaning that the words "creation" and "drawing" had for Angelo Mangiarotti. And from the bottom of my heart I raise an emotional tribute of esteem in his regard as an architect and designer.

アルツァーテ・ブリアンツァのレマの工場の屋上からの眺め　1969-1979年
View of the roofing of the Lema factory in Alzate Brianza, 1969-1979.
(Rodolfo Facchini, AAM, Milano).

フランツ・グラフ、フランチェスカ・アルバーニ

Franz Graf, Francesca Albani

建築の組み立て方
10のバリエーション

Assembling to Build:
Ten Variations on a Theme

　本稿はアンジェロ・マンジャロッティが1961年から1979年に建てた10作品を分析し考察したものである。[1] 建築作品の選考ではマンジャロッティが1960年に独立するまでブルーノ・モラスッティと協働した初期の活動は考慮しなかった。彼らのパートナーシップからミラノのクアドロンノ通りの集合住宅、ガヴィラーテ通りの集合住宅や、バランザーテの教会など戦後の建築的景観に深い刻印を記した作品が生まれた。これらの作品においてマンジャロッティの貢献とモラスッティの仕事を分けられないので、マンジャロッティの第二期の作品に焦点を当て、前章でも多く扱ったテーマを再び取り上げて各個人が解釈した。マンジャロッティの仕事には幅広い様々な面がある。彼は金持ちの住居や仕事場や展示場といったテーマに取り組んだ。完成した建築作品のみを分析し、非常に面白いが実現しなかった数々の研究の基本的段階を示すプロジェクトはここでは除外する。その理由は多岐にわたる。

　そもそも、マンジャロッティの研究の中心を占めるのは、建築作品の設計から制作の段階で成熟した統合化と工業化とプレハブ工法である。このプロセスでのみ、複雑なダイナミクスと、作品に最終的な意味と特徴を与えるものを解釈することができる。モラスッティと別れた後、おそらくマンジャロッティの性格と個人的な傾向から、時には頑固なまでに独力で建築を研究したと考えられている。実際にはマンジャロッティは事務所で有能なチーム[2]に加えて、アルド・ファヴィーニ、ジュリオ・バリオ、ジョバンニ・コロンボ、アルベルト・ヴィンターニといった非凡な腕前を持つ構造エンジニアと働いてい

The reflections presented in the following pages are based on an analysis of ten works by Angelo Mangiarotti built from 1961 to 1979.[1] In selecting these architectural works, no consideration has been given to the first part of Mangiarotti's activity conducted with Bruno Morassutti, from whom Mangiarotti separated in 1960. Their partnership led to the creation of works that left a profound mark on the architectural landscape of the postwar period, such as the Residential buildings in Via Quadronno and Via Gavirate in Milan and the Church of Mater Misericordiae at Baranzate. Since Mangiarotti's contribution cannot be separated in these works from Morassutti's, we have chosen to focus on the second phase of his production, in which many of the themes previously dealt with were taken up again and reinterpreted in personal ways. Mangiarotti's work is wide-ranging and many-faceted. He measured himself with the themes of the bourgeois residence, workplaces and exhibition spaces. Our analysis takes into account only built architectural works, so excluding his projects, numerous and extremely interesting, which still represent a fundamental stage of his research. The reasons are various and different in kind.

In the first place, many issues central to Angelo Mangiarotti's research, such as unification, industrialization and prefabrication, came to full maturity only within the process from design to production of the architectural work. Again, only within this process is it possible to interpret the complex dynamics and the contributions that gave the works their final meanings and characteristics. It is often supposed, perhaps because of Mangiarotti's character and personal bent, that after his parting from Morassutti he conducted his architectural research single-handed, perhaps at times stubbornly on his own. Actually Mangiarotti surrounded himself in his office with a large and capable team,[2] in addition to working

_ 1. The names of the works adopted is that used in the Studio Mangiarotti: see www.studiomangiarotti.com. In the literature on Angelo Mangiarotti there appear many different versions, probably due to the fact that they better express the intended use, the clients or the typology. The architectural works, however, are always easily and uniquely identifiable.
_ 2. Among them the historical memory of the office until his death in January 2015 was Enrico Malli. Much of this work it is also due to his generous patience, in the first place with the students and then with us. His stories of a past life at the side of a man like Angelo Mangiarotti, very often in the shadows, helped us to read and interpret different events and situations. His passion for work, his devotion to study and his refined kindness conveyed his enthusiasm and pride at the all he had achieved in over sixty years. It was an honour to work with him.

た。
　構造エンジニアとの相乗効果があった事例としてメストレにあるスプリューゲン・ブロイ社倉庫が挙げられる。特に屋根の根源的な形は実験と研究から決定した。最初の図面から屋根材の下端に梁の構造を組み込み、柱と接続する構造だった。ファヴィーニとのコラボレーションの後で部材は優雅に細くなった。この形は静的な機能から生じた。協働実験によって倉庫の屋根は、建築的造形とプレハブ工法とポストテンション方式の技術的要件を融合した見事な例へと変わった。
　建築を決定する過程においてしばしば蚊帳の外に置かれるが、実際の出来事で深い印象を残すのは依頼主である。マンジャロッティの依頼主のほとんどはイタリア北部ブリアンツァやフリウリ地方の上流階級やビジネスクラスに属していた。マンジャロッティはまたジェノヴァのIRIの展示パヴィリオンや、ミラノ通行線（ミラノの地下鉄交通システム）の鉄道駅の公的組織とも仕事をした。概要の草案作成に限らず、建築作品の定義において依頼主は重要な役割を果たす。例えばIRIグループのフィンシーデル社とイタルシーデル社はマンジャロッティとコラボレーションを重ねた。最初はジェノヴァの海の見本市展示館で、次はピオンビーノの住宅街だったがこちらは実現しなかった。依頼主には明らかな意図があり、マンジャロッティが使う金属材料を指定した。ジェノヴァのパヴィリオンの場合、フィンシーデル社金属構造の技術局の構造エンジニアのファブリツィオ・デ・ミランダが構造計算で貢献した。軽さと流動性を実現するのに必要な厚さと寸法の「限界」を見つけてアーチ推力を排除

with structural engineers of rare skill, such as Aldo Favini, Giulio Ballio, Giovanni Colombo and Alberto Vintani.

An example of applications introduced by the synergy with the structural engineers is the Splügen Bräu complex in Mestre, in particular in the definition of the roofing, the fundamental object of experimentation and study. From the first drawings, the form of the single roofing segment used to compose the structure appears on the soffit looking squat with columns set close together. Only after the work carried out in collaboration with Favini did the element become slender and elegant. The formal aspect found its reasons in the static functioning: the work of experimentation conducted together turned the roofing of the depot into a masterful example of the relation between the form of the architecture and the technical requirements of prefabrication and post-tensioning.

Another actor in the process of defining the architecture, whose role has often been left in the margins, but who in fact made a deep impression on events, was the client. Most of Angelo Mangiarotti's clients were private members of the upper bourgeoisie and business class in Brianza and Friuli. He also worked with public commissioning bodies, as in the case of the IRI exposition pavilion in Genoa and the railway stations of the Passante Ferroviario (Milan's underground cross-rail system). A significant example of the role of the client in the definition of the architectural work, not limited only to the drafting of the brief, was the case of Finsider and Italsider in the IRI Group, with which Mangiarotti collaborated on several occasions, firstly on the exposition pavilion at the Fiera del Mare in Genoa and then on the residential centre in Piombino, which was never built. The client specified, for obvious reasons, the metal materials which Mangia-

– 3. To explore this topic more fully, see the essay by Franz Graf, *The Ethics of Prefabrication: Archaism and Universality* in the present volume.
– 4. A. Mangiarotti, *Architettura oggi*, in E.D. Bona, *Mangiarotti*, Sagep Editrice, Genova 1988, p. 9.

し、象徴と商業的表現のはざまで、海と陸の間に完璧なバランスで見本市展示館を設置した。

　ここに選出した建築10作品はマンジャロッティが追求した建築言語の見事な例である。機能と結びついているわけではなく、組み立ての構造作用で強さとユニークさを引き出そうとしたものだ。[3] 1988年のエッセイで建築家は「建築言語」の意味を非常に明解に説明した。「建築言語とは第一にコミュニケーションの兆し、または建築的行為の物理的対象、その扱い、その構成、つまり設計の意図を物理的現実に変換するすべての手段を意味する。しかしこの建築言語とは建築の制作に付随する言葉でもある。この言語の兆しは頻繁に提案の場に変わるからだ。よって、兆しの具体化という支えがなければ、言葉は建築特有の現実、つまり建物とは何の関係もない空しい知的憶測であり続ける」[4] 私たちが設定したテーマの主題を読み解くカギは3つある。

　最初のカギは「実験」で、マンジャロッティの形態の研究と、新しく複雑な構造の解がもたらす可能性の関係を調査することが目的だ。メストレの倉庫とジェノヴァの見本市展示館を例に挙げた。審美的かつ技術的な認識から前者ではコンクリート、後者では鉄鋼を材料に用いて、象徴的、造形的、文化的に達成すべき結果を限界まで押し広げた。マンジャロッティの作品では特定の好みの素材は見受けられないが、むしろ各素材に内在する論理と戯れるかのように素材の限界に挑む。ジュゼッペ・パガノは建築の定義において材料が果たす役割を1931年に次のように記した。「素材とは建築家が建築的に想像するために用いるもので、その形態の結果には明らかな影響が及ぶ。木や花崗岩やレンガで設計した建築や、鉄や鉄筋コンクリートで設計した建築もある。素材にはその外観だけでなく、選択した素材固有の形態的な傾向が

rotti was to use. In the case of the pavilion in Genoa the structural engineer, Fabrizio de Miranda of the technical office at Finsider Metal Construction, contributed through the calculation of the arch with the thrust eliminated to locating the "limit" of its thicknesses, and the dimensions, necessary to achieve that lightness and fluidity that set this object in a perfect balance between land and sea, between symbol and commercial interests.

The ten selected architectural works are masterful examples of Mangiarotti's search for an architectural language, not necessarily linked to function, which would draw its strength and uniqueness from the tectonics of the assemblage.[3] In a 1988 essay the architect explained very clearly what he meant by "language in architecture": «Language in architecture firstly means communicating with signs, or the physical objects of architectural action, their treatment, their composition, in short, all those instruments that allow one to translate a design intent into a physical reality. But the language is also that of the words that accompanies the making of architecture, because very often the language of signs becomes the field of suggestion; so also words, without the support of the tangible reality of signs, may remain a futile intellectual speculation that has nothing in common with the only reality that is peculiar to architecture, namely building».[4] There are three keys for reading the subject with which we have decided to address the theme.

The first, "Experimentation", aims to investigate the relation between Mangiarotti's formal research and the possibilities offered by the use of new and complex structural solutions. The examples selected are the Mestre warehouse and the exposition pavilion in Genoa. The materials, concrete in the first instance and steel in the second, are used with skilful aesthetic and technical awareness and are pushed to the limits in relation to the symbolic, formal and cultural results to be achieved. In his work there is no observable preference for any material, but rather an urge to push each material to its limit, as if playing with the logic intrinsic to it. Gi-

– 5. G. Pagano, *I materiali della nuova architettura*, in "La Casa Bella", June 1931, p. 14.
– 6. F. Albani, *The Prefabrication in Italy after the World War II. Zanuso versus Camus*, in *5th Congress of Construction History*, Chicago (Ill.) 2015, pp. 39-46.
– 7. Words uttered at a lecture in Chicago between 11 and 18 June and quoted in E.D. Bona, *Mangiarotti*, Sagep editrice, Genova 1988, p. 71.

存在する」⁵この言葉はマンジャロッティが新素材と伝統的な素材の両方を研究して抱いた情熱と愛を良く表している。彼は再構成した木のような石、プレストレストコンクリートのような従来のコンクリート、鋼鉄のような大理石、合成材料のような礫岩に魅了された。

2番目の「重力」では、マンジャロッティの目的であったプレハブ工法のテーマをまとめる。構成上の限界と建築的な限界と三石塔式システムの可能性と共に、複雑な理由からイタリアで主に「鉄筋コンクリートのプレハブ工法」⁶ という形をとった。「このプロジェクトでは過去と現在の類似性は戻らないが、比喩は戻る」⁷ というマンジャロッティの言葉を思い出す。古典的な三石塔とは単純で機能的な形を成す柱、梁、屋根というわずかな要素から成り、重力で固定しあう仕組みである。様々な方法や手段で、特に建築から家具の構成部品まで様々なスケールで解釈されている。リッソーネのエルマグ社工場、アルツァーテ・ブリアンツァのレマ社工場、ジュッサーノのフェグ社エントランス棟、ブッソレンゴのフィアット販売店の4つの建築作品と、インカス、エチェントリコ、エロスというテーブルを例に挙げた。主梁が構造的な役割を果たしているのが形態から読み取れる、古典的な三石塔はリッソーネの工場とブッソレンゴのフィアット販売代店で開発されたテーマだった。

ファチェプ社が製造した鉄筋コンクリートのプレハブ工法と、新しい可能性に満ちたプレストレスコンクリートによるプレハブ工法は、マンジャロッティの巧みで洗練された感性と相まって、これらの仕事場を重要で魅力的な場に変えた。特にエントランスには建築的、構造的、実践的な重要性がたくさんつまっている。エルマグ社の素晴らしい柱廊式玄関の特徴的な構造はマグナ・グラエキアの寺院を思い起こさせる。そしてブッソレンゴのフィ

useppe Pagano wrote in 1931 of the role that materials play in the definition of architecture: «Materials are the matter which the architect's imagination uses in order to think architecturally, and as such it has evident influences on the formal consequences. There are architectures that are designed in wood, granite or bricks, just as there exist architectures that are designed in iron or reinforced concrete. In the material there exists something that is not just the external appearance but a formal tendency potentially inherent in the chosen material».⁵ These words well describe the passion and love that Mangiarotti had for the study of materials, both new and traditional. He was fascinated by stone as by re-composed wood, by traditional concrete as by pre-stressed concrete, by marble as by steel, by conglomerates as by synthetic materials.

The second section, "Gravity," sums up Mangiarotti's purpose of combining the theme of prefabrication – which in Italy, for complex reasons, took the form primarily of "prefabrication in reinforced concrete"⁶ – with the compositional and architectural limits and potential of the trilithic system. «In the project, the analogy between past and present does not return, but its metaphor»,⁷ Mangiarotti reminds us. The scheme of the classic trilith consists of a few basic elements with simple, functional forms (pillar, beam, roofing segment) held together by gravity. It is interpreted using different ways and means, but above all on different scales, from the architectural to that of the furniture complement. Examples of this are on the one hand the four architectural works analysed (the Elmag factory in Lissone, the Lema factory at Alzate Brianza, the Feg entrance pavilion in Giussano and the Fiat dealership at Bussolengo) and on the other the "Incas", "Eccentrico" or "Eros" tables. The classic trilith, where the structural role played by the main beam is formally legible, is the theme developed in the Lissone factory and the Fiat dealership at Bussolengo.

The two prefabricated systems in reinforced concrete produced

– 8. For the difference between "open system" and "closed system", see the chapter *Sistemi chiusi e aperti* in E.D. Bona, *Angelo Mangiarotti, il processo del costruire*, Electa, Milano 1980, pp. 12-13.

アット代理店にある見事な片持梁は、単体では何の特徴もない一つの構造部材が、組み立ての過程で初めて意味を持つことを強調している。屋根から差し込む光を巧みに制御し、建物の中で交錯する光が部材を照らし出す。アルツァーテ・ブリアンツァのレマ社工場では三石塔式のプレハブ工法のテーマにさらなる意味を加えて具現化した。屋根の下面を一定に揃える空間を作ろうと研究し、構造ではなく、形態的な理由から屋根材と梁の形態を逆転した。屋根の厚みを揃えたことで、寸法の揃った屋根材と梁を設置するなど幾つかの利点が生まれた。この空間的、造形的な成果はイタリアのプレハブ工法建築の一つの頂点を確かに表している。

ジュッサーノにある、フェグ社エントランス棟はブリオナ72システムを用いて建てた、マンジャロッティの建築の研究で「オープンエンドシステム」と解釈した概念の頂点を示している。⁸ 一定の建設部材を組み合わせて自由に拡張できる多方向構造だ。正方形と長方形のグリッドのバリエーションがあり、従来の鉄筋コンクリートで作るシステムである。丸い柱や梁の窪み、ガラスの外皮が特徴的だ。洗練されたデザインによって、この名もなき小さな構造物は地域の宝石として位置づけられている。

3番目は「組み合わせ」だ。多数あるいは少数の構成部材からほぼ無限のバリエーションを生みだす建築の組み合わせ構法を網羅した。このテーマはマンジャロッティの作品全体に通じる。例えば次の例では特に建物の外皮と、部材の組み合わせが建築を形作る意味合いを強調した。ミラノ郊外のチニゼッロ・バルサモにあるアルミタリア社工業施設と、マイアーノにあるスナイデロ社工業施設、モンツァの住宅建築とアロジオの住宅建築である。二つの工業施設の最終的な形態からは、見る者を驚かせ

by Facep and the new possibilities of prestressing, together with Mangiarotti's masterly and refined sensibility, led to the definition of these workplaces possessing great charisma and significance. The entrance areas in particular concentrate many of their principal architectural, constructional and practical significances. The great portico at Elmag, in which the structure is emphasized as if to recall a temple in Magna Grecia, and the stunning cantilevered beam at Bussolengo, emphasize how a single structural component, in itself anonymous and inexpressive, becomes charged with meanings only in the process of assemblage. The emphasis on the elements is also created by the interplay of light and shade that are determined within the buildings by the expertly controlled overhead lighting. In the Lema factory at Alzate Brianza the theme of the trilith and prefabrication is embodied by adding a further implication. The research in this case sought to define spaces with a coplanar intrados, which leads to the reversal of the morphological relations, though obviously not the structural ones, between the roofing segment and the beam. The solution with the coplanar intrados has several advantages, including the possibility of integrating the installations in the roofing and of having infill elements all of the same size. The spatial and formal result achieved certainly represents one of the summits of Italian prefabricated architecture.

The Feg entrance pavilion in Giussano was built using the Briona 72 system, which represents the pinnacle of Mangiarotti's research into a conception of architecture understood as the "open-ended system."[8] It is a question of a pluridirectional structure capable of being expanded freely by repeating a constant structural module. The variants include both the square grid and the rectangular one, and the system is built out of traditional reinforced concrete. In this case, the refined design, characterized by curved lines that define the chamfers, roundings and shutters, make this small structure a jewel in a region characterized by the anonymity of its architecture.

ようとする意図が明確に見て取れる。前者は電車の世界、後者では他より高く抜きんでたオフィス棟が、意識的または無意識的にSFのイメージを喚起する。建物の外皮は張力が集中する場所である。アルミタリア社の外皮は施設を構成する部材を統合する役割を果たす。異なる基準を元に設計し建設した。正方形では二方向で定数値を示すが長方形では矛盾することを考慮し、マンジャロッティは施設内で標準のグリッドを用いず、正方形のグリッドの可能性と限界に取り組むことを決めた。しかしマイアーノではそれが逆転した。オフィスとショールームと幾つかの建物では意図的に設計と素材と意味が変えられている。スナイデロ社の複合施設は、材料と構造技術の研究、象徴と表現力の限界の追求という点で、マンジャロッティの作品の集大成である。モジュラーの構成が優れた多様性における不変性を表している。

二つの住宅建築では、組み合わせのテーマにさらなる意味合いが加わった。全体の構成はユニットの組み合わせから決まる。建築の役割という倫理的な概念を具体化して見せた。私たちのゴールや夢は、住人が「プロデューサー」と新たな関係を築いて、各自の住居ユニットの機能や形態や美的な特徴を決める機会を与えてもらい、積極的に設計の仕事に関わることだ。組み合わせ構成による建物では単純な間取りや家具のレイアウトが可能となる。それどころか、通常の要素に代えて、建築そのものを定義するという大志にたどり着く。

この研究ではミラノにあるアンジェロ・マンジャロッティ・アーカイブに保管されたスケッチと図面と写真を資料に用いた。鉛筆、クレヨン、マーカー、時には水彩絵の具を用いて素早くしっかりと手を動かして描いたスケッチは彼の継続的で目まぐるしい活動の証だ。[9] また、彼は建物や複合施設を設計する際に、工業製品に専心し

The third issue addressed is that of "Module". The theme of the modular coordination of architecture, comprising a greater or lesser number of components whose assembly gives rise to almost endless variations, is present throughout Mangiarotti's output. In the examples given, the emphasis is placed particularly on the envelope of the buildings and on the implications that its modularity has in relation to the definition of the architecture. The examples are two industrial complexes – Armitalia in Cinisello Balsamo, on the outskirts of Milan, and Snaidero at Majano – and two residential buildings, the first in Monza and the second at Arosio. In the two industrial complexes we can observe the explicit intention of arousing wonder through the final image of the architecture. The first recalls the world of trains and the second, in particular in the office block, which rises higher than the rest, consciously or unconsciously evokes the collective imagery of science fiction. The building's envelope is the place where the tensions are concentrated. In Armitalia its role is to unify the parts that make up the complex. These are designed and built with different criteria, since Mangiarotti decided not to use a standard grid within the complex and to deal with the potentials and limitations of the square grid compared to the rectangular one, considering that the constant values in the two directions of the former were contradicted by the latter. In the case of Majano, however, the opposite happened. The offices, the showroom and the service building are intentionally different in their designs, materials and meanings. This second complex is in some ways a culmination of Mangiarotti's work in terms of research into materials, construction techniques and research into their symbolic and expressive limits. Modular coordination represents a constant within the great diversity.

In the two residential buildings, the theme of the module is charged with an additional meaning. Here the modular coordination that governs the whole composition is embodied in an ethical conception of the role of architecture. The goal, or perhaps we

– 9. For a detailed discussion, see the essay by Kinue Horikawa in this volume.
– 10. Two sketches for the Exposition pavilion at the Fiera del Mare in Genoa come from the collection of Professor Alberto Sposito of Palermo, to whom we wish to express our gratitude.
– 11. It appears impossible at present to date the sketches of Angelo Mangiarotti as they bear no dates, but above all no written documents useful to this process of dating have been conserved within the archive. For these reasons it has been decided to indicate as the initial date the year given on the first drawings made by the office.

たのと同様に心を砕き、スケールや機能の大小や機能や素材にこだわらず、シンプルかつ基本的な形を追求する姿勢を貫いたことがわかっている。彼のスケッチや、彼とジョルジョ・カザーリや建設中または竣工時に撮った写真は知名度があり出版もされているが、前もって彼のオフィスで描かれた決定的な実施設計図は余り知られていない。[10] その大半はもっぱらトレーシングペーパー上に墨汁で描いた図面で、その順番から設計過程の異なる段階を詳述することが可能だ。これまでのマンジャロッティ関する文献は事務所から提供された重要な日付だけに絞ってまとめているので、最初の図面[11]から建物の竣工までの期間をじっくりと再構成した点が新しい。この時期の活動を特定すると、それぞれの作品は線形に改善の一途をたどらなかったことがわかった。ほとんどのプロジェクトは同時進行で、さまざまなニュアンスや意味を含んだ可能性をいろいろ研究しようとしていた。

私達は写真、図面、スケッチ、モデルといった間接的な情報源から得た情報を、直接の情報源である建築と比較してきた。何度も実施した現場検査[12]では、事務所に管理されることなく、制作の過程で他にバリエーションは作られなかったことが検証できた。数々の正確な詳細図がそれを裏付けている。実際に、各プロジェクトに関する様々なフォルダを調べて、たいてい20分の1の縮尺で、たまに5分の1から2分の1、時折1分の1の縮尺の図面を発見した。アーカイブには様々な資料が豊富に保管されているが、ここで紹介したのはその一部である。アーカイブ資料と実際の建築を比較する過程はまさしく新しく重要な研究の一段階だった。この研究はメンドリシオ建築アカデミーにおける4年生と5年生の授業とその理論を論文に執筆する様々な段階から成る。巨視的レベルでの調査と分析と観察は新たな考察への道を拓いたが、

could say the dream, is to define a new relation between the inhabitants and the "producer", in which the inhabitants should become active in the design work, being given the opportunity to define the functional, morphological and aesthetic features of their own home units. This possibility is offered by the building's modular coordination, which goes far beyond a simple layout of the plan or the furniture and that, while superseding the usual factors, has the ambition to reach to the definition of the architecture itself.

The sources used for this study are the sketches, drawings and photographs preserved at the Angelo Mangiarotti Archive in Milan. The sketches, made with a firm, rapid hand in various media with pencils, crayon, markers and sometimes watercolours, are evidence of his unflagging, fast-paced activity.[9] It is also clear that when designing a building, or an architectural complex, Mangiarotti devoted the same care and used the same approach that he devoted to the objects of industrial production, seeking restrained, elementary forms capable of transcending differences of scale, function and materials. While his sketches and photographs taken by Giorgio Casali or Mangiarotti himself during the phases of construction or of the completed building are well known and have been published, less well known are the preliminary, definitive and executive drawings produced by his office.[10] They are almost exclusively drawings in Indian ink on tracing paper, whose sequence is capable of recounting the different phases of the design process. A novelty compared to the literature on Angelo Mangiarotti, characterized by the time indication supplied by the office, which is reduced to a significant date, is the reconstruction of the period of time extending from the first drawing[11] to the completion of the building. The identification of this period of time has enabled us to understand that the works do not follow each other forming a linear sequence of improvements, but that in most cases the projects were carried out simultaneously, showing the intention of investigating the potential of various issues

– 12. We wish to express our gratitude to the owners of the works, who have always welcomed the students and ourselves enthusiastically. In particular, the Meroni family, the Snaidero family, and Renza Beinat.
– 13. See the essay by Francesca Albani in this volume.

1950年代から60年代にかけてイタリアで活動した複雑な人物の一人の作品に見られる矛盾と連続性に光を当てることを目的とした新たな大志も生まれた。時には時の試練に耐え、時には耐えられなかった、つまり解体された建築作品の偵察は第一歩に過ぎない。そしてこれは設計を通じ人類と資源への懸念を明らかにする、倫理的で敬意に満ちたアプローチの産物である。[13]

with different nuances and meanings.

The information derived from indirect sources – photographs, drawings, sketches and models – have been compared with the direct source, namely the architectural work itself. Site inspections,[12] conducted at different times, have made it possible to verify that in general no variants were ever made in the course of the work without being controlled by the office. This is borne out by the numerous drawings that define exactly how every detail was to be implemented. In fact, by consulting the various folders related to each project, it was discovered that there are always present drawings on a scale of 1:20 and often drawings on a scale of 1:5 to 1:2, and sometimes even of 1:1. The material preserved in the archives is rich and varied and only a small selection of it is presented here.

This process of comparison between the archival sources and the built architecture is certainly one of the new and significant phases of this work. It was carried out during different phases of the research, as well as during the teaching activities conducted with students at the Academy of Architecture in Mendrisio, both within courses for students in the fourth and fifth years and in their theoretical papers. The surveys, the analyses on the macroscopic level and the observations that were made paved the way to new considerations, but they also gave birth to the ambition that this study, which aims to highlight the contradictions and continuity in the work of one of the most complex Italian figures active in the fifties and sixties, will be just one step in a process aimed at reconnoitring those architectural works that have sometimes stood the test of time well, and sometimes not – some have even been demolished! – and which are the product of an ethical and respectful approach to design which reveals a concern for humanity and its resources.[13]

EXPERIMENTATION

1 スプリューゲン・ブロイ社倉庫およびオフィスビル
メストレ（ベネチア）
1961–1964

Splügen Bräu warehouse and office building
Mestre (Venezia), 1961–1964

2 海の見本市展示館
ジェノヴァ
1962–1963

Exposition pavilion at the Fiera del Mare
Genova, 1962–1963

1

Splügen Bräu warehouse and office building
Mestre (Venezia), 1961–1964

スプリューゲン・ブロイ社倉庫およびオフィスビル
メストレ（ベネチア）、1961–1964

倉庫と2階建てのオフィスとサービス部門で構成されている複合施設は、ヴェネツィアの潟へと続く運河沿いに建っている。マンジャロッティは三石塔式の可能性を研究し、ここで鉄筋コンクリート製の倉庫の重要性と新規性を実験した。アルド・ファヴィーニがこの大胆な試みのパートナーとして構造計算を担当した。この二人のいつもの挑戦的なコラボレーションから、1960年までのブルーノ・モラスッティと協働した作品に加え、1957年のバランザーテの教会や、1959–1960年のミラノのガヴィラーテ通りの集合住宅、クアドロンノ通り集合住宅など重要な作品が作られてきた。

この倉庫は、梁と屋根材を組み合わせ一体化した屋根ユニットを、現場で打設した先端の欠けた4本の円錐状の柱で支える構造である。単純化した水平方向の部材は耐荷重構造と屋根の両方の役割を果たし、ポストテンション技術とプレハブ部材による設計と共に、建設の進化を物語っている。この特徴的な構成は必ずしも機能とは結びついてはいないが、建設の論理と密接に結びついている。いずれ拡張する必要性が予測できたが、22m四方の二つのプレートを現場にてプレハブ工法で製作し、8本の梁をポストテンションの鋼線で一体化した。

まだ飲料の倉庫として用いられているが、維持管理の不足に加え、改修を無秩序に繰り返したせいで構造の劣化が進行している。

The complex consists of a storage facility and a two-story office and service building located on the bank of a canal leading to the lagoon of Venice. The interest and novelty of the experiment lie in the reinforced concrete structure of the warehouse, which is a variation on Angelo Mangia-rotti's research into the potential of the trilithic system. His companion in this adventure was Aldo Favini, who was responsible for the structural calculations. The (not always easy) collaboration between the two – which included Bruno Morassutti down to 1960 – had already produced some important works: in 1957 the Church of Mater Misericordiae at Baranzate and between 1959 and 1960 the Residential buildings on Via Gavirate and Via Quadronno in Milan.

The structure of the deposit consists of four truncated-conical columns cast *in situ*, supporting a single element that combines beam and roofing segment. The simplification of the horizontal elements, which act as both load-bearing structure and roof, together with the use of the technique of post-tensioning and the design of the prefabricated element, represent an advance in the search for a compositional vocabulary not necessarily linked to function, but that defines its characteristic features in close connection with the constructive logic. Although the project envisaged the possibility of future expansion, only two square plates measuring 22 m per side were built, each consisting of 8 beams, prefabricated and shaped on the construction site and held together by post-tensioning cables.

Still used as a deposit for beverages, the structure is in a state of advanced decay, not only because of the lack of maintenance but also because of a chaotic succession of alterations and additions.

4本の柱と単一構造の陸屋根　アンジェロ・マンジャロッティによるスケッチ
Four pillars and a roof deck form a single unit, sketch by Angelo Mangiarotti. (AAM, Milano).

幾つもユニットを並列して拡張した建物の検証　アンジェロ・マンジャロッティによるスケッチ
Potential for extending the complex by juxtaposing different units, sketch by Angelo Mangiarotti. (AAM, Milano).

EXPERIMENTATION 1 — Splügen Bräu warehouse and office building

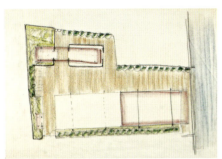
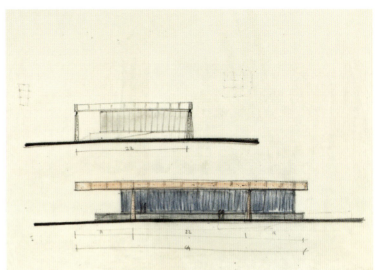

倉庫の正面図と断面図
アンジェロ・マンジャロッティによるスケッチ
Frontal views and section of the warehouse,
sketches by Angelo Mangiarotti.
(AAM, Milano).

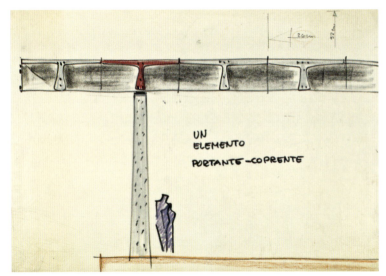

倉庫とオフィスの複合体の
スケッチ、平面図、模型、縮尺1:200
マンジャロッティ事務所、1961年9月8日
Sketch, plan and model of the complex, scale 1:200,
Studio Mangiarotti, 8 September 1961.
(AAM, Milano).

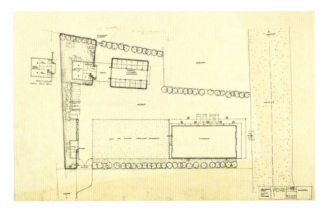

対向ページ
メストレのアンジェロ・マンジャロッティ
Opposite page:
Angelo Mangiarotti in Mestre.
(Giorgio Casali, AAM, Milano).

EXPERIMENTATION 1 | Splügen Bräu warehouse and office building

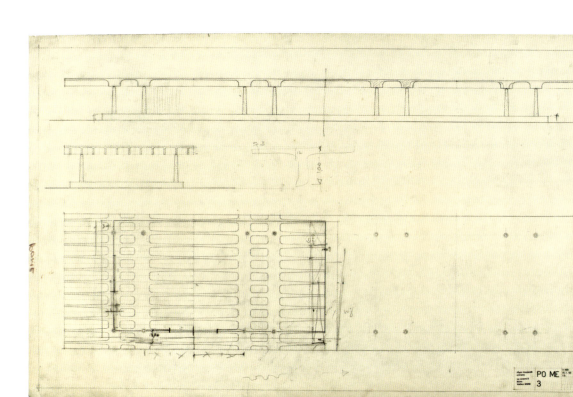

平面図と断面の構造図、縮尺1:100
1962年1月15日、マンジャロッティ事務所のR.B.による製図
Plan and sections of the structure, scale 1:100,
drawing by R.B., Studio Mangiarotti, 15 January 1962.
(AAM, Milano).

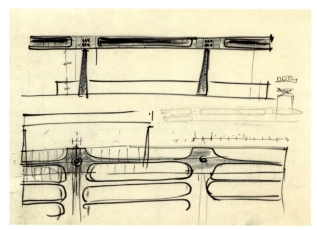

構造計画
アンジェロ・マンジャロッティによるスケッチ
Scheme of the structure,
sketch by Angelo Mangiarotti. (AAM, Milano).

対向ページ
Opposite page:

プレハブ工法の屋根構造の平面図と断面図、
縮尺1:50および1:10
スタジオ・ファヴィーニ、1962年2月25日
Plan and sections of the prefabricated roofing structure,
scale 1:50 and 1:10, Studio Favini, February 25, 1962.
(AAM, Milano).

屋根の平面図、断面図、立面図、詳細図
1962年3月3日、マンジャロッティ事務所のエンリコ・マッリ
による製図
Plan, sections, elevations and details of the roofing,
drawing by Enrico Malli, Studio Mangiarotti, 3 March 1962.
(AAM, Milano).

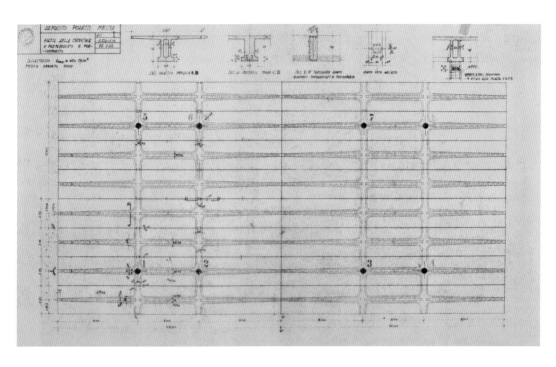
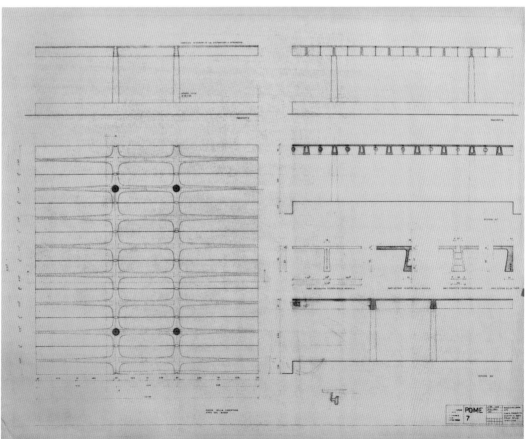

| EXPERIMENTATION | 1 | Splügen Bräu warehouse and office building | | 88 |

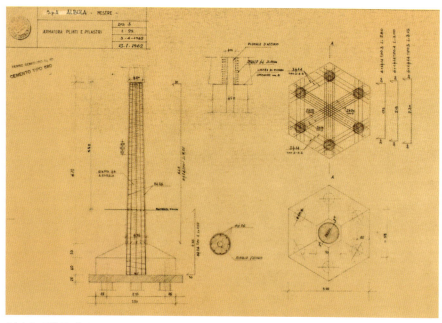

柱と台座の配筋図、縮尺1:25
スタジオ・アルド・ファヴィーニ、1962年4月3日、1962年7月13日に更新
Reinforcement of plinths and pillars, scale 1:25,
Studio Ing. Aldo Favini, 3 April 1962, updated on 13 July 1962. (AAM, Milano).

柱を設置した後の工事現場
View of the construction site
after completion of the pillars.
(AAM, Milano).

柱と屋根材の配筋の解析
Analysis of reinforcement of the pillar
and the roofing element.
(Enrico Venuda, Accademia di architettura, USI).

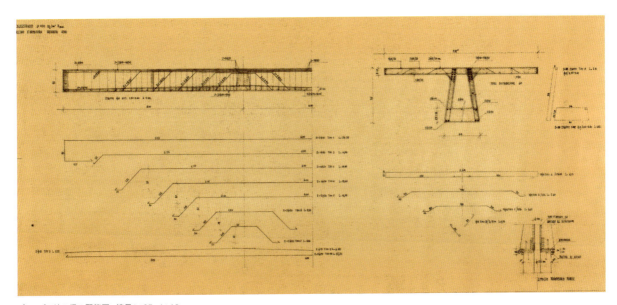

プレハブ工法の梁の配筋図、縮尺1:25、1:10
スタジオ・アルド・ファヴィーニ、1962年3月27日
Reinforcement of the prefabricated beam, scale 1:25
and 1:10, Studio Ing. Aldo Favini, 27 March 1962.
(AAM, Milano).

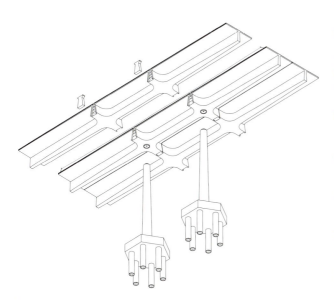

構造部材の分解図
Assembly of the elements of the structure.
(Riccardo Cola, Accademia di architettura, USI).

梁が一体化した屋根ユニット下面
View of the intrados of the roofing "deck".
(Giorgio Casali, AAM, Milano).

EXPERIMENTATION 1 — Splügen Bräu warehouse and office building

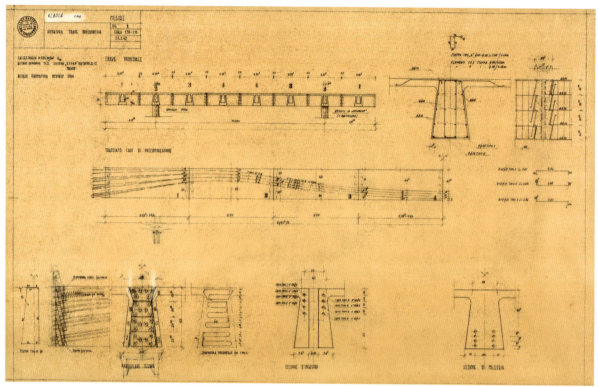

ポストテンションと梁の配筋図、縮尺1:50、1:10
スタジオ・アルド・ファヴィーニ、1962年3月27日
Reinforcement of the post-tensioned "beam", scale 1:50 and 1:10, Studio Ing. Aldo Favini, 27 March 1962. (AAM, Milano).

梁のポストテンションケーブル部分の詳細
Details of the head of the "beam" with post-tensioning cables. (AAM, Milano).

現場打ち鉄筋コンクリート造屋根ユニットの
施工状況
Stages of fabrication on-site of
a roofing element made of reinforced concrete.
(AAM, Milano).

コンクリートを打設前の梁・屋根ユニットの型枠と配筋
Formwork and reinforcing bars of the beam/roofing segment
before pouring the concrete. (AAM, Milano).

成形された梁・屋根ユニットの敷設
Laying of the shaped beam/roofing segment.
(Giorgio Casali, AAM, Milano).

屋根の建設段階とその詳細
Stages and details of construction of the roof.
(Giorgio Casali, AAM, Milano).

EXPERIMENTATION 1 | Splügen Bräu warehouse and office building

屋根ユニット敷設のため倉庫に足場を組む
The warehouse during construction
with the temporary structure for laying the roofing segments.
(Giorgio Casali, AAM, Milano).

倉庫のスケルトンを運河から望む
View from the canal of the warehouse structure. (Giorgio Casali, AAM, Milano).

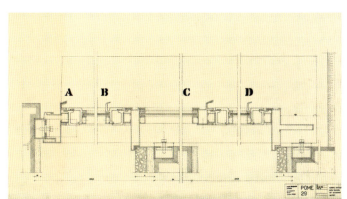

ファサードの開閉可能開口部の詳細、縮尺1：1
Enr.B.による製図、マンジャロッティ事務所、1962年12月19日
Details of the openable part of the façade, scale 1:1,
drawing by Enr. B., Studio Mangiarotti, 19 December 1962. (AAM, Milano).

倉庫　波形鉄板による外装
The warehouse with the corrugated iron sheathing.
(Giorgio Casali, AAM, Milano).

| EXPERIMENTATION | 1 | Splügen Bräu warehouse and office building | | 96 |

建物の増築と変更を青で示す
In blue the later additions and alterations to the complex.
(Alice Francesconi, Accademia di architettura, USI).

1964年の竣工直後と現在の比較
Image of the recently built warehouse in 1964 and present state.
(Giorgio Casali, AAM, Milano; Francesca Albani, 2014).

劣化の兆候が見られる屋根ユニットの下面
Intrados of the roofing with advanced signs of decay.
(Francesca Albani, 2014).

使用中の倉庫内部
Inside the warehouse still in use.
(Francesca Albani, 2014).

倉庫の床面積を拡張するため運河の上に張り出した片持ち張り
Overhang area on the canal enclosed to increase
the floor space of the warehouse. (Francesca Albani, 2014).

Exposition pavilion at the Fiera del Mare
Genova, 1962–1963

海の見本市展示館
ジェノヴァ、1962–1963

ジェノヴァの展示場の東側の海沿いに位置する展示館は、イタルシーデル社の依頼で「鋼から船まで」の製造過程を見せる目的で建てられた。見学者に示す展示構成は、その象徴性と重要性は異なるが、バランザーテの教会と良く似ている。見学者は片持ち梁の屋根に覆われた階段を下りて、鉱石の採掘過程を展示した地下階に入る。そして海の水平線が見える地上階へ上って、IRIグループ16社の活動を示した凹面状のガラスの6つ展示台の傍を通り、海の上に最終製品である船を眺めることができる。

曲線を描く屋根がこの建築の際立った特徴である。来場者の視線が海に向くように空間を切り開いた形は、マンジャロッティが精巧な建設技術を用いて追及した形態と象徴の表現の代表例である。曲線の屋根は「非推力」アーチの原理に基づいて建てられた。38本の鉄製アーチで構成し、鎖のカテナリー曲線が推力を打ち消す。厚さ2 mm、幅1 mの金属板で構成した各アーチを三角形の支柱で固定した。この解決方法から、屋根の下面は構造に不可欠だが、上面はただ屋根の役割を果たせばよいことがわかる。全体の構造はアーチが架かる縁梁と上に向かって細くなる4本の柱から成る。フィンシデール社の鉄骨構造技術部門のファブリツィオ・デ・ミランダが構造計算を行った。

倉庫として長年使用していたが、その価値を顧みることもなく、2000年に展示館の拡張のため取り壊された。

Located on the east side of the Fiera di Genova, on the seafront, the pavilion was commissioned by Italsider with the aim of representing the whole production cycle "From steel to ship." The layout of the exhibition presented to visitors is very similar – though naturally not in its symbolism and significance – to that of the Church at Baranzate. Through a scale partially sheltered by the cantilever, the visitors descend into an underground space with an exhibit displaying the processes of mining the ore. Then they come up from the underground level to the horizon of the sea, passing by the six large concave glass cases that illustrate the activities of sixteen companies in the IRI group, and so can watch the finished product, the ship.

The curvilinear roofing is the dominant feature of this architecture, not only because it opens up the space, forcing us to turn our gaze to the sea, but also because it represents in an exemplary way Mangiarotti's pursuit of formal and symbolic expression through the use of sophisticated construction techniques. The curvilinear roofing was built on the basis of the principle of the "non-thrusting" arch. It consists of 38 metal arches with the thrust eliminated by means of a chain with an obligatory outline. The latter consists of a sheet of metal 2 mm thick and 1 m wide, held in position by a series of triangular struts. This solution means that the lower surface of the pavilion becomes an integral part of the structure, while the upper surface only fulfils the function of a roof. The structure is completed by an edge beam, on which rest the arches, and four columns tapered as they rise. The structural calculations for the metal structure were made by Fabrizio de Miranda at the technical office of Finsider's metal-building division.

After being used for many years as a deposit, the pavilion was demolished in 2000 to make way for an extension to the fair, in ignorance of its value.

海の地平線、アンジェロ・マンジャロッティによるスケッチ
Horizon of the sea, sketch by Angelo Mangiarotti. (Collezione A. Sposito, Palermo).

「鋼から船へ」展示館のプロジェクト・モデルのサイドビュー
Side view of the exhibition pavilion "From Steel to the Ship", project model. (Giorgio Casali, AAM, Milano).

EXPERIMENTATION 2 | Exposition pavilion at the Fiera del Mare

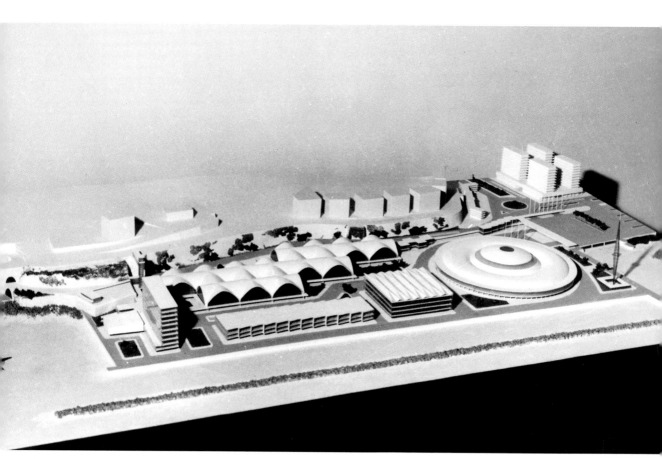

海の見本市展示館が作られる前の見本市会場模型
Fiera del Mare in Genoa before completion of the pavilion, model. (AAM, Milano).

展示館の模型を正面から見る
Front view of the pavilion, project model. (AAM, Milano).

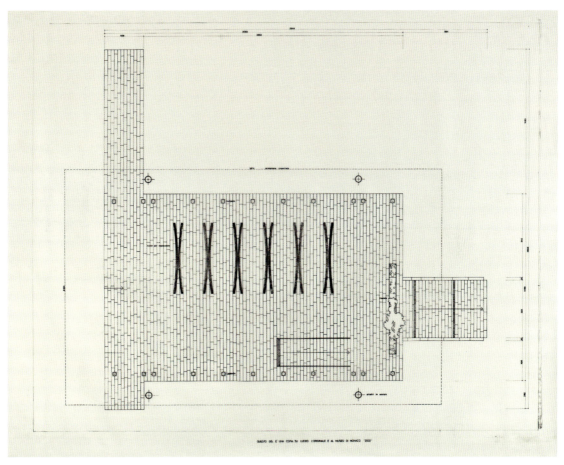

1階の平面図の写し、ミュンヘン工科大学建築博物館が原本を所蔵
Plan of the raised ground floor, copy of the original preserved in the Architecture Museum at the Technische Universität in Munich. (AAM, Milano).

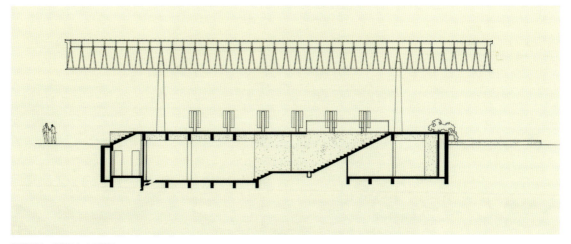

縦断面図　出版のための製図
Longitudinal section, drawing for publication. (AAM, Milano).

| EXPERIMENTATION | 2 | Exposition pavilion at the Fiera del Mare | | 102 |

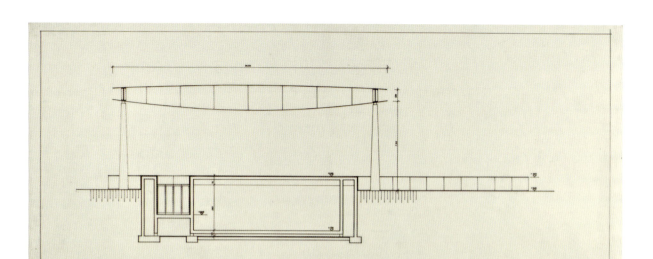

横断面図、縮尺1:50
Bobによる製図、マンジャロッティ事務所、1962年8月6日
Cross section, scale 1:50, drawing by Bob, Studio Mangiarotti, 6 August 1962. (AAM, Milano).

海からの眺め
アンジェロ・マンジャロッティによるスケッチ
View from the sea, sketch by Angelo Mangiarotti.
(Architecture Museum at the Technische Universität, Munich).

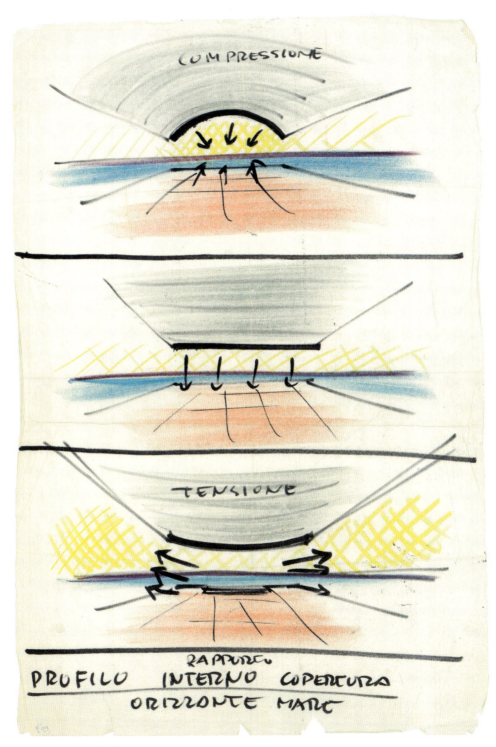

屋根の下面と海の水平線の関係のスタディ
アンジェロマンジャロッティによるスケッチ
Study of the relation between the intrados of the roofing
and the sea horizon, sketch by Angelo Mangiarotti. (Collezione A. Sposito, Palermo).

EXPERIMENTATION 2 | Exposition pavilion at the Fiera del Mare

建設中の展示館
View of the pavilion under construction. (AAM, Milano).

海の見本市展示館の入り口を望む昼景と夜景
View by day and by night from the entrance to the Fiera del Mare.
(Giorgio Casali, AAM, Milano).

| EXPERIMENTATION | 2 | Exposition pavilion at the Fiera del Mare | | 106 |

海と港
View of the sea and the port. (Giorgio Casali, AAM, Milano).

対向ページ 建設中の屋根の下面
Opposite page: Intrados of the roof during construction. (AAM, Milano).

EXPERIMENTATION 2 Exposition pavilion at the Fiera del Mare

側景
Side view. (Giorgio Casali, AAM, Milano).

夜間、屋根の下側で拡散する光と、展示台が発する光のコントラスト
At night light diffused by the intrados of the roofing contrasts
with direct light from the display cases. (Giorgio Casali, AAM, Milano).

地下空間から凹面の展示台が設置された地上階への展示ルート
The exhibition itinerary from underground space
to the ground level with the concave display cases.
(Giorgio Casali, AAM, Milano).

80年代には港の学校の倉庫として用いられた展示館
The pavilion used as a storage facility for the port school in the eighties. (AAM, Milano).

「非推力」アーチの鉄骨造
The metal structure of the "non-thrusting" arch. (AAM, Milano).

海の水平線
The horizon of the sea. (Giorgio Casali, AAM, Milano).

Column

EXPERIMENTATION

河合俊和　　　　　　　　　　　　　Kawai Toshikazu

その素材で何ができるのであろうか？　　## What will be completed with that material?

Casta

　加工技術やガラスの成分による違いによって世の中には様々なクリスタルガラスの表現が存在する。マンジャロッティにとってその表現は、表層の美しさだけではなく、素材特性の考察に基づいた三次元立体として造形の可能性を追求したものと言って過言ではない。それは建築の思考の延長線上にもあることは言うまでもない。プロダクトデザインは機能を無視して考えることはできない。例えばグラスの飲み口は円形でないと飲みにくいため用途によって適切な形が必要とされる。必要とされる機能性そしてその使い易さに眼を背けたものは、正しいデザインではなく、マンジャロッティにとって無意味な行為であると断言できる。

　初期の作品の多くは幾何学の形態操作による手法を用いている。幾何学形態の「位相」によって生まれる空間造形だ。円形から正方形へ、また円形から三角形への位相、三角形から三角形あるいは四角形から四角形への回転を伴う位相など様々な試

There are various expressions of crystal glass in the world according to the processing technology and the differences of components of the glass. For Mangiarotti, it was no exaggeration to say that the expression was to pursue not only the beauty on the surface but also the possibility of modeling a three-dimensional shape based on a consideration of material characteristics. Needless to say, it was also based on an extension of architectural thinking. The product design must not be completed without thinking of its function. For example, unless the rim of the glass is round, it is hard to drink from. The appropriate form is required depending on the use. It is not the right design that ignores the required functionality and ease of use, and it can be asserted that this is a meaningless act for Mangiarotti.

Many of his early glassworks used geometric manipulation measures. Forms were born from the topology of geometry. Various methods have been used for a series of works, such as circular to

Psikebana

Ergo

みが一連の仕事に用いられている。この幾何学の位相の過程で生まれる形態は自由であり、いかなる形にもクリスタルガラスは成形可能である。例えばグラスの飲み口から底に至るまでの形及び底の形は自由なのである。これがクリスタルガラスという素材の特性である。ここにマンジャロッティ固有の造形の考え方が色濃く反映されている。

　カスタ（Casta）はテーブルの中央で果実を置いたり花を置いたり様々なものの器として機能する。外円と内円の大きさの変化と中心のズレを利用することによって厚みが生じる。この厚みが重さになってデザインとしての傾きを生み、同時にクリスタルガラスの輝きの変化を生む。直径35cmという大きさに加えて厚みを持たせることは成形過程での難しさも同時に有することになり、ガラス職人の技術が重要となってくる。それ故に職人との綿密な対話によってこの作品は出来上がっている。

　シケバナ（Psikebana）は三角形の幾何学形態の位相を手法として用い用いた花器である。独特の形態の表現と共にバランスによって成り立っている。水を入れ花を生けることによってこのデザインは完結する。重力を意識したマンジャロッティ独自の哲学思考が読み取れる作品である。

　エルゴ（Ergo）は蝋燭立てである。手に持って移動できると言うアイデアによって、支柱の曲線が生まれてくる。クリスタルガラスの自由な造形を表現したもので、その曲線に素材の柔らかさと同時に力強さと安定感そして存在感を感じる。クリスタルガラスに映り込む蝋燭の炎の揺らぎは本当に美しい。複数並んだ立ち姿は独創的であり、エレガントである。

square, circular to triangular, triangular to triangular, or square to square with rotation. The various forms were created in the process of the topology, and crystal glass can be shaped into any form. For example, the shape of the rim of the glass can be different from the shape of the bottom. This is the characteristic of the material of crystal glass on which Mangiarotti's unique ideas on molding are strongly reflected.

"Casta" is a vessel that can contain fruits, flowers, and various things in the center of the table. The thickness was generated by utilizing the change in the size of the outer and inner circles and the displacement of the center. This thickness gives weight and produces inclination as design, at the same time causing a change of brilliance of crystal glass. In addition to achieving a size of 35 cm in diameter, giving thickness is difficult in the forming process, so the glass technique of the craftsman was important. Therefore, this work was completed via close dialogue with the craftsman.

"Psikebana" is a flower vase that uses the topology method of a triangle. It consists of balance with a unique form of expression. This design is completed by putting water and flowers in it. It is a work in which we can read Mangiarotti's gravity-conscious, unique, and philosophical thinking.

"Ergo" is a candleholder. A curved post was generated with the idea of carrying the work by hand. It expresses the free form of crystal glass. In the curve, we can feel the softness of the material as well as senses of stability and presence. The flickering of the candle flame reflected in the crystal glass is really beautiful. The series of candleholders standing in a row appear original and elegant.

Intermezzo

Onda

All photo provided by Fatto ad Arte

Stelo

　インターメッツォ（Intermezzo）とオンダ（Onda）とステロ（Stelo）は前述の作品とは考え方を異にするが、素材感の表現とその独特なフォルムと美しい線に魅了される。自然の中に存在する現象を取り込み、凹凸や切り込みが幾重にも重なって見え、クリスタルガラス独特の美しい輝きが表現されている。ここに記したクリスタルガラスはすべてファットアダルテ・エディション（Fatto ad Arte Editions）として発表されている。

　素材を知ることが形を導く。また素材が変われば形が変わる。方法論としての形態操作の過程は形式的な思考に陥りやすいが、マンジャロッティが結果として導き出した形は、人の手に触れるものは柔らかさを表現し、自然と共に在るものはそこに寄り添って存在している。そのデザインは、人を幸福にするために在る。

"Intermezzo", "Onda", and "Stelo" were created with a different idea from those of the above works but fascinated us with their material expressions, unique forms, and beautiful lines. They incorporate natural phenomena, show multiple layers of unevenness and incisions, and express a beautiful brilliance unique to crystal glass. All of the crystal glasses listed here are announced as Fatto ad Arte Editions.

Knowing the material leads to creating the form. Changing the material leads to forming a different shape. Although the process of morphological operation as methodology tends toward formal thinking, the forms that Mangiarotti created express softness of an object that people touch by hand and the presence of objects that are with nature. His design aims to make people happy.

GRAVITY

3 エルマグ社工場
リッソーネ（モンツァ・エ・ブリアンツァ）
1963–1966

Elmag factory
Lissone (Monza e Brianza), 1963–1966

4 レマ社工場
アルツァーテ・ブリアンツァ（コモ）
1969–1979

Lema factory
Alzate Brianza (Como), 1969–1979

5 フェグ社エントランス・パヴィリオン
ジュッサーノ（モンツァ・エ・ブリアンツァ）
1976–1979

Feg entrance pavilion
Giussano (Monza e Brianza), 1976–1979

6 フィアット代理店
ブッソレンゴ（ヴェローナ）
1976–1979

Fiat dealership
Bussolengo (Verona), 1976–1979

3

Elmag factory
Lissone (Monza e Brianza), 1963–1966

エルマグ社工場
リッソーネ(モンツァ・エ・ブリアンツァ)、1963–1966

　この工業施設はオフィス、展示室、生産施設から構成されている。ファチェプ社の構造システムに基づき、16×8mのグリッドに沿って設計された。一連のプレハブ工法システムの先駆けとなるファチェプ社のシステムにおいて、マンジャロッティは三石塔式を単に形態から選択したのではなく、建設方式に結びついた建築的表現としての可能性を研究した。

　三石塔式の古典的な要素である、むき出しの鉄筋コンクリートの柱部、梁部、屋根部をあらかじめ工場で作り、現地では簡単な支えで組み立てた。柱は上端に向かって細くなり、中間や外側など設置される場所ごとに異なる種類の補強材と組み合わさる。柱の柱頭はドリス式のような形を成し、梁を支える。この梁の長さは普通のトラックで輸送できるように14mに抑えられている。柱頭の上面はプレストレストコンクリート製の屋根材の幅と一致する。8mの長さの屋根材の上面は凹面状、下面は平で、中央にリブがあるのは剛性を高めるためだ。連結した屋根材に一定間隔で設けたポリエステルファイバー製の天窓は室内に直接光が差し込むのを防ぐ。この建築の主な特徴は、細身でありつつ荷重に耐える構造で、正面の柱廊式玄関と、側面の縦の隙間によって柱が金属製の壁から離れて立った特徴的な姿が、耐荷重構造と外皮が分離したコンセプトを際立たせている。

　現在、建物の所有権はエルマグ社から他に移り、内部に一通りの変更が加えられたが、基本的な特徴はまだ十分に維持されている。

The industrial complex comprises offices, exhibition rooms and production facilities. Designed as a grid measuring 16 x 8 m, it is based on the FM system produced by Facep, the first of a series of prefabricated systems in which Mangiarotti investigated the potential of trilithic systems not as a purely formal choice, but as an architectural expression bound up with the construction process.

The classic elements of the trilithic system (pillar, beam, roofing segment), in exposed reinforced concrete, were prefabricated in the factory and assembled *in situ* with simple supports. The pillar, whose shaft tapers as it rises, is given different kinds of reinforcement depending on whether it is intermediate or perimetric; at the summit it widens until it almost forms a capital, so creating a support for the beam. This device reduces the length of the pre-compressed beam to 14 m, so that it can be transported on trucks of normal size. The upper part of the capital also corresponds to the width of the prestressed concrete roofing segment: the latter, about 8 m long, has a concave extrados and flat intrados with a central rib to enhance its rigidity. A series of skylights in polyester fibre interrupts the sequence of roofing segments, so shedding overhead lighting in the rooms below. The main feature of this architecture is the slender but at the same time powerful load-bearing structure, emphasized in the main elevation by the front portico and at the sides by a series of vertical openings that visually divide the pillar from the metal infill panels, accentuating the conceptual separation between the load-bearing structure and the envelope.

Today the ownership of the building has changed and it has undergone a series of internal alterations, but it is still well preserved in its basic features.

柱、梁、および屋根材、ファチェプ社の三石塔式システムの模型
Pillar, beam and roofing segment
making up the FM trilithic system, model.
(Giorgio Casali, AAM, Milano).

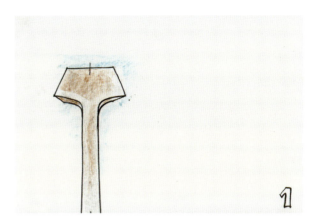

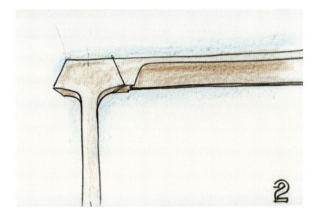

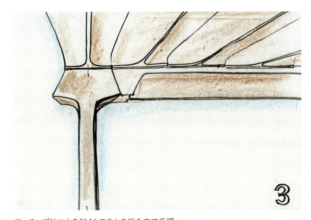

ファチェプ社によるFMシステムの組み立て手順
アンジェロ・マンジャロッティによるスケッチ
Assembly stages of the FM system produced by Facep,
sketches by Angelo Mangiarotti. (AAM, Milano).

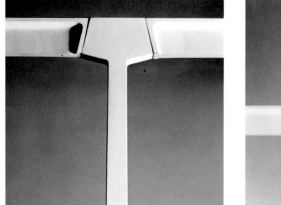
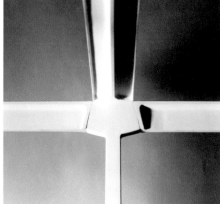

部材を組み立てる簡単な仕組みの模型
Elements of the system assembled in simple support, model.
(Giorgio Casali, AAM, Milano).

アンジェロ・マンジャロッティによるエルマグ社施設のスケッチ
View of the Elmag industrial complex, sketch by Angelo Mangiarotti. (AAM, Milano).

部材の組み立て
Assembly of the elements. (AAM, Milano).

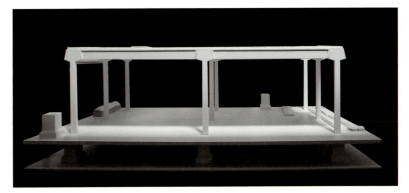

ファチェプ社のマンジャロッティ・システムの解析のスタディ・モデル
Analysis of the Facep Mangiarotti system, study model.
(Yizheng Chen, Matteo Frangi, Jacopo Irace, Jacopo Mandelli,
Tommaso Sartorio, Leonardo Vantini, Accademia di architettura, USI).

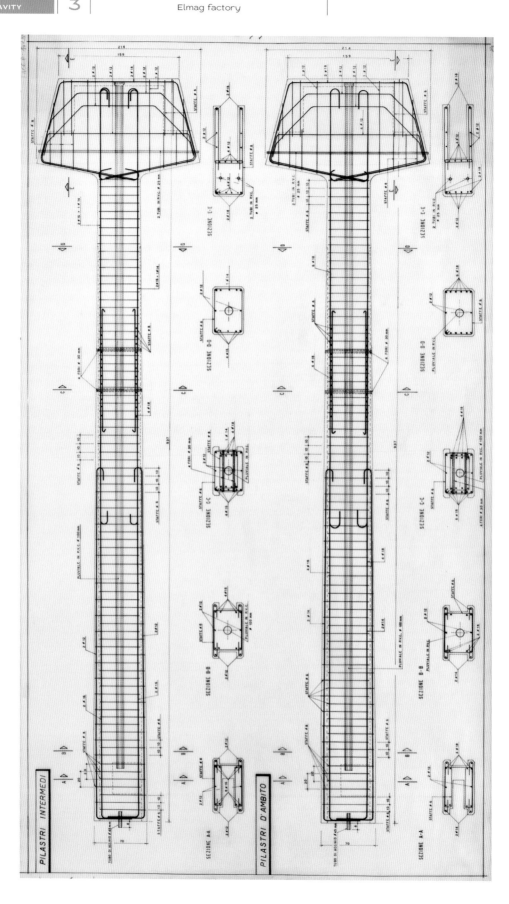

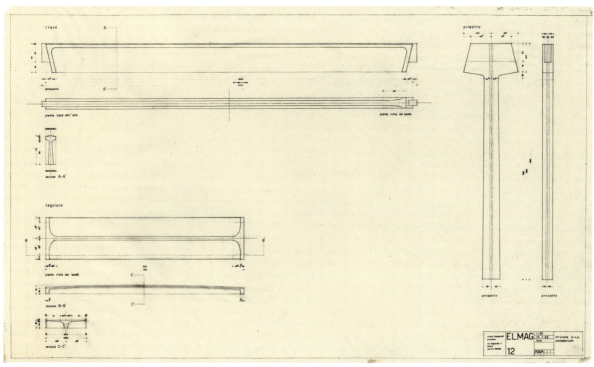

プレハブコンクリートの柱、梁および屋根ユニット、縮尺1：25
トーレによる製図、マンジャロッティ事務所、1963年7月15日
Pillar, beam and roofing segment in prefabricated concrete,
scale 1:25, drawing by Tore, Studio Mangiarotti, 15 July 1963. (AAM, Milano).

プレハブ柱の配置
Positioning the prefabricated pillar. (AAM, Milano).

対向ページ　外側の柱と中間の柱の配筋図
Opposite page: Reinforcement of the perimetric pillar and intermediate pillar.(AAM, Milano).

梁を取り付ける前の工事現場
View of the construction site before laying the beams. (AAM, Milano).

足場を使用せずにプレストレストビームを取り付ける
Laying of the prestressed beam without using scaffolding. (TFAM, Milano).

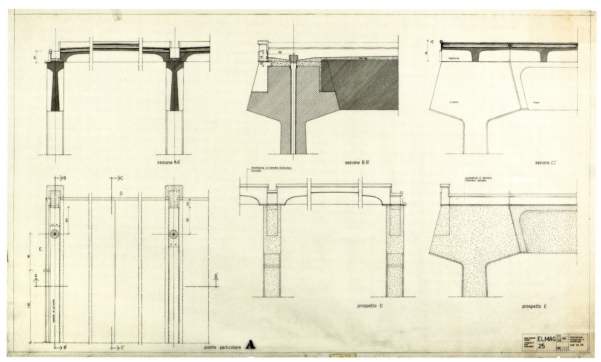

屋根の詳細、縮尺1:10、エンリコ・マッリによる製図、マンジャロッティ事務所
1964年3月11日
Details of the roofing, scale 1:10, drawing by Enrico Malli, Studio Mangiarotti,
11 March 1964. (AAM, Milano).

プレキャスト・プレストレスト屋根材の輸送と敷設
Transport and laying of a precast
prestressed roofing segment. (AAM, Milano).

対向ページ　柱材、梁材、屋根材の詳細
Opposite page: Detail of assembly of the pillar, beam and roofing segment. (AAM, Milano).

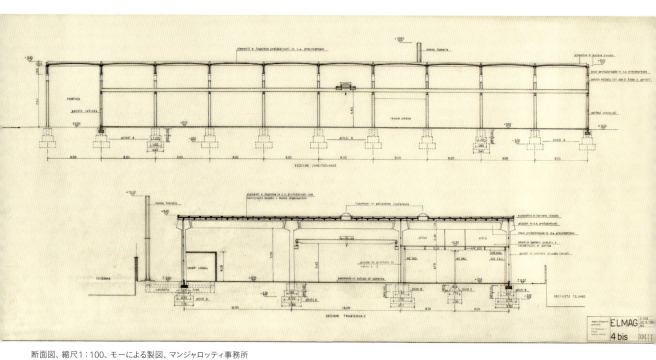

断面図、縮尺1:100、モーによる製図、マンジャロッティ事務所
1963年3月22日
Cross section, scale 1:100, drawing by Mo,
Studio Mangiarotti, 22 March 1963. (AAM, Milano).

側面
Side elevation. (AAM, Milano).

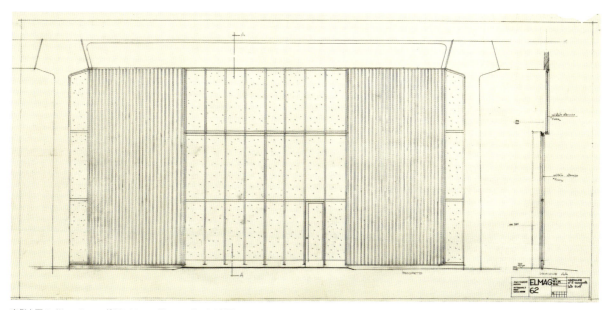

南側立面のバリエーション、縮尺1:20、エンリコ・マッリによる製図
マンジャロッティ事務所 1965年1月19日
Variant of the south elevation, scale 1:20, drawing by Enrico Malli,
Studio Mangiarotti, 19 January 1965. (AAM, Milano).

完成した建物の外観と内観
Exterior and interior view of the completed building. (Giorgio Casali, AAM, Milano).

正面立面
Main elevation. (AAM, Milano).

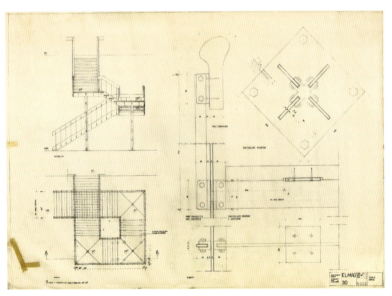

内部の金属製の階段、縮尺1:20および1:1
ペープによる製図、マンジャロッティ事務所　1964年6月23日
Internal metal staircase, scale 1:20 and 1:1, drawing
by Pep, Studio Mangiarotti, 23 June 1964. (AAM, Milano).

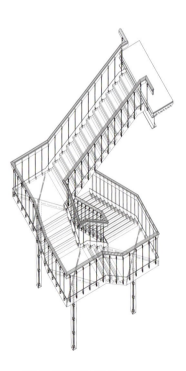

事務所に通じる階段の解析
Analysis of the staircase leading to the offices.
(Irene Giubbini, Accademia di architettura, USI).

入り口の柱廊の詳細
Detail of the entrance portico. (AAM, Milano).

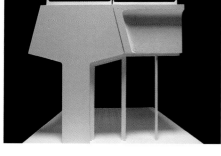

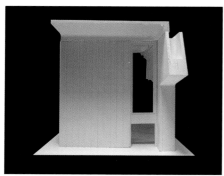

軸受構造と外皮の関係のスタディモデル
Relation between the bearing structure and envelope, study model.
(Yizheng Chen, Matteo Frangi, Jacopo Irace, Jacopo Mandelli,
Tommaso Sartorio, Leonardo Vantini, Accademia di architettura, USI).

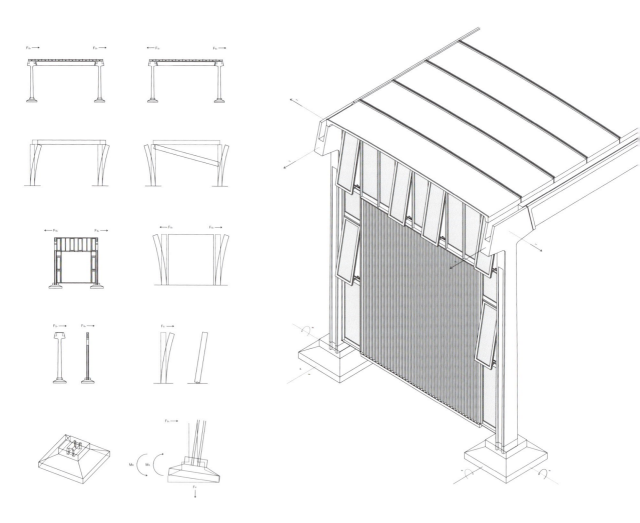

地震時の崩壊メカニズムの解析
Analysis of collapse mechanisms in case of earthquake.
(Paolo Marchiori, Accademia di architettura, USI;
We wish to thank prof. Mario Monotti and Stefano Miccoli).

現在の工場施設内部
Views of the complex today. (Francesca Albani, 2014).

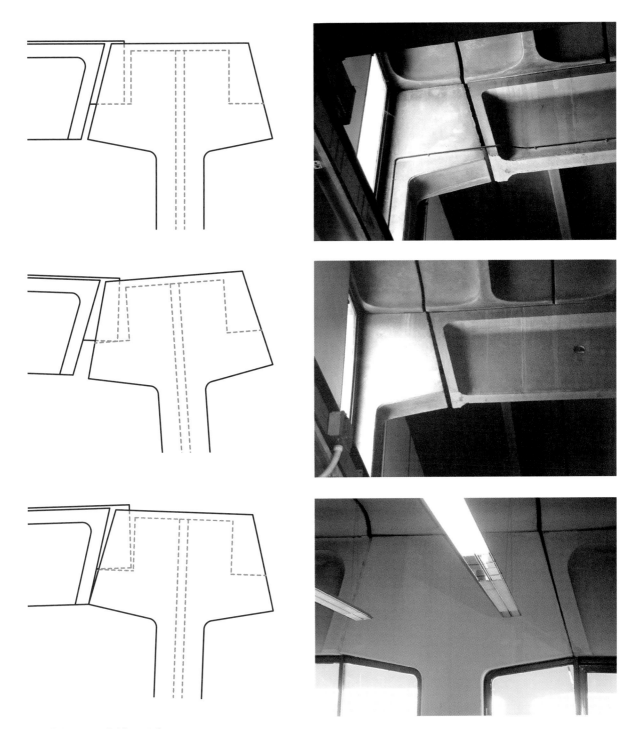

構造に見込む不安定性のスタディ
Study of the possible instability of the structure.
(Riccardo Paolin, Accademia di architettura, USI;
We wish to thank prof. Mario Monotti and Stefano Miccoli).

4

Lema factory
Alzate Brianza (Como), 1969–1979

レマ社工場
アルツァーテ・ブリアンツァ(コモ)、1969–1979

U70イゾチェルプレハブシステムを用いた工業施設では、サイロと煙突に加え特別室のある屋根の形態が特徴的で、一見に値する風景を作り出している。

マンジャロッティはプレキャストコンクリート部材を研究し、屋根の下部が平面的に連続した内部空間を作るという目的をU70イゾチェルシステムで体現した。梁の寸法と屋根材の関係を逆転して、構造の建設方法も入れ替えることにした。成型した屋根材よりも短い梁を台形の柱頭に架けた。柱の端部をU字型にして部材同士をしっかり結合させようとした初期の案は却下され、より単純なデザインに変わった。プレストレスト梁と屋根材の両方に凹んだ部分があり、簡単な支えで組み立てられる。設備の配線を接合部の間に収めた。梁と屋根材を同じ面に揃えることで、プレハブ工法で製作する4種の内装材および外装材は同じ長さになった。内部空間の基本的な特徴は、屋根材の間の天窓から差し込む光で、構造材の間に光の交錯が生まれた。

継続的な維持管理によって施設は良い保存状態にある。プラスチック製の小さな天窓と加熱室と塗装室の屋根材は、近頃、単純でありふれた形に取り換えられたが、この工業施設は間違いなくアルツァーテ・ブリアンツァ地区のランドマークである。

The industrial building built with the U70 Isocell prefabricated system, together with a number of elements with a strong formal character – a silo, chimney and the roofing of the special purpose rooms – gave rise to a complex with a marked landscape value.

In the course of Mangiarotti's research, the U70 Isocell system embodied his purpose of examining how precast concrete elements could be used to define interior spaces with a continuous and coplanar intrados. This intention determined a reversal of the constructional logic of the structure, with the inversion of the relation between the dimensions of the beam and the roofing segment. The beam, which is shorter than the shaped roofing segment, rests on top of the pillar, which is trapezoidal in form. An early version of the pillar envisioned a U-shaped termination so as to ensure better cohesion between the elements, but this was discarded in favour of a simpler design. The prestressed beam and the roofing segment both have a concave section and are assembled in simple support. The housings for the utilities are set between the joints. Thanks to the coplanarity of the beam and the roofing segment, the four typologies of infill elements of external and internal division, also prefabricated, are the same height. A fundamental characteristic of the interior space is the zenithal lighting shed through the skylights set in the roofing segments, resulting in an interplay of light between the elements of the structure.

Subjected to continuous maintenance, the complex is in a good state of preservation. The small skylights in plastic materials and the elements of the roofings of the heating and the paint rooms have been replaced recently with elements with the simplest and most obvious forms. The industrial complex is definitely a landmark in the Alzate Brianza area.

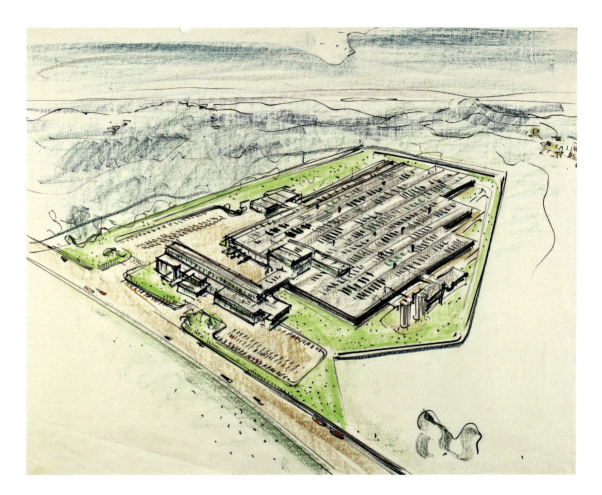

工場施設の俯瞰とメインのファサードを望む　アンジェロ・マンジャロッティによるスケッチ
View of the industrial complex and main elevation, sketches by Angelo Mangiarotti. (AAM, Milano).

GRAVITY 4 Lema factory

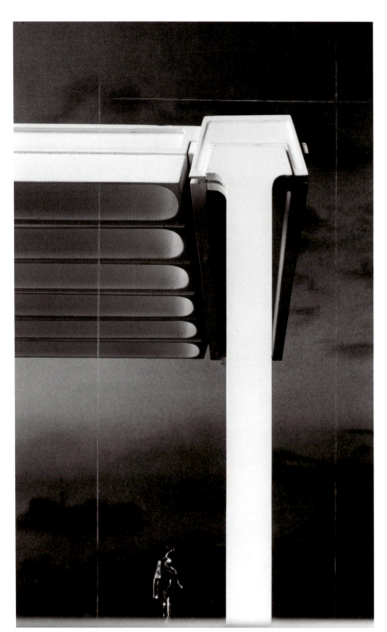

梁材と屋根材の下端が揃ったU70イゾチェルシステムの模型の詳細
Detail of the U70 Isocell system with coplanar beam and roofing segment, model.
(Giorgio Casali, AAM, Milano).

柱と梁の接合部を見上げる初期スタディ
アンジェロ・マンジャロッティによるスケッチ
Preliminary studies, view from below of the pillar-beam connection, sketch by Angelo Mangiarotti.
(AAM, Milano).

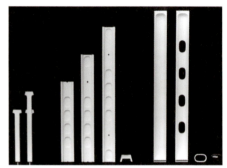

システムを構成するプレハブ部材の模型
Prefabricated elements that make up
the system, model. (Giorgio Casali, AAM, Milano).

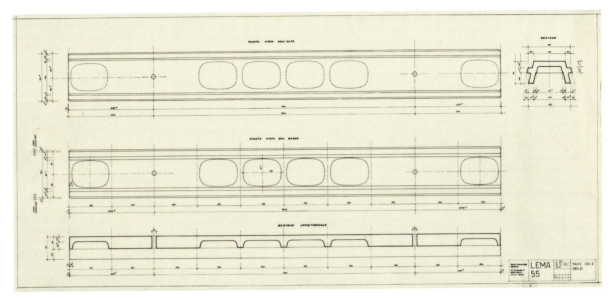

下面に凹みがあるプレハブ工法の梁、縮尺1:20
サグによる製図、マンジャロッティ事務所　1969年10月8日
Prefabricated beam with shaped intrados, scale 1:20,
drawing by Sag, Studio Mangiarotti, 8 October 1969. (AAM, Milano).

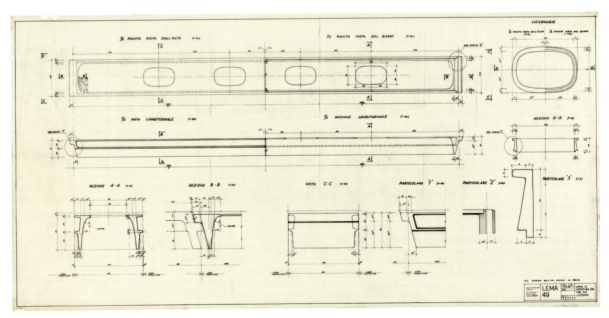

天窓の付いた屋根材、縮尺1:20、縮尺1:10
サグによる製図、マンジャロッティ事務所　1969年9月4日
Roofing segment with skylights, scale 1:20 and 1:10,
drawing by Sag, Studio Mangiarotti, 4 September 1969. (AAM, Milano).

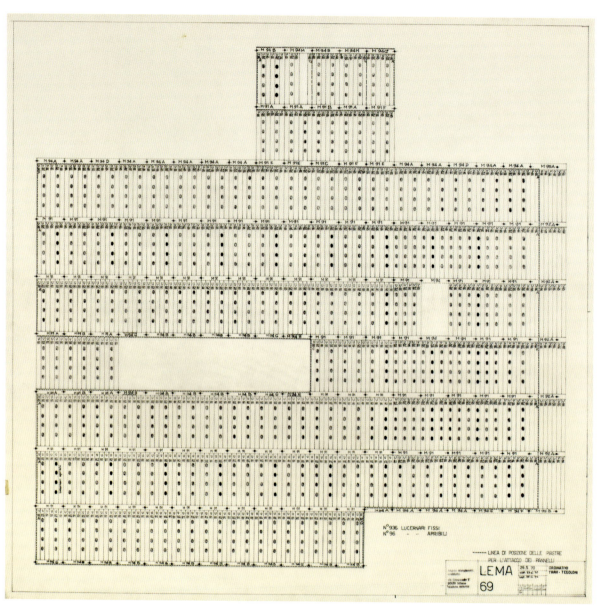

梁材の頂版と屋根材
マンジャロッティ事務所　1970年5月26日、他
Abacus of the beams and roofing segments,
Studio Mangiarotti, 26 May 1970 and later variants. (AAM, Milano).

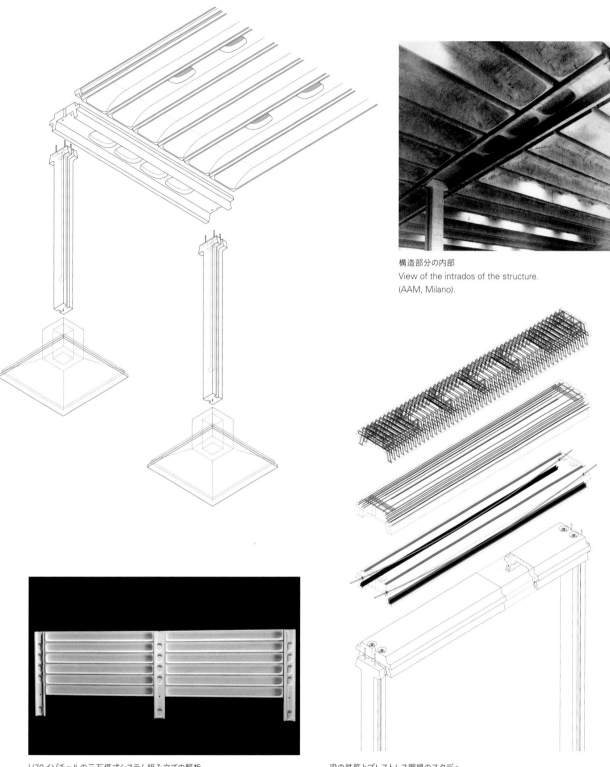

構造部分の内部
View of the intrados of the structure.
(AAM, Milano).

U70イゾチェルの三石塔式システム組み立ての解析
Analysis of assembly of the U70 Isocell trilithic system.
(Italo Edilberto Ortega Zumaran,
Accademia di architettura, USI).

梁の鉄筋とプレストレス鋼線のスタディ
Study of the reinforcing bars and the prestressing
cables of the beam. (Michael Svantner,
Accademia di architettura, USI;
We wish to thank prof. Mario Monotti.).

U字型柱頭が描かれた初期のU70イゾチェルシステム
アンジェロ・マンジャロッティによるスケッチ
First version of the U70 Isocell system with the pillar
showing a U-shaped head, sketch by Angelo Mangiarotti. (AAM, Milano).

柱の形状が決め手となった最終的なスタディモデル
Definitive solution with the spare forms of the pillar, study models.
(Luciana Cuciovan, Marija Urbaite, Gion Balthasar Von Albertini,
Accademia di architettura, USI).

プレストレストコンクリートのプレキャスト梁を支える
柱頭の詳細
Detail of the head of the pillar supporting
the precast beam in prestressed concrete.
(Giorgio Casali, AAM, Milano).

屋根材の製造と梁の敷設
Production of a roofing segment and laying of a beam. (Giorgio Casali, AAM, Milano).

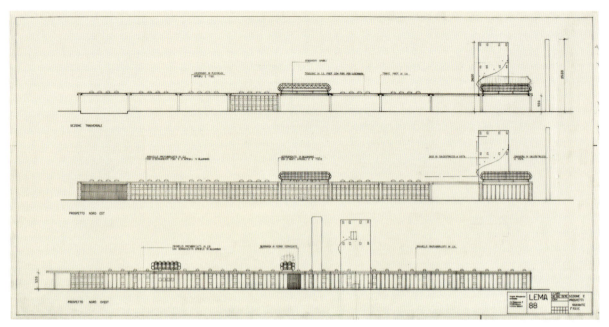

断面図と立面図、縮尺1：200
Camによる製図、マンジャロッティ事務所　1970年12月21日
Section and elevation, scale 1:200, drawing by Cam,
Studio Mangiarotti, 21 December 1970. (AAM, Milano).

工場施設と景観
View of the industrial complex and the landscape. (Rodolfo Facchini, AAM, Milano).

対向ページ　ファサードの詳細
Opposite page: Detail of the façade. (Rodolfo Facchini, AAM, Milano).

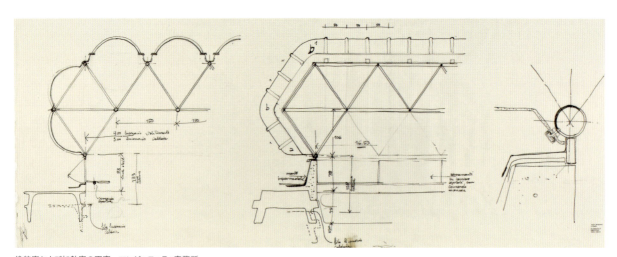

塗装室および加熱室の天窓　マンジャロッティ事務所
Skylights of the painting and heating room, Studio Mangiarotti. (AAM, Milano).

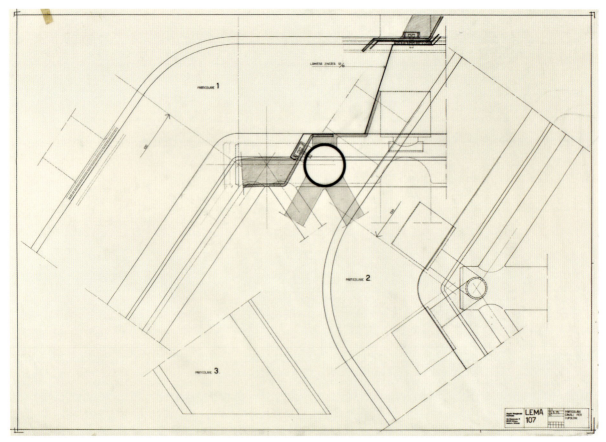

天窓の金属構造図、縮尺1：1
Tiによる製図、マンジャロッティ事務所　1971年5月11日
Metal structure of the skylights, scale 1:1,
drawing by Ti, Studio Mangiarotti, 11 May 1971. (AAM, Milano).

サイロと煙突と加熱室の屋根がある工業施設の眺め
View of the industrial complex with silo, chimney and roof of the heating room. (Rodolfo Facchini, AAM, Milano).

サイロの基部から望む
View from the bottom of the silo. (Rodolfo Facchini, AAM, Milano).

天窓のある屋根と加熱室の曲線状の部材
View of the roofing with skylights and curved element of the heating room. (Rodolfo Facchini, AAM, Milano).

プレハブ構造物の上部に現れたアルカリ骨材反応と付着物。現在、配筋は腐食していない
Mineral deposits and incrustations affecting the top of the prefabricated structure; to date there the reinforcing bars are not corroded. (Francesca Albani, 2014).

サイロの劣化図。青はアルカリ骨材反応、黄色は漏水、赤はコンクリート表面の剥離
Mapping of the decay of the silo: in blue the mineral deposit, in yellow trickling, in red the spalling of the concrete cover. (Roberto Roncoroni, Accademia di architettura, USI).

北西側の写真立面図
Photoplan of the northwest elevation. (Irene Giubbini, Pimpipat Hongdulaya, Elisa Segata, Accademia di architettura, USI)..

加熱室の屋根の下からの眺め
View from below of the roof of the heating room. (Francesca Albani, 2014).

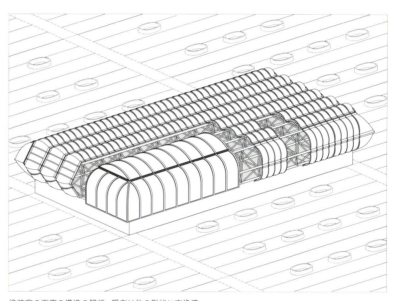

塗装室の天窓の構造の解析。現在は他の形状に交換済
Analysis of the three-dimensional elements of the skylight of the painting room, now replaced. (Leonardo Vinti, Accademia di architettura, USI).

Feg entrance pavilion
Giussano (Monza e Brianza), 1976–1979

フェグ社エントランス棟
ジュッサーノ(モンツァ・エ・ブリアンツァ)、1976–1979

フェグ社の管理人室と宿泊施設を備えたエントランス棟は、マンジャロッティの拡張式プレハブ工法の傑作である。圧縮応力を加えていない鉄筋コンクリートを三石塔式の部材に用いた。

1972年にサーチ社と共同で開発したブリオナ72システムは、シンプルな部材を少ない点数で構成している。精巧な正方形の柱頭がついた柱、梁、そして屋根材から成る。1.2m単位のグリッドを7.2mまで拡張した。基本的な構造パターンは4本の柱と露出した梁から出来ており、この幾何学的構造をどの方向にも繋げていくことができる。あらかじめ屋根材の長さや配置を変えた場合も想定してシステムを設計した。

エントランス棟全体の組み立ての構造計算をジュリオ・バリオ、ジョバンニ・コロンボ、アルベルト・ヴィンターニが担当した。ガラス面や不透明なはめ込みパネルを内側に設置し、支持構造物を強調している。これまでは梁の存在によって高さに変化が生じたが、屋根の下側が一定の高さを保つように設計し、構造内に照明を組み込む空間を確保した。コンクリートに圧縮応力を加えないと決めたため、単純な支えで組み立てる構造部材の重さが増したが、現場でのプレハブ工法の作業は簡単になった。このシステムは梁と屋根材の幾何学に合わせたプレハブ工法のファサードによって完成した。解決のカギとなったのは四方に連結できる角の収まりである。エントランス棟の保存状態は優れている。

Entrance pavilion to the Feg company, a caretaker's lodge with accommodation for the caretaker, is a masterful example of Mangiarotti's reflection open-ended prefabrication using trilithic elements in non-prestressed reinforced concrete.

The elements that make up the Briona 72 system, developed with the Sacie company in 1972, are few and simple: the column with a square capital of a refined design, the beam and the roofing segment. The metric coordination grid was equal to 1.20 m, giving rise to a grid of 7.20 x 7.20 m. The basic structural pattern consists of four pillars and perimetric beams with the same geometric characteristics, which determine the structure's multi-directionality. The system envisaged a series of variations in the length or arrangement of the roofing elements.

In the overall composition of the pavilion, designed to structural calculation by Giulio Ballio, Giovanni Colombo and Alberto Vintani, the emphasis was placed on the supporting structure by setting back the glazing or opaque perimetric infill panels. The structure was designed so that the intrados was set at a constant height, without the changes in grade usually associated with the presence of the beam, so making it possible to define a uniform spatiality with the lighting incorporated in the structure. The decision not to use prestressing for this system on the one hand determined an increase in the weight of the components, assembled by means of simple support, and on the other made it possible to simplify the operations of prefabrication *in situ*. The system was completed by the prefabricated façade elements that reflected the geometry of the beams and the roofing segment, which had a refined solution with an open angle at the point of connection of the two adjacent sides. The pavilion is in an excellent state of preservation.

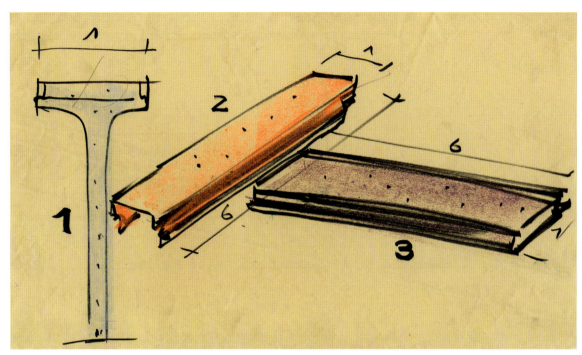

プレキャストシステムの打放しコンクリートの部材　アンジェロ・マンジャロッティによるスケッチ
Elements of the precast system in exposed concrete, sketch by Angelo Mangiarotti. (AAM, Milano).

ブリオナシステムの初期スタディ　アンジェロ・マンジャロッティによるスケッチ
Preliminary studies for the Briona system, sketch by Angelo Mangiarotti. (AAM, Milano).

正方形の柱頭で梁を支える模型の詳細
Detail of the support of the beams on the square capital
of the column, model. (Giorgio Casali, AAM, Milano).

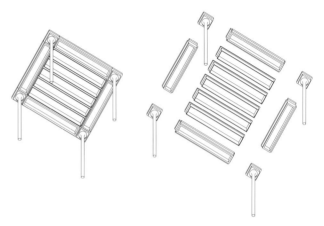

プレストレストコンクリート以外の部材の組み立てのスタディ
Study of the assembly of elements
in non-prestressed concrete.
(Joyce Victoria Rossi, Accademia di architettura, USI).

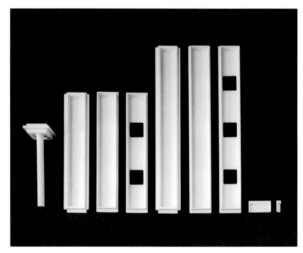

ブリオナ72システムの部材
Elements of the Briona 72 system.
(Giorgio Casali, AAM, Milano).

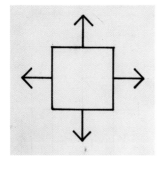

構造の多方向性を示す、正方形と長方形の平面の構造スキーム
Structural scheme with a square and rectangular plan,
showing the multi-directionality of the structure. (AAM, Milano).

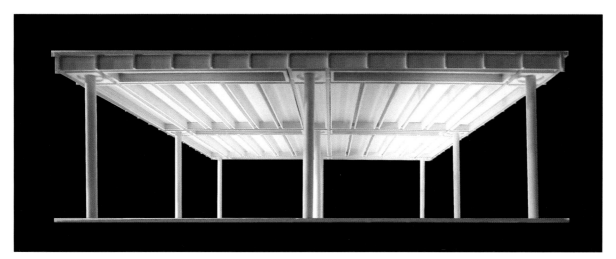

梁材と屋根材が同一平面上にある構造の下面の眺め、スタディモデル
View of the intrados of the structure with coplanar beams
and roofing segments, study model.
(Giulia Bastogi, Aminah Costantini, Nadia Kronauer,
Valentina Luvini, Alice Piazzoli, Accademia di architettura, USI).

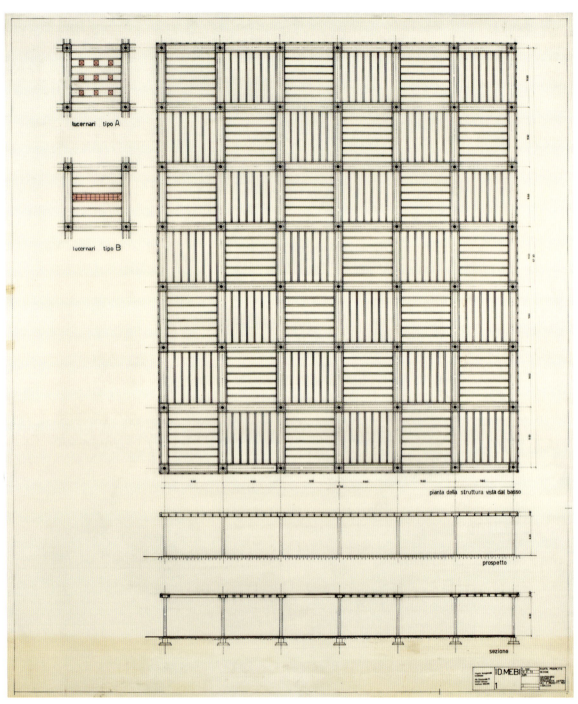

プリオナ72システムで建てた展示場の平面図、立面図、断面図
縮尺1:100、ユリによる製図、マンジャロッティ事務所　1973年2月12日
Plan, elevation and section of a pavilion built with the Briona 72 system,
scale 1:100, drawing by Yuri, Studio Mangiarotti, 12 February 1973, AAM, Milano.

プレハブシステムの端部と角の収まりの模型
Model of the corner solution with prefabricated curtains closing the system. (Giorgio Casali, AAM, Milano).

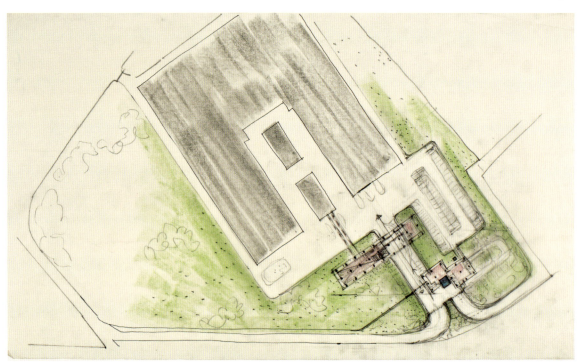

フェグ社の工業施設とエントランス棟　アンジェロ・マンジャロッティによるスケッチ
Feg industrial complex with entrance pavilions, sketch by Angelo Mangiarotti. (AAM, Milano).

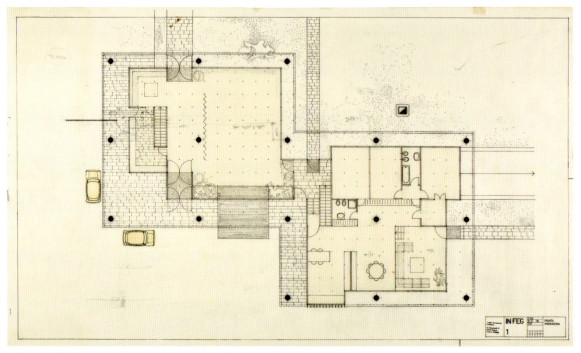

梁間二つ分をずらした管理人室の平面図、縮尺1:50、Chによる製図、マンジャロッティ事務所　1976年2月9日
Plan of the caretaker's lodge with staggered double span, scale 1:50, drawing by Ch, Studio Mangiarotti, 9 February 1976. (AAM, Milano).

足場を使用せずに梁を設置する
Laying of the beams without using scaffolding. (Giorgio Casali, AAM, Milano).

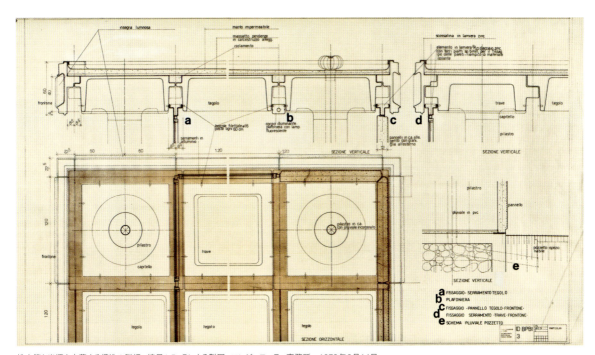

排水管と光源を内蔵する構造の詳細、縮尺1:5、Eによる製図、マンジャロッティ事務所 1973年2月14日
Details of the structure with built-in drainpipes and light sources, scale 1:5, drawing by E., Studio Mangiarotti, 14 February 1973. (AAM, Milano).

耐力構造に組み込まれた人工照明システム アンジェロ・マンジャロッティによるスケッチ
Artificial lighting system built into the load-bearing structure, sketch by Angelo Mangiarotti. (AAM, Milano).

対向ページ 組み立てた梁材と屋根材の下面と柱頭
Opposite page: Detail of the capital of the column and shaped intrados of the beams and roofing segments. (Giorgio Casali, AAM, Milano).

組み立てた部材の詳細
Detail of assembly of the elements. (Giorgio Casali, AAM, Milano).

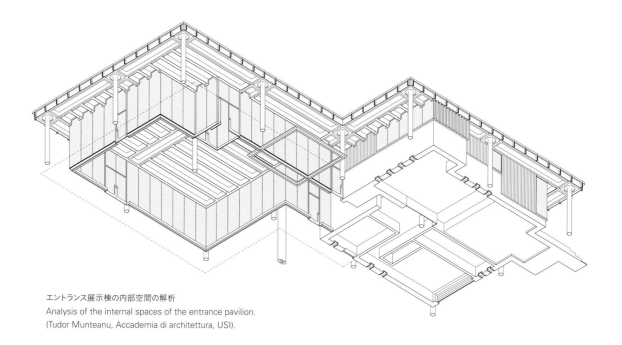

エントランス展示棟の内部空間の解析
Analysis of the internal spaces of the entrance pavilion.
(Tudor Munteanu, Accademia di architettura, USI).

エントランス棟外観。ガラス窓に囲まれた管理人室と高い土台に建った宿泊室
View of the entrance pavilion completed with the glazed envelope
of the caretaker's office and the accommodation envelope with the base in aggregate. (AAM, Milano).

定期的な維持管理によって完璧に保たれたエントランス棟
The entrance pavilion perfectly preserved
thanks to regular maintenance. (Francesca Albani, 2013).

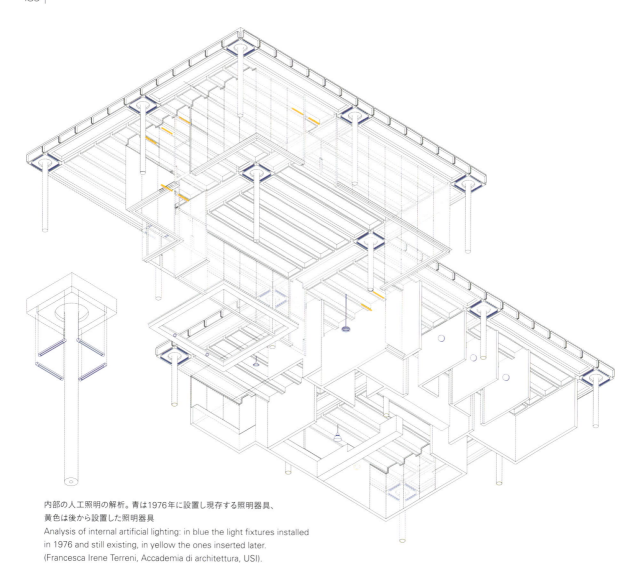

内部の人工照明の解析。青は1976年に設置し現存する照明器具、黄色は後から設置した照明器具
Analysis of internal artificial lighting: in blue the light fixtures installed in 1976 and still existing, in yellow the ones inserted later.
(Francesca Irene Terreni, Accademia di architettura, USI).

柱頭と梁の間の溝に照明器具はまだ設置されている
The light fixtures still preserved, set in the groove between the capital of the column and the beams.
(Francesca Albani, 2013).

Fiat dealership
Bussolengo (Verona), 1976–1979

フィアット代理店
ブッソレンゴ(ヴェローナ)、1976–1979

工場、展示場、オフィス、整備部門を備えたブッソレンゴのフィアットの建物は、多くの点で進化したファチェップ社の構造システムを用いて建てられた。

長方形の10.6×20mのグリッドで構成した三石塔式の鉄筋コンクリート構造がマンジャロッティの研究した梁と屋根の新しい関係を表している。梁を屋根裏のスラブの一定の厚さの中に納める方法を断念し、露出した梁から耐荷重構造がわかる。合成材料を塗布した木製型枠で鋳造したH字型断面の柱が屋根を支える。細くなった柱の上端がくさびとなって屋根材が滑り落ちるのを防ぐ。この建設方式を特徴づける梁の形状は構造の論理に基いており、多くのスケッチが粘り強く研究したことを示している。梁の逆Y字形の形状は分岐したフランジでPC鋼材を収容するために作られた。ひときわ寸法の長い2本の梁を用いて、柱廊式玄関の上に劇的に突き出す特徴的な屋根を作り出した。

非常に薄い屋根材(厚さわずか3.5cm)を、わずかに上部が凹んだ部材に留めて金属型枠で固定した。明かり取りの空間と屋根材を交互に並べて設備ダクトを配置した。この複合施設の基本テーマである上からの自然光が、建物の内部に光と影の交錯を作り出す。

ここ数年はメルセデスの販売店として使われている。建物はかなり良い状態にあるが、オーナーの交代にともない改修が進めば、単なる倉庫と化して構造はおそらく埋もれてしまうだろう。

The Fiat complex in Bussolengo includes a workshop, an exhibition space, offices and services and was built using a system that was, in many respects, an evolution of the Facep system.

The trilithic structure in reinforced concrete, organized as a rectangular grid measuring 10.60 x 20 m, represents a new relation between the beam and the roofing segment in Mangiarotti's research. The beam retains the legibility of the load-bearing structure, since he had abandoned the idea of the beam set in the thickness of the slab with a constant intrados. It is supported by an H-shaped pillar cast in wooden formwork and faced with a synthetic material, which tapers upwards and terminates in a pin that prevents it from overturning. The form of the beam – sought tenaciously, as the numerous sketches reveal – is the element that characterizes the construction system, with its reasons based on constructional logics. Its inverted Y section is determined by the fact that in the flanges which diverge are housed the prestressing tendons. Using two beams with larger dimensions than the others created the dramatic overhang that characterizes the portico of the entrance area.

The particularly slender roofing segments (only 3.5 cm thick) and slightly concave at the top, stiffened by four ribs and cast in metal formwork, were positioned so that they alternated with the skylights and the ducts for housing the utilities. A fundamental architectural theme was natural zenithal light, which produces a sophisticated interplay of light and shade within the complex.

The building, used as a Mercedes dealership for many years, is in a fairly good condition, although the recent changes in ownership will lead to alterations and modifications that will probably be aimed at concealing the facility by turning it into a simple container.

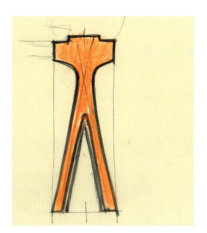

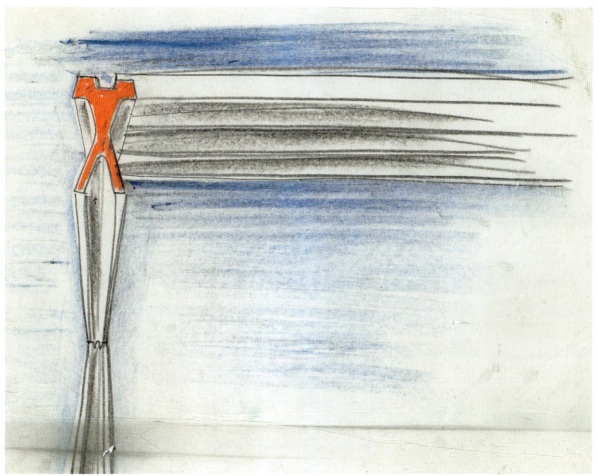

梁の先端形状の習作
アンジェロ・マンジャロッティによるスケッチ
Studies for the form of the head of the beam, sketches by Angelo Mangiarotti.
(AAM, Milano).

上からの自然光による内部の光と影のスタディ、試験装置
Study of internal lights and shadows cast
by natural zenithal illumination, project model.
(Giorgio Casali, AAM, Milano).

プレハブ工法による三石塔システムの正面図、試験装置
Front view of the prefabricated trilithic system, project model.
(Giorgio Casali, AAM, Milano).

構造の下部の透視図、マンジャロッティ事務所
Perspective sketch of the intrados of the structure, Studio Mangiarotti. (AAM, Milano).

非常に薄いプレストレストコンクリート製の屋根の組み立て部分詳細、4本のリブで固定
Detail of the assembly of the very thin prestressed concrete
roofing segment stiffened by four ribs, project model. (Giorgio Casali, AAM, Milano).

Fiat dealership

入り口から望むフィアット代理店　アンジェロ・マンジャロッティによるスケッチ
Entrance to the Fiat dealership, sketch by Angelo Mangiarotti.
(AAM, Milano).

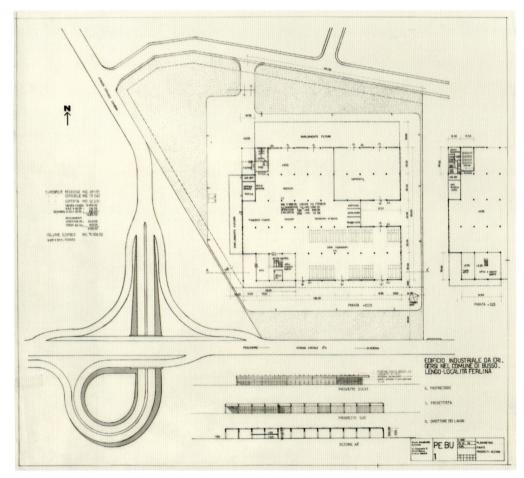

平面図、立面図、断面図、縮尺1：500　ユリによる製図、マンジャロッティ事務所　1976年10月15日
Floor plan, elevations and section, scale 1:500,
drawing by Yuri, Studio Mangiarotti, 15 October 1976. (AAM, Milano).

入口の屋根が突き出た側面観
Side view of the entrance with overhung beams. (Giorgio Casali, AAM, Milano).

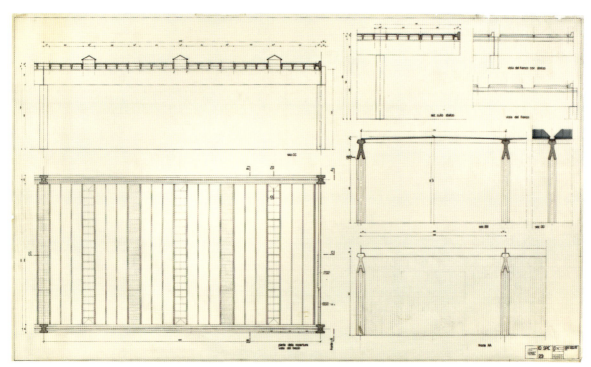

屋根の見上げ図、立面図、断面図、
縮尺1:25、MFによる製図、マンジャロッティ事務所　1978年2月16日
Plan of the roofing seen from below, elevation and sections,
scale 1:25, drawing by MF, Studio Mangiarotti, 16 February 1978.
(AAM, Milano).

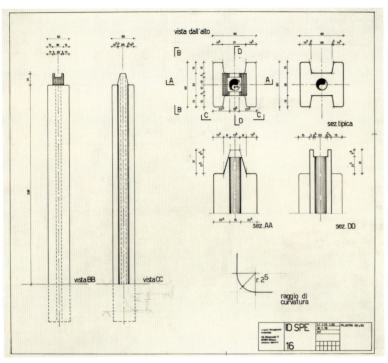

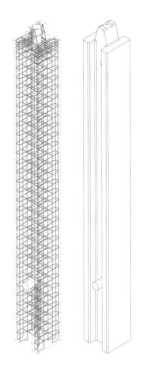

プレハブ鉄筋コンクリートの露出した柱
MFによる製図、マンジャロッティ事務所　1978年1月30日
Pillar in exposed prefabricated reinforced concrete,
drawing by MF, Studio Mangiarotti, 30 January 1978. (AAM, Milano).

H字型柱の内部の排水管と傾斜を防ぐ端部のスタディ
Study of the H-shaped pillar, inner drainpipe
and terminal element that prevents tipping.
(Francesca Peruzzi, Accademia di architettura, USI).

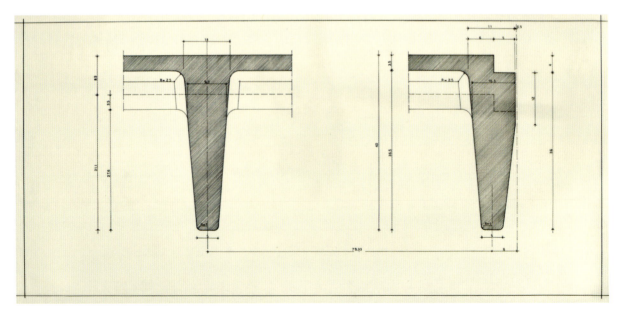

屋根の部材に固定するリブの詳細図　縮尺1:1、マンジャロッティ事務所
Detail of a stiffening rib in the roofing segment,
scale 1:1, studio Mangiarotti. (AAM, Milano).

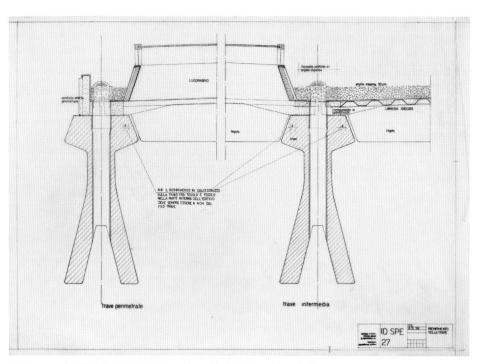

屋根のコーナーと中間梁の詳細図　縮尺1:5、マンジャロッティ事務所　1978年11月8日
Details of the roofing for the corner and intermediate beams, scale 1:5, Studio Mangiarotti, 8 November 1978. (AAM, Milano).

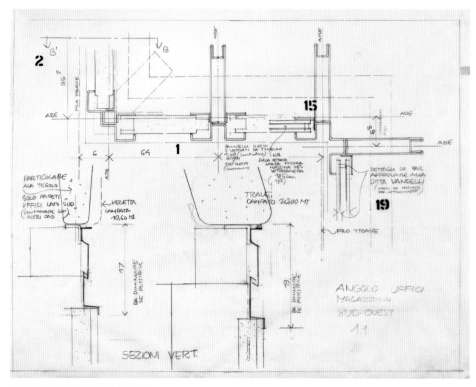

オフィスと倉庫の南西の角の外皮詳細図
Details of the envelope of the south-west corner of the offices and warehouse. (AAM, Milano).

突き出た屋根とガラス面が見える柱廊式入り口の外観
Views of the entrance portico with overhung beams and glazed elevations.
(Giorgio Casali, AAM, Milano).

建物側面の遠景
View of rear and side façades. (Giorgio Casali, AAM, Milano).

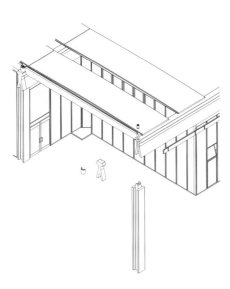

施設の北西の角の分解図
Analysis of the north-west corner of the complex.
(Francesco Lingeri, Accademia di architettura, USI).

フィアット代理店内部
Interior of the Fiat dealership. (Giorgio Casali, AAM, Milano).

施設の西側の写真立面図
Photoplan of the west elevation of the complex.
(Celine Bianchi, Beatrice Carolina Muzi,
Andrea Schiavio, Accademia di architettura, USI).

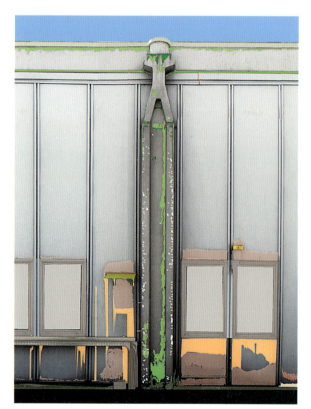

劣化した柱の分析。緑色に苔など付着物、白にコンクリート表面の剥離、
オレンジ色にアルカリ性骨材反応を示す。
Analysis of deterioration of a pillar: in green biological growth,
in white spalling of the concrete cover, in orange mineral deposits.
(Lucrezia Rapillo Victoria, Accademia di architettura, USI).

定期修理を施した鉄筋コンクリート構造
Regular maintenance of the reinforced concrete structures.
(Francesca Albani, 2014).

近年の改修でガラスが新たに加えられ構造が隠れている
Operations carried out recently include replacement
of the glazing and concealment of the structure.
(Francesca Albani, 2014).

Column

諸角 敬　　　　　　　　　　　　　　　Morozumi Kei

重さがデザインになる

Weight is the design

Eros, Photo provided by Agapecasa

　エロス（Eros）シリーズのテーブル（1971）は学生時代から雑誌でよく見かけていたので、その官能的なジョイントや曲線とネーミングに心惹かれていた。
　その後イタリア、ミラノでマンジャロッティ事務所に入ることになるとは思ってもいなかった。ある日、図面を描いているとアルキテットが片手にアゾロ（Asolo, 1981）の写真を持って話しかけてきた。
　「このテーブルをどう思う？」
　私の勉強不足で、発表から2年経っていたそのテーブルを目にするのは初めてであった。両者とも天板と脚が全て石製で天板にあいた穴に脚が差し込まれており、同じ考え方で作られたテーブルだ。エロスの女性的な重厚感のある曲線のデザインとは対照的に、アゾロは直線を強調し、天板や脚板も薄くシャープで、「私はこの軽やかなデザインが好きだ」と答えたと思う。その時アルキテットは言った。
　「この石だからできるデザインだ。重さがデザインの重要な要素になっている」
　正直、この一言ではよく理解できなかった。
　「この石の重さがあるからテーブルが安定する。木ではこの形状は作れないだろう」
　確かに木のような軽い素材では安定感が損なわれ、何か複雑な機構を足さないと同じ形状は成立しないだろう。さらに
　「エロスは大理石製、このアゾロは御影石。石の強度と硬さが違うから自ずからデザインも変わってくるのだよ」と、石がどのような形になりたいのか語っているようだった。
　アルキテットは、ほかにインカス（Incas, 1978）というシリーズも作っている。イタリアで石畳や外壁などによく使われるグレーの砂岩系の石が使われている。屋外で使用することを前提に素材と表面仕上げが選ばれている。エロスのような艶っぽさはなく、アゾロのようなシャープさもなく、まさにセレーナ石が望んだ形状に全体のフォルムとジョイント部のデザインが落ち着いている。

When I was a student, I often happened upon the "Eros" table series (1971) on magazines and was attracted to their sensual joints, curves, and names. I had never imagined that later, I would join Studio Mangiarotti in Milan, Italy. One day, while I was drawing, the architetto (Mangiarotti) approached me with a photo of "Asolo" (1981) in his hand.
«What do you think of this table?»
It was first time I had seen that table, though two years have passed after its release. Both tables are made of stone table tops and legs. The legs are inserted into holes in the table tops. In contrast to the feminine, curvy, and massive design of "Eros," "Asolo" emphasises straight lines, and the table top and legs are thin and sharp.
I think I replied, «I like this light design».
The architetto said, 'This stone allowed this design. Weight is an important element of design.'
Honestly, I could not understand this.

Asolo, Photo taken by Kei Morozumi

Incas, Photo provided by Agapecasa

He continued, «The weight of this stone stabilises the table. This shape can't be realised with wood».

Certainly, light materials such as wood achieve neither stability nor certain shapes without the addition of some complex mechanisms. Further, the architetto spoke as if he had known the shape that the stones wanted to form.

«"Eros" is made of marble, and "Asolo" is made of granite. The differences in strength and hardness spontaneously produce different designs».

The architetto also produced a table series named "Incas" (1978), made of grey sandstone, which is often used in Italy for pavement and exterior walls. The material and surface finish are chosen for outdoor settings. It has neither a glossy surface like "Eros" nor sharpness like "Asolo". The entire form and the design of the joints are settled into the shape, as if wished by the Serena sandstone.

天板に穴を開けてその穴に脚を差し込みテーブルにする

　3つのテーブルで天板に開けられた穴の大きさ、形状、ジョイントの方法が各々違った回答になっているのは、気まぐれで変えられているはずもなく、各々の素材の持つ性質を忠実にデザインに反映した結果だ。素材の持つ重さ、強さ、硬さでデザインが決まる。またその素材を知り尽くさなくてはマンジャロッティが考える本当のデザインにならないのである。

　柔らかい大理石でできたエロスでは円錐状の脚と天板の穴の内周が接触して天板を支えている。御影石で作られたアゾロでは台形状の脚と、天板の長穴の両端の半円部分だけがぶつかり天板を支えており、強靭な素材でないとできないジョイントの方法がとられている。インカスでは台形の脚の厚みの長辺2辺が天板を支えている。

　重さで安定させる方法として私が建築で最初に思いつくのはアーチの中央にはめ込まれたキーストーンであるが、生まれた時からイタリアの街中で日常的にキーストーンを見ている彼らには「重さで安定させるデザイン」は自然と湧き出る発想なのかもしれない。

　マンジャロッティの初期のプレハブシステムのデザインでも重さが重要なファクターとなっている。建築、家具というジャンルを超えた発想の展開が、より総合的なデザインの質と深さを作り出している。建築家は建築を設計し、デザイナーはプロダクトを作り出す役割を分担する「木と紙の建築文化」の中で育った私たちにとっては、発想の原点と広がりが違うことを思い知らされた。

　2009年よりアガペカーザ（agapecasa）によってマンジャロッティデザイン家具の殆どが復興されている。

Make holes in the table top
and insert legs into theholes to make a table

Among the three tables, the sizes and shapes of the table top holes as well as the joint methods differ because these were designed not from caprice but as a result of faithfully reflecting the nature of each material. The design of each table is determined by the weight, strength, and hardness of the material. Without sufficient knowledge of the materials, it can't be a real design of Mangiarotti's.

"Eros" is made of soft marble. The conical legs contact the inner circumference of the hole in the table top, supporting it. "Asolo" is made of granite. The trapezoidal legs contact only semi-circular parts at both ends of the long holes in the table top and hold it using a joint method applicable only to strong materials. In "Incas," two long sides of the sections of the trapezoidal legs support the table top.

The stabilisation method that uses weight in the architecture reminds me of keystone insets in the centre of arches. For those who have long observed keystones, commonly used in cities in Italy, the idea of a design using weight for stabilisation may come up spontaneously.

Weight was also an important factor for Mangiarotti in his early design of the prefabricated system. The development of an idea beyond the field of architecture and furniture creates quality and deepness of a more comprehensive design. We Japanese grow up in the 'culture of buildings using wood and paper', where the roles of the architect (designing buildings) and the designer (creating products) are separate. I have always known that his origin and his spreading of the idea were fundamentally different.

Most of the furniture designed by Mangiarotti has been reproduced by Agapecasa since 2009.

MODULE

7 アルミタリア社の工場及びオフィス
チニセッロバルサモ（ミラノ）
1968–1971

Armitalia offices and factory
Cinisello Balsamo (Milano), 1968–1971

8 スナイデロ社のオフィス、展示場とサービス施設
マイアーノ（ウディネ）
1971–1978

Snaidero offices, showroom and services
Majano (Udine), 1971–1978

9 集合住宅
モンツァ
1968–1975

Residential building
Monza, 1968–1975

10 集合住宅
アロジオ（コモ）
1974–1978

Residential building
Arosio (Como), 1974–1978

7

Armitalia offices and factory
Cinisello Balsamo (Milano), 1968–1971

アルミタリア社の工場及びオフィス
チニゼッロ・バルサモ(ミラノ)、1968–1971

ミラノ郊外の高速道路のジャンクションの傍に、高さの異なる3つの建物で構成された複合施設がある。

地上4階建てのオフィスと2階建ての倉庫が8.75×4.37mの長方形のグリッドでつながっている。1階建ての工場は一辺8.75mの正方形のグリッドを成す。現場で製造したコンクリート製の屋根を柱で支える構成が特徴的だ。この建物は20枚のプレートで出来ている。浅くくぼんだプレートの中央には天窓があり、2辺のリブは空調と照明を収納する。この複合施設はマンジャロッティが研究した四角いグリッド案の金字塔である。屋根材は四方どちらにも連結できる。

各施設をまとめ特徴づけているのは、建物の丸みを帯びた輪郭と、ファサードパネルに並ぶ角の丸い窓だ。ピンク色がかった厚さ14cmの鉄筋コンクリート製プレキャストパネルの骨材で多様なファサードを構成している。2本の出っ張ったリブで固定し、内部には絶縁材を組み込み漆喰で仕上げている。建物のストライプと丸い輪郭は鉄道車両を思わせる。わずかに持ち上がった建物の下端が地面の上に横長の影を作り出す。

この複合施設は様々な改修にさらされている。最近、この建物の特徴である優雅さとシンプルさを実質的に損なう改修が行われた。オフィス棟の上部に新たな窓を設け、ファサードを塗り替え、工場の窓の形を変更し、倉庫の屋上に手すりが追加された。数々の小さな変更から建築の体現する重要性が完全に変わってしまう悪い手本である。

The complex, located close to a motorway junction on the outskirts of Milan, consists of three buildings with heights and different features.

The offices and warehouse, with four and two storeys above ground, are articulated by a rectangular grid measuring 8.75 x 4.37 m. The one-storey building that houses the workshop has a square grid of 8.75 m per side and is characterized by a concrete roof cast *in situ* supported by columns. It consists of twenty plates – whose intrados recalls a very shallow pavilion vault – each with a central perspex skylight, whose lateral ribs house the air conditioning and lighting running in the two directions. This complex was a milestone in Mangiarotti's research into the square grid plan with a plate roof in which there were no priority values between the two axes.

The element that unifies and characterizes the complex is the façade panel, with its curvilinear profile and windows with rounded corners. The rich range of façade elements consists of precast panels in reinforced concrete of pinkish aggregates 14 cm thick, stiffened by two protruding ribs and incorporating the insulation and the plaster of the interior finish. The complex, whose lines and soft curves are reminiscent of railway carriages, has a single large horizontal line determined by the shadow created at the base of the panels raised slightly off the ground.

The complex has been subjected to various restructuring operations. The most recent, in particular, resulted in a substantial loss of the elegance and simplicity that characterized it. The apertures of the windows in the upper part of the office block, the paintwork of the façades, the changes to the form of the windows of the workshop, the addition of a parapet on the roof of the warehouse and a number of internal changes are examples of how numerous small alterations can radically alter the significance embodied in a building.

3つの建物から成るアルミタリア社屋とオフィス入り口の眺め
アンジェロ・マンジャロッティによるスケッチ
View of the three buildings forming the complex
and of the entrance to the offices, sketches by Angelo Mangiarotti. (AAM, Milano).

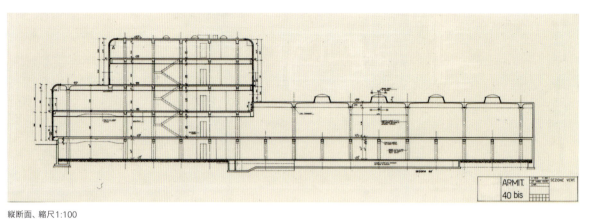

縦断面、縮尺1:100
エンリコ・マッリによる製図、マンジャロッティ事務所　1970年3月27日
Longitudinal section, scale 1:100, drawing
by Enrico Malli, Studio Mangiarotti, 27 March 1970. (AAM, Milano).

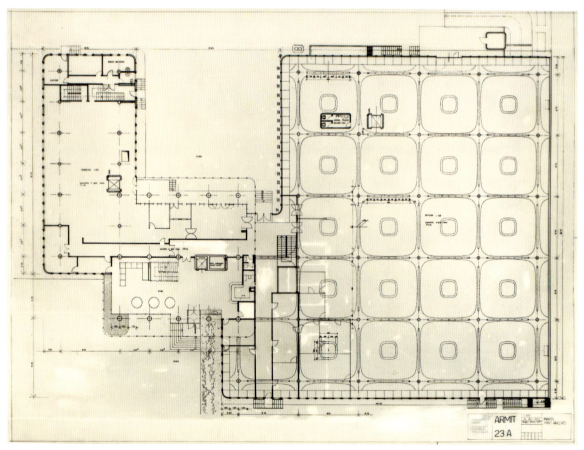

持ち上がった1階の平面図、縮尺1:100、マンジャロッティ事務所　1970年7月4日
Plan of the raised ground floor, scale 1:100, Studio Mangiarotti,
4 June 1970 and updated on May 1971. (AAM, Milano).

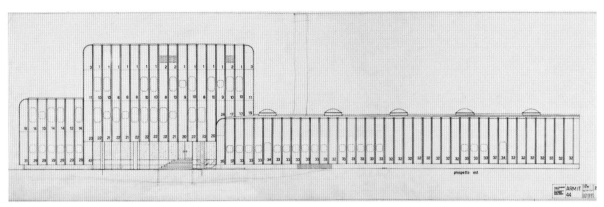

東側ファサードのパネルの類型を示す立面図、縮尺1:50、
マンジャロッティ事務所　1970年7月4日
East elevation with typology of the façade panels, scale 1:50,
Studio Mangiarotti, 3 February, updated on 29 May 1970. (AAM, Milano).

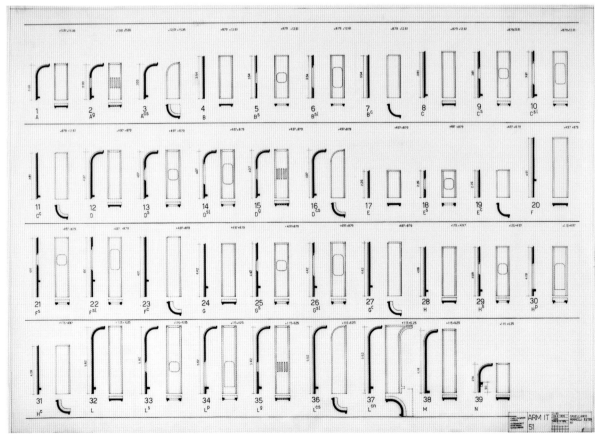

プレキャスト鉄筋コンクリート製ファサードパネル頂部
エンリコ・マッリによる製図、マンジャロッティ事務所　1970年2月25日、修正3月9日
Abacus of the façade panels precast in reinforced concrete, scale 1:50, drawing
by Enrico Malli, Studio Mangiarotti, 25 February and updated on 9 March 1970. (AAM, Milano).

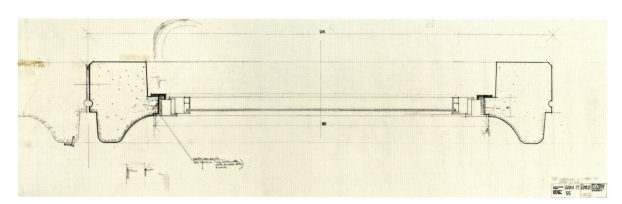

ファサードパネルと窓枠の詳細図、縮尺1:1、
マンジャロッティ事務所　1970年3月4日、修正5月14日
Detail of the façade panel with window frame, scale 1:1, Studio Mangiarotti,
4 March 1970 and updated on 14 May 1970. (AAM, Milano).

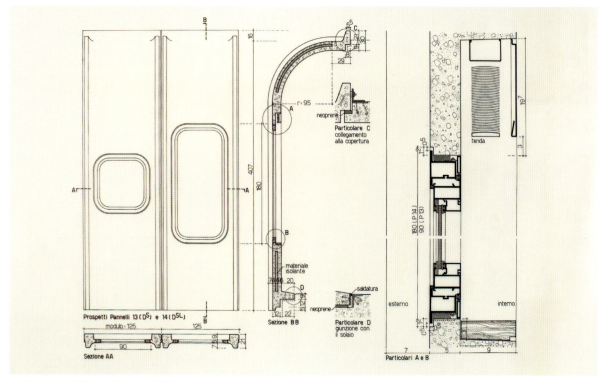

ファサードパネルの詳細、マンジャロッティ事務所
Details of the façade panel, Studio Mangiarotti.
(AAM, Milano).

高速道路のジャンクションから見たアルミタリア社屋
View of the complex from the motorway junction.
(Giorgio Casali, AAM, Milano).

ファサードパネルの設置の分析
Analysis of the placing of the
façade panels. (Juri Schoenenberger,
Accademia di architettura, USI).

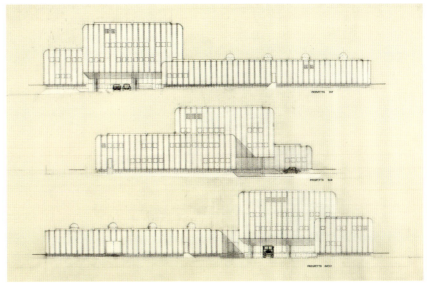

東側、南側、西側立面図、縮尺1:100
エンリコ・マッリによる製図、マンジャロッティ事務所　1968年12月5日
East, south and west elevations, scale 1:100,
drawing by Enrico Malli, Studio Mangiarotti, 5 December 1968. (AAM, Milano).

屋根スラブと湾曲したファサードの組み立て
Assembly of the curvilinear façade panel with the roofing slab.
(Giorgio Casali, AAM, Milano).

オフィス棟の丸みを帯びた上部と開口部とグレーチング
Top of the office building with rounded corners apertures and gratings.
(AAM, Milano).

MODULE 7 | Armitalia offices and factory

アルミタリア社屋の外観
View of the industrial complex.
(Giorgio Casali, AAM, Milano).

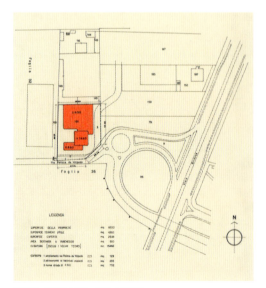

平面図、縮尺1:1000、GPによる製図、
マンジャロッティ事務所　1969年2月28日
Plan, scale 1:1000, drawing by GP, Studio Mangiarotti,
28 February 1969. (AAM, Milano).

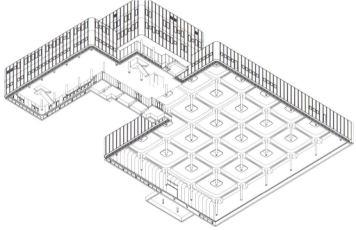

1階天井の分析図
Analysis of the internal spaces on the first floor.
(Caterina Pedo, Accademia di architettura, USI).

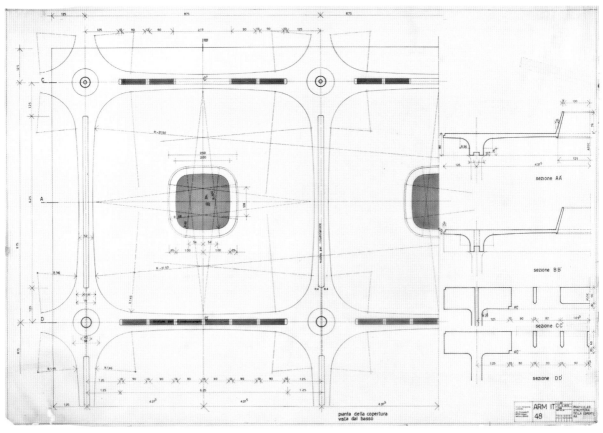

工場の屋根の詳細図、縮尺1:20
エンリコ・マッリによる製図、マンジャロッティ事務所　1970年2月17日、4月修正
Details of the workshop roof, scale 1:20, drawing by Enrico Malli,
Studio Mangiarotti, 17 February 1970, updated April 1970, AAM, Milano.

内部が浅く窪んだ四角い鉄筋コンクリート製プレートの製造段階
Phases in the fabrication of the reinforced concrete plates
with intrados in the form of a pavilion vault with shallow arches.
(AAM, Milano).

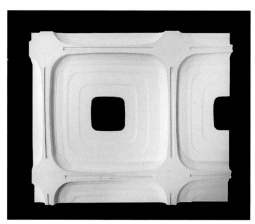

屋根材のスカイライトのスタディモデル
Skylights in the roofing plate, study model.
(Antoine Contour, Antoine De Champs, Fabienne Morath,
Anda Cristina Popescu, Marc Anton Ros Garganté,
Accademia di architettura, USI).

屋根材のリブに埋め込まれた空調と照明
Air conditioning and lighting built
into the ribbing of the plates.
(AAM, Milano).

工場の内部
Interior of the workshop.
(Giorgio Casali, AAM, Milano).

対向ページ　建設中のファサードの詳細
Opposite page: Detail of a façade under construction. (Giorgio Casali, AAM, Milano).

近年の改修で上部に開口部が設けられ
余計な設備が追加された
Recent restructuring: new apertures in the
upper part and new elements added.
(Giulio Sampaoli, 2013).

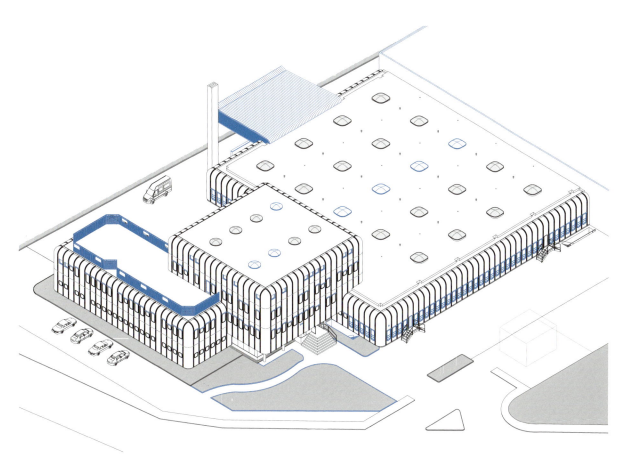

改修が加えられた部分を青色で示す
In blue the additions and alterations made over time.
(Luca Suriano, Accademia di architettura, USI).

工場の窓を拡張した場合の建物の予想図
Images of the complex with the workshop windows already enlarged.
(Francesca Albani, 2010).

Snaidero offices, showroom and services
Majano (Udine), 1971–1978

スナイデロ社のオフィス、展示場とサービス施設
マイアーノ(ウディネ)、1971–1978

　管理人室のあるスナイデロ社の複合施設は、アルミタリア社屋の解決策と形態を彷彿とさせる。展示場、サービス施設、オフィス棟という用途の異なる3棟で構成されている。建物全体がアンジェロ・マンジャロッティの形態と構造と建築の研究の集大成だ。

　展示場棟とサービス棟からモジュラー構成の可能性と建設工程を厳密に研究したことが良くわかる。三角形の断面を成す6本の鋼鉄トラスで展示場棟を建設した。トラスの補助梁からサービス棟の屋根のモジュールと揃えた展示場棟の屋根の四角いグリッドを吊り下げている。周囲の三角形の断面の梁を逆三角形の鋼鉄製の柱で支えている。

　革新性と伝統を融合したオフィス棟は、予期せずマイアーノの郊外に不時着した宇宙船のようだ。初期の案ではアルミ製だったファサードはファイバーグラスとポリウレタンフォーム製のパネルになった。楕円形の窓が並び、基部の粗い石壁、入り口のスロープと外壁、傾斜した道との調和を見せる。角の丸い長方形の建物の中央に自然光を取り入れる中庭を配した。洗練された建物の構造計算はジュリオ・バリオ、ジョバンニ・コロンボ、アルベルト・ヴィンターニが担当し、ジュゼッペ・グランドリとヴィンチェンツォ・ペトリーニが耐震構造を確認した。4本の鉄筋コンクリートの柱で屋根の大梁を支え、そこから中空コアのコンクリート製スラブを引張棒で吊り下げている。

　この複合施設は大手キッチン設備製造メーカーの社屋として良い状態を保っている。時が経つにつれて、オフィス棟には象徴的な価値観が生じ、文化と伝統とこの土地固有の職業倫理と結びついた。

The complex, with access by a caretaker's lodge which recalls the forms and solutions adopted in the Armitalia plant, consists of three buildings with very different characteristics: showroom, service building and office building. The whole work is a culmination of Angelo Mangiarotti's formal, constructional and architectural research.

The showroom building and the one housing the services are the clear expression of a rigorous study of the compositional potential of modularity and the legibility of the construction process. The showroom is built out of six large steel portals with triangular sections: from these are suspended the secondary beams that support the square grid roofing whose module is coordinated with that of the roofing of the service building, characterized in its turn by steel pillars with inverted pyramidal capitals supporting truss beams with triangular sections.

The office building, combining innovation and tradition, looks like a spaceship that has unexpectedly touched down in the Majano countryside. The façade panels with elliptical portholes in fiberglass and polyurethane foam – in a first version they were made of aluminium – interact with the rough-stone walls of the base, the ramp and outer wall, which root the composition to the ground. The building, rectangular in shape with bevelled corners, is organized around a central courtyard lit by a skylight. The sophisticated load-bearing structure was built to calculations by Giulio Ballio, Giovanni Colombo and Alberto Vintani and checked for earthquakes by Giuseppe Grandori and Vincenzo Petrini. It consists of four reinforced concrete columns that support the cross beams of the roofing, from which the slabs in hollow-core concrete are suspended by tie rods.

The complex, which still houses the leading manufacturer of fitted kitchens, is well preserved. Over time, the office building above all has acquired symbolic values related to culture, tradition, but also the work ethic that characterizes this land.

入り口のスロープから建物をのぞむ　アンジェロ・マンジャロッティによるスケッチ
Entrance ramp to the complex, sketch by Angelo Mangiarotti.
(AAM, Milano).

スナイデロ社の丸みを帯びたオフィス棟と低層ビル　アンジェロ・マンジャロッティによるスケッチ
Snaidero complex with office building and a low-rise building
with rounded forms, sketch by Angelo Mangiarotti. (AAM, Milano).

| MODULE | 8 | Snaidero offices, showroom and services | | 194 |

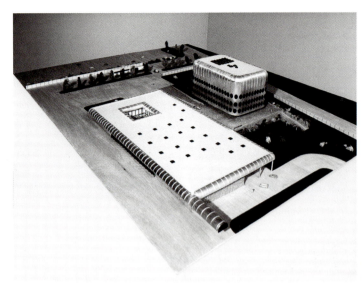

アルミニウムに覆われたオフィス棟の初期モデル
Model of the first project with the office building faced with aluminium. (AAM, Milano).

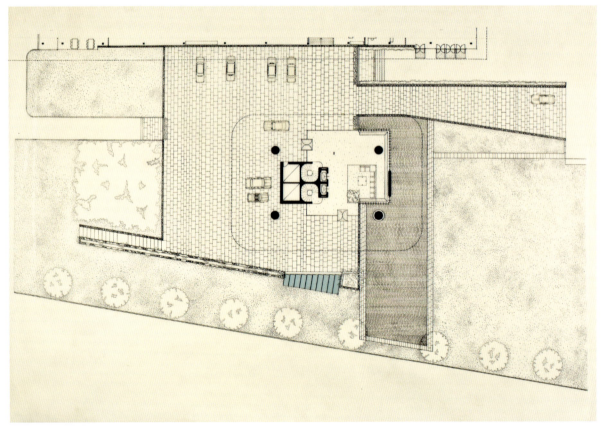

1階の入り口からオフィスまでの平面図
マンジャロッティ事務所による掲載用の設計図
Plan of the ground floor with the entrance to the offices,
Studio Mangiarotti, drawing for publication. (AAM, Milano).

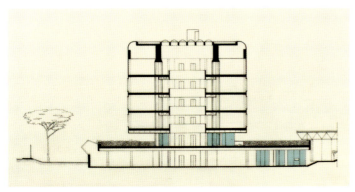 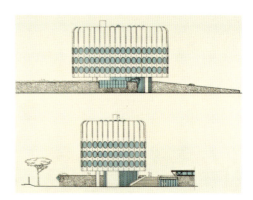

オフィス棟の断面図と立面図
マンジャロッティ事務所による掲載用の設計図
Section and elevations of the office building,
Studio Mangiarotti, drawing for publication.
(AAM, Milano).

オフィス棟の中庭
アンジェロ・マンジャロッティによるスケッチ
Central courtyard of the office building, sketch by Angelo Mangiarotti.
(AAM, Milano).

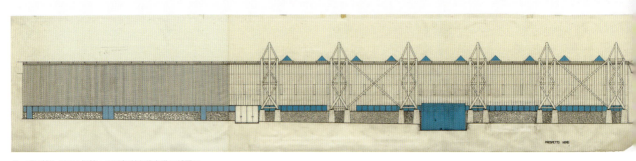

サービス棟から展示場棟への屋根付き遊歩道の断面図
Section of the covered walkway connecting the service building to the showroom, scale 1:50, Studio Mangiarotti, 2 May 1977. (AAM, Milano).

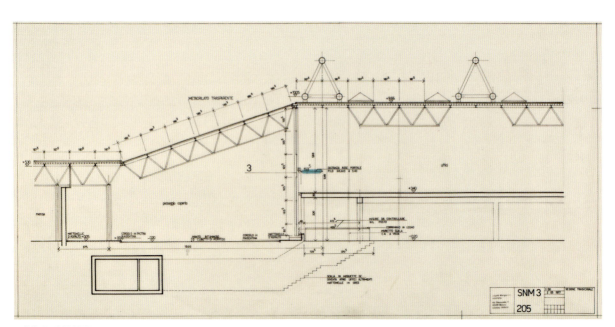

工業施設の北側立面図
マンジャロッティ事務所
North elevation of the industrial complex,
Studio Mangiarotti. (AAM, Milano).

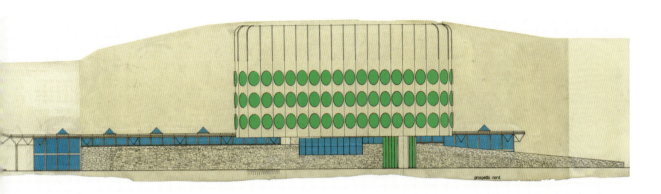

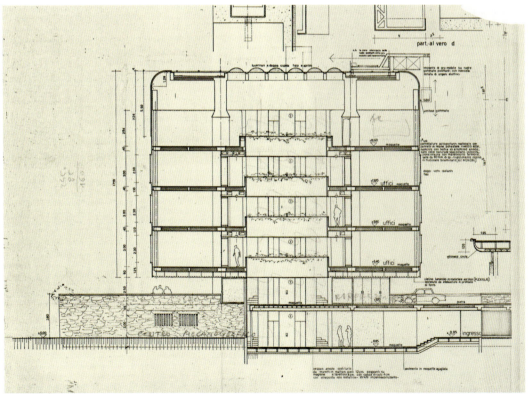

オフィス棟と中庭の断面図
マンジャロッティ事務所
Section through the central courtyard
of the office building, Studio Mangiarotti.
(AAM, Milano).

Module 8 — Snaidero offices, showroom and services

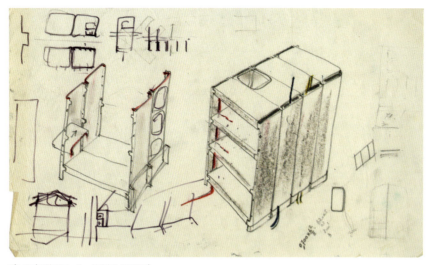

プレハブ工法のファサードパネルのスタディ
アンジェロ・マンジャロッティによるスケッチ
Study of prefabricated façade panels, sketch by Angelo Mangiarotti.
(AAM, Milano).

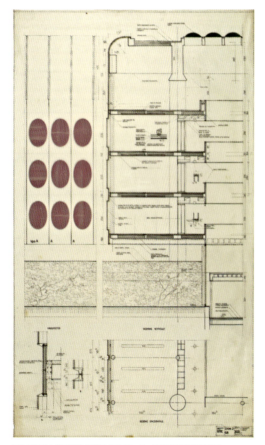

アルミニウム製パネルで覆われたファサードの立面図と断面図
縮尺1:20と縮尺1:5、マンジャロッティ事務所
Elevations and sections of the façade covered
with aluminium panels, scale 1:20 and 1:5, Studio Mangiarotti.
(AAM, Milano).

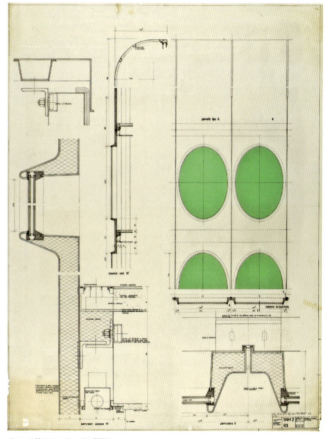

オフィス棟のファサードの詳細
Eによる製図、マンジャロッティ事務所
Details of the façade of the office building,
drawing by E., Studio Mangiarotti. (AAM, Milano).

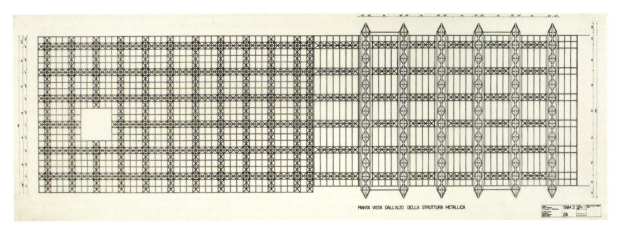

サービス施設と展示場棟の金属構造の平面図
縮尺1:100　マンジャロッティ事務所
Marによる製図、マンジャロッティ事務所　1978年4月18日
Plan of metal structure of the service and showroom buildings, scale 1:100, drawing by Mar, Studio Mangiarotti, 18 April 1978. (AAM, Milano).

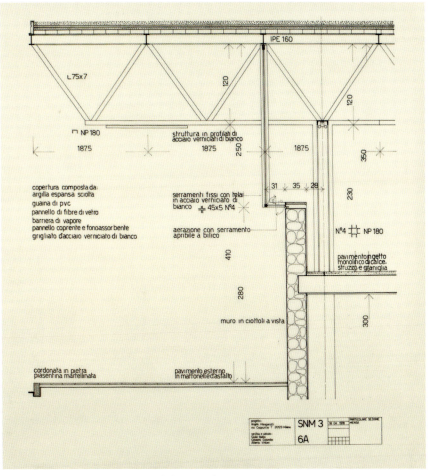

食堂のファサードの断面図　マンジャロッティ事務所　1978年4月18日
Section of the façade of the canteen, Studio Mangiarotti, 18 April 1978. (AAM, Milano).

ファイバーグラスとポリウレタンフォーム製のファサードの設置
Placing of façade panels in fiberglass and polyurethane foam.
(Giorgio Casali, AAM, Milano).

複合施設の建設段階
Construction stages of the complex.
(F.lli Di Leno, AAM, Milano).

Module 8 — Snaidero offices, showroom and services

鋼鉄のトラスに覆われた展示場
View of the showroom with the great triangular steel portals.
(AAM, Milano).

サービス棟の内部と外部
Extrados and intrados of the structure of the service building.
(F.lli Di Leno, AAM, Milano).

サービス棟の金属柱
Metal pillar in the service building.
(AAM, Milano).

ショールーム棟のトラスのヒンジ詳細図
マンジャロッティ事務所　1978年4月18
Detail of the hinge of a metal portal of
the showroom building, Studio Mangiarotti,
18 April 1978. (AAM, Milano).

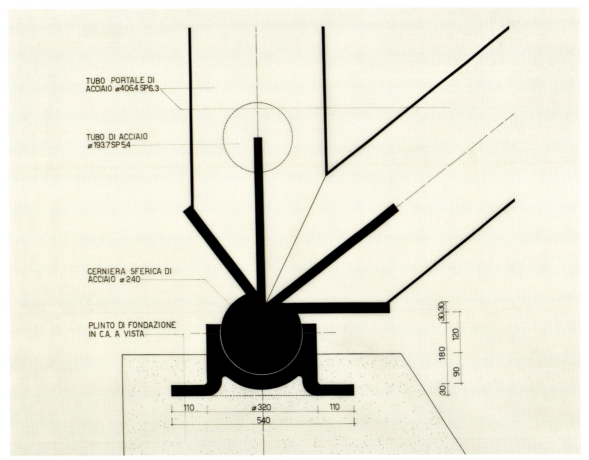

サービス棟の柱の接地面　マンジャロッティ事務所　1978年4月18日
Attachment to the ground of the pillar of the service building, Studio Mangiarotti, 18 April 1978.
(AAM, Milano).

オフィスの昼景と夜景
Daytime and night-time views of the office building.
(Giorgio Casali, AAM, Milano).

オフィス内部
Interior of the offices.
(Giorgio Casali, AAM, Milano).

MODULE 8 | Snaidero offices, showroom and services | 206

複合施設の南側の写真立面図
Photoplan of the south elevation of the complex.
(Pietro Brugo, Davide Etter, Bjorn Klingenberg, Jacopo Josiah Mazzucchelli,
Francesco Tadini, Accademia di architettura, USI).

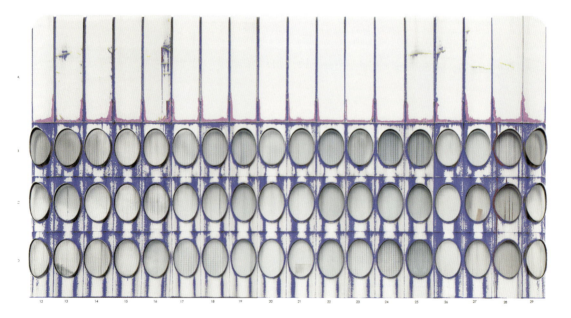

南側立面の劣化図。青は漏水、ピンクはアルカリ骨材反応、黄色は亀裂
Mapping of deterioration on the south elevation: in blue trickling,
in pink mineral deposit, in yellow crack.
(Michele Zanuso, Accademia di architettura, USI).

展示場棟の外観
View of the showroom building.
(Francesca Albani, 2014).

コンクリートの台座と鋼鉄トラスのヒンジの詳細
Detail of the concrete plinth
and the hinge of the steel portal.
(Francesca Albani, 2014).

Residential building
Monza, 1968–1975

集合住宅
モンツァ、1968–1978

ブリアンツァの二つの集合住宅計画のうち最初に建てた建物である。アンジェロ・マンジャロッティは室内とファサードの柔軟な構成をテーマに掲げ、住人が設計段階から参加できるようにした。

周辺の建物とは違って、8階立てのコンパクトな建物は不規則な形である。32cmのグリッドに基づき、コンクリート製の耐荷重構造を現場で製作した。階段とエレベーターをのぞいて集合住宅の自由な構成が可能となった。各戸の内部の構成がファサードのデザインに反映されている。96cmのグリッドに基づきプレハブ工法で作成した透明または不透明なパネルと、開口部と、金属製の手すりがついたバルコニーを配置し、巧みな分割による立派な構成が完成した。断熱材のポリウレタンフォームをはさんだ不透明なパネルや、ビチェンツァ産の石を砕いて仕上げた石材、C字型の形状のモールディングを用いた。特筆すべきはエントランスのスロープから地下の駐車場に入る構成である。角が丸みを帯びた四角い管理人部屋は黒く塗装した鋼鉄シートで柱を覆い、住宅との区切りを示した。

様々な種類の管理が行き届き、建物は良い保存状態にある。窓と木製の目隠しは現在も維持管理が必要だ。

This building is the first of two residential projects built in Brianza, through which Angelo Mangiarotti continued to explore the theme of the flexibility of the interiors and façades with a view to fostering participation by the inhabitants already in the design phase.

The building has a compact plan, consisting of eight floors. It stands isolated on a lot of irregular form and without any relation to the surrounding buildings. The load-bearing structure made of concrete cast on site, whose only fixed elements are the stairwell and the elevator, determines a free plan organized on the basis of a 32cm grid, which makes for complete freedom in the configuration of the apartments. The internal organization of each apartment is reflected in the overall design of the façade, which is also based on a modular grid of 96 cm, in which opaque or glazed or openwork prefabricated panels or balconies with metal parapets alternate, so defining an elegant and highly articulated composition. The opaque panels are made of reinforced concrete with interposed polyurethane foam insulation, an outer cladding of Vicenza gritstone and string courses with C-shaped profiles. Particularly refined are the plan of the basement level with the garages, with access provided by a ramp, and that of the entrance floor, with the concierge's lodge fully glazed with pillars sheathed in sheet steel painted black, delimiting rectangular elements with rounded corners.

Subjected to maintenance work of various kinds, the building is in a good state of preservation. At present the windows and wooden shutters are in need of repair and conservation.

透視図、マンジャロッティ事務所　1968年5月20日
Perspective view, Studio Mangiarotti, 20 May 1968.
(AAM, Milano).

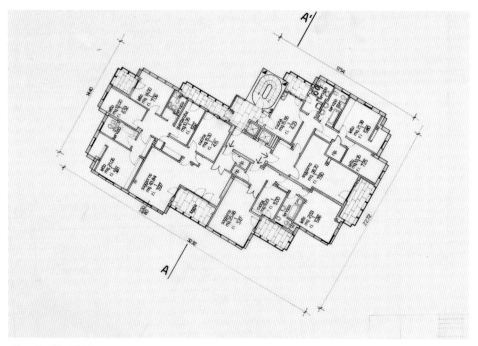

3階、5階、6階の平面図
Marによる製図、縮尺1:100、マンジャロッティ事務所　1974年1月22日
Plan of floors 3, 5 and 6, scale 1:100,
drawing by Mar, Studio Mangiarotti, 22 January 1974. (AAM, Milano).

竣工直後の外観
Views of the recently completed building.
(Giorgio Casali, AAM, Milano).

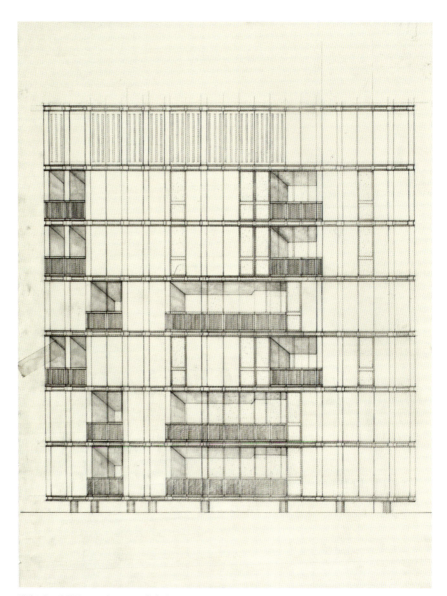

道路からの立面図、マンジャロッティ事務所
Elevation towards the street, Studio Mangiarotti. (AAM, Milano).

| Module | 9 | Residential building | | 212 |

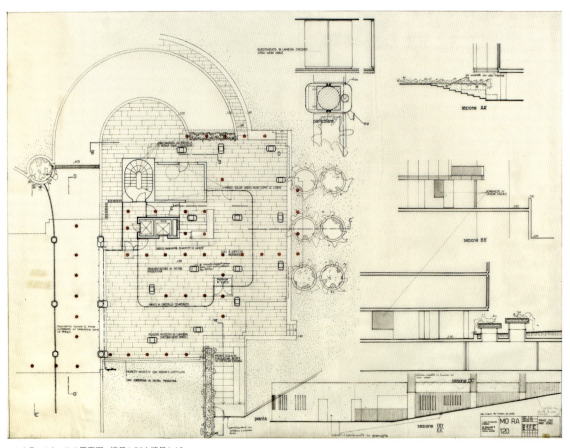

エントランスホールの平面図、縮尺1:50と縮尺1:10
マンジャロッティ事務所　1975年3月26日ほか
Plan of the entrance floor, scale 1:50 and 1:10,
Studio Mangiarotti, 26 March 1975 and variants.
(AAM, Milano).

ファサード詳細、エントランスから地下に向かう
Detail of a façade and entrance to the basement level.
(Giorgio Casali, AAM, Milano).

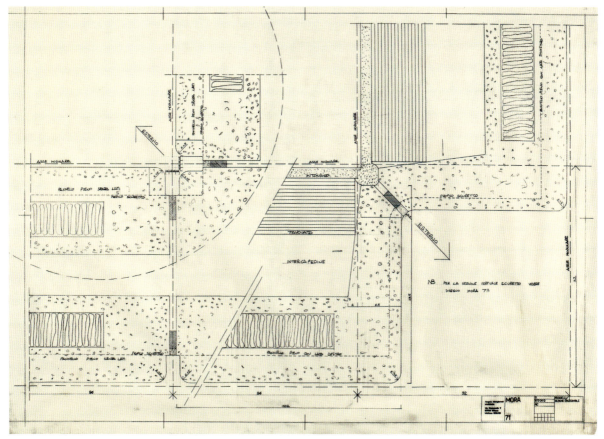

ファサードパネルの水平断面、縮尺1:1　Ricによる製図、マンジャロッティ事務所　1973年4月13日
Horizontal section of the façade panels, scale 1:1,
drawing by Ric, Studio Mangiarotti, 13 April 1973. (AAM, Milano).

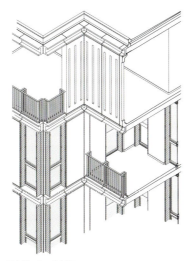

最上階の角の分析図
Analysis of the top of the corner.
(Leander Bulst, Accademia di architettura, USI).

不透明および透明パネルと開口部が交互にファサードを構成する
Opaque, transparent and openwork panels alternate
in the composition of the façade. (Giorgio Casali, AAM, Milano).

角の収まりの模型
Model of the corner solution.
(Maria Cristina Luisa Bongiovanni, Giovanna Moccia, Andrea Neri, Accademia di architettura, USI).

鉄筋コンクリートの中空コアの耐力構造
コンクリートスラブとプレキャストの外皮のスタディーモデル
The load-bearing structure of reinforced concrete,
with hollow core. concrete slabs and precast envelope, study model.
(Francesca Facchini, Filippo Viano,
Francesca Zanella, Accademia di architettura, USI).

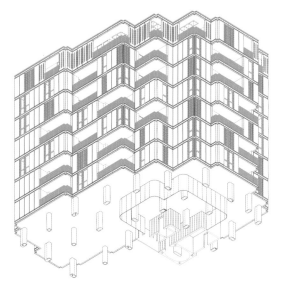

エントランス階の空間分析
Analysis of the internal spaces
of the entrance floor. (Francesco Meroni,
Accademia di architettura, USI).

東側の写真立面図　2015年
Photoplan of east elevation, 2015.
(Luciano Ricci, Accademia di architettura, USI).

管理が行き届いた現在の状態
Present state of the carefully preserved building.
(Francesca Albani, 2014).

10

Residential building
Arosio (Como), 1974–1978

集合住宅
アロジオ(コモ)、1974–1978

　上から見て蛇腹状の四角形を成すアロジオの集合住宅は、モンツァの集合住宅の様々な要素を下敷きにしている。同じテーマのもと、柔軟な設計、組み合わせの構成、住人による参加、プレハブ工法の外皮が用いられた。

　バルコニーの設置と大きなセットバックによって、6階建ての建物の構成はモンツァの時よりも複雑さを増した。建物に入るには敷地を対角線上に横切り、スロープを降りて遠近感を感じながら管理人室がある半地下階へと進む。今まで通り中空コアコンクリートのスラブを用いて現場で鉄筋コンクリートを打ち込む耐力構造だが、ファサードのパネルはレンガ粉体を混ぜたプレキャスト鉄筋コンクリートで製作した。モンツァに比べてパネルの種類が減った。設計の最終段階で上部に開口部を設けるのをやめて、耐久性を高めるためにモールディングを厚くした。モンツァと同様に断熱材をはさんだ不透明なパネルや室内のレンガ製のカウンターを用いる一方で、作り付けの木製窓枠に雨戸と開き窓を設けた。

　予め建物の凹凸を深く設けたため建物は良い保存状態にあり、これまで鉄筋の腐食は起きていない。さもなければコンクリート表面が剥離していただろう。

The residential building in Arosio, built on a lot with a trapezoidal shape, is in many ways a variation on the one in Monza. The themes are the same: flexibility, modular coordination, participation by the inhabitants, prefabrication of the envelope.

The building, laid out on six storeys, has a more complex floor plan than its predecessor because of the presence of balconies and more pronounced setbacks. Access is provided by a path that traverses the diagonal of the lot and along a ramp that leads scenically to the semi-basement level, where the concierge's lodge is located. The load-bearing structure is in traditional reinforced concrete cast *in situ* with slabs in hollow-core concrete, while the façades are made of panels precast in reinforced concrete with brick powder aggregate, a simplification of the typologies compared to the residential building in Monza. In the last version of the project the openwork element was eliminated in the upper part and the string course was made thicker to ensure greater durability. The opaque panel in concrete with incorporated insulation envisaged, as in Monza, a brick counter-wall on the inside, while the wooden window fixtures had casements in natural wood with external shutters.

The building is in a good state of preservation thanks to the precautions taken in the string courses, which to date have not presented any problems caused by corrosion of the reinforcing bars, which would otherwise have led to the detachment of the concrete cover.

対向ページ　集合住宅の立面図
アンジェロ・マンジャロッティによるスケッチ
Opposite page: Elevation of the residential building, sketch by Angelo Mangiarotti. (AAM, Milano).

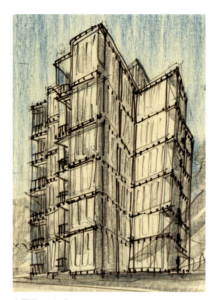

立面図のスタディ
アンジェロ・マンジャロッティによるスケッチ
Studies of the elevations, sketches by Angelo Mangiarotti.
(AAM, Milano).

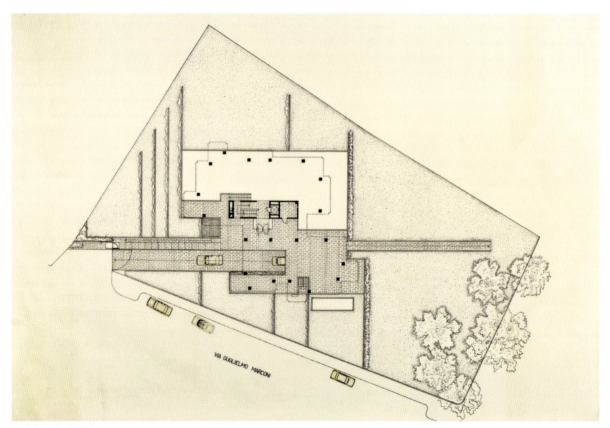

エントランス階の平面図
掲載用の設計図、マンジャロッティ事務所
Plan of the entrance floor, drawing for publication, Studio Mangiarotti.
(AAM, Milano).

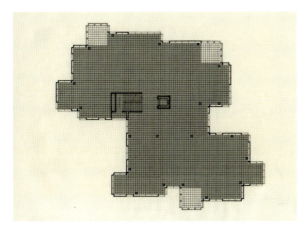

モジュールのグリッドとバルコニーの計画案
Plan scheme with modular grid and balconies.
(AAM, Milano).

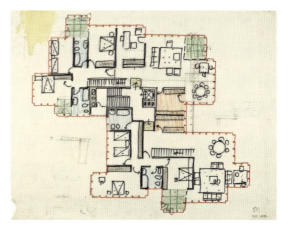

家具の配置図
アンジェロ・マンジャロッティによるスケッチ
Plan with furniture, sketch by Angelo Mangiarotti.
(AAM, Milano).

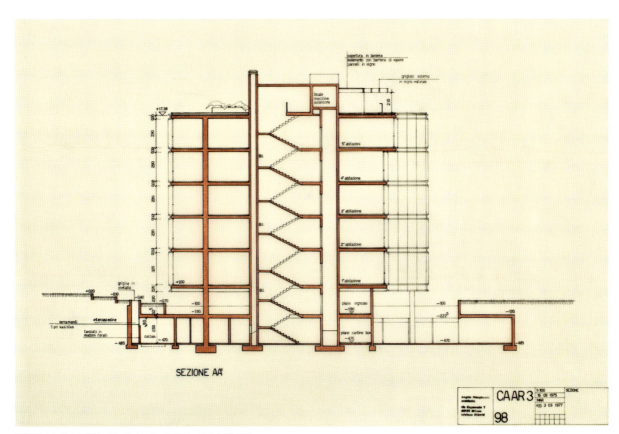

断面図、Marによる製図　マンジャロッティ事務所　1977年3月3日
Section, drawing by Mar, Studio Mangiarotti,
16 September 1975 and updated on 3 March 1977.
(AAM, Milano).

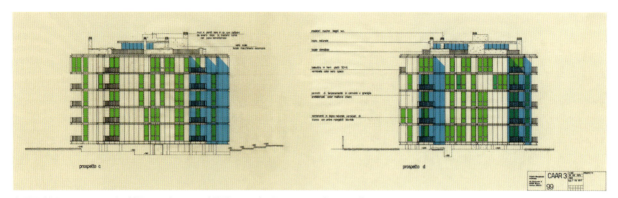

立面図、縮尺1:100　Marによる製図、マンジャロッティ事務所　1975年9月18日、1977年3月7日修正
Elevations, scale 1:100, drawing by Mar, Studio Mangiarotti,
18 September 1975 and updated on 7 March 1977. (AAM, Milano).

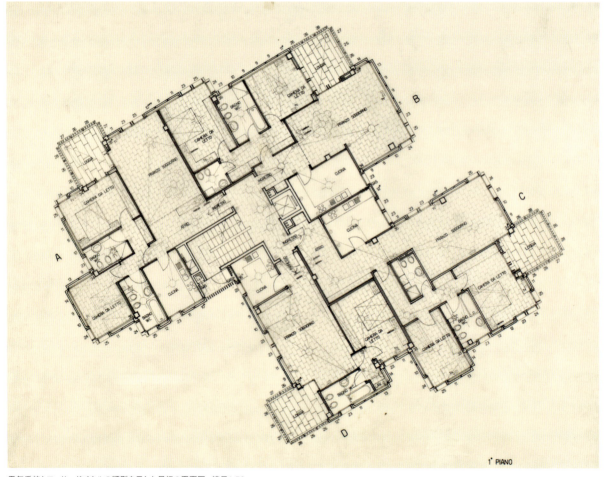

電気系統とファサードパネルの類型を示した最初の平面図、縮尺1:50
マンジャロッティ事務所　1975年3月25日、繰り返し修正
First-floor plan with electrical system and typology of the façade panels, scale 1:50,
drawing by Mar, Studio Mangiarotti, 25 March 1975 and successive updates. (AAM, Milano).

透明および不透明パネルと開口部が交互にファサードを構成するスタディモデル
Transparent and opaque panels alternate in the composition of the façades, study model.
(Ernest Robert Babyn, Matteo Defendini, Angelica Moioli, Giulia Rapizza,
Mateusz Zaluska, Accademia di architettura, USI).

プレキャストコンクリート製パネルをレンガ粉体に打ち込む
Placing of a precast concrete panel faced
with brick powder aggregate. (AAM, Milano).

Module 10 — Residential building

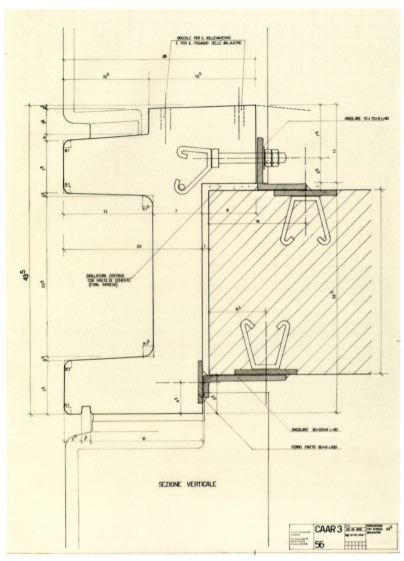

バルコニーの手すりを備えた蛇腹状の外壁の詳細図、縮尺1:1
マンジャロッティ事務所　1975年1月20日、2月1日修正
Detail of the string course with attachment of the balustrade of the balconies, scale 1:1, Studio Mangiarotti, 20 January 1975, updated 1 February 1975. (AAM, Milano).

蛇腹状の外壁の角の設営
Laying of the corner solution of the string courses. (AAM, Milano).

建物正面の立面と入り口のスロープ
Main elevation with the entrance ramp.
(AAM, Milano).

| Module | 10 | Residential building | | 224 |

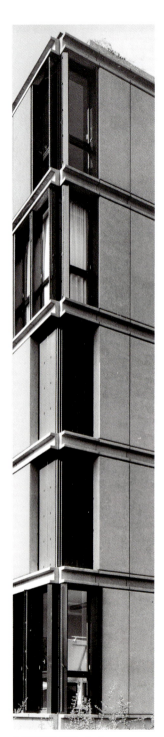
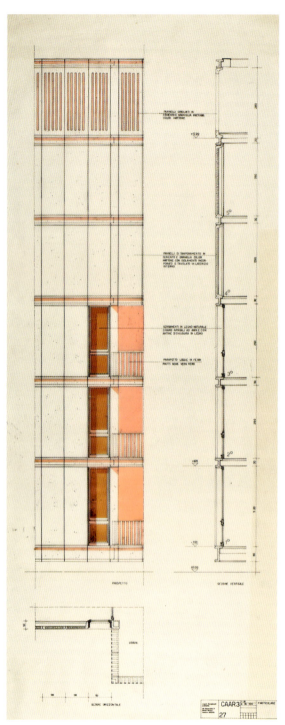

角の収まりのバリエーション
Views of different corner solutions.
(Giorgio Casali, AAM, Milano).

最上階に残るファサードのパネルの開口部、縮尺1:20
マンジャロッティ事務所　1974年6月6日
Façade solution with the openwork panels still present on the top floor, scale 1:20, Studio Mangiarotti, 6 June 1974.
(AAM, Milano).

ファサードを構成するプレハブパネルの分析
Analysis of the prefabricated
panels forming a portion of the façade.
(Piera Barabino, Accademia di architettura, USI).

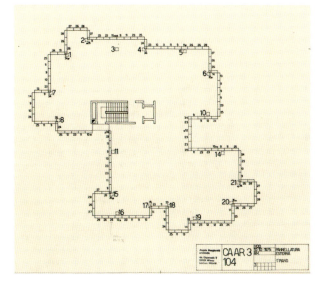

一階のプレハブパネルの設計図
縮尺1: 100、AMによる製図、
マンジャロッティ事務所
Drawing of the prefabricated
panels on the first floor,
scale 1:100, drawing by
AM, Studio Mangiarotti.
(AAM, Milano).

最上階のバルコニーと角の収まり
Corner solution with a balcony
on the top floor.
(Giorgio Casali, TFAM, Milano).

| Module | 10 | Residential building | | 226 |

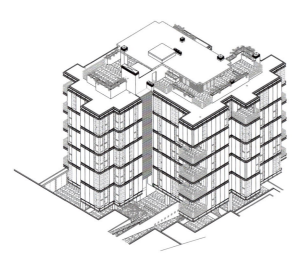

等角投影図
Axonometric projection from above.
(Michelle Badrutt, Accademia di architettura, USI).

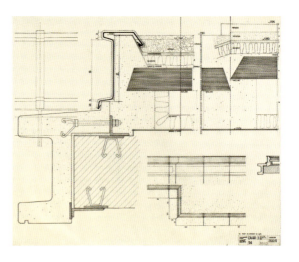

屋根の詳細図、縮尺1:1と縮尺1:10
AMによる製図、マンジャロッティ事務所　1975年10月23日
Details of the roof, scale 1:1 and 1:10,
drawing by AM, Studio Mangiarotti, 23 October 1975. (AAM, Milano).

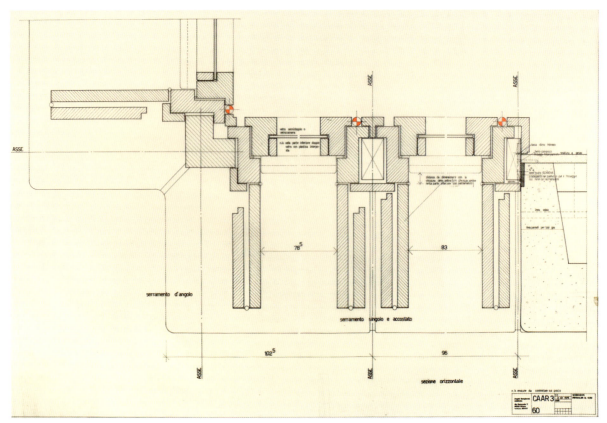

窓のフレームの詳細図、縮尺1:1
Marによる製図、縮尺1:1、マンジャロッティ事務所　1975年2月3日
Details of window frames, scale 1:1,
drawing by Mar, Studio Mangiarotti, 3 February 1975. (AAM, Milano).

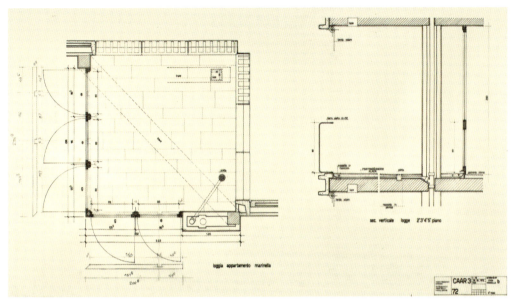

5階バルコニーの平面図と断面図、縮尺1:10
Marによる製図、マンジャロッティ事務所　1975年5月26日
Plan and section of the fifth-floor balcony, scale 1:10,
drawing by Mar, Studio Mangiarotti, 26 May 1975, AAM, Milano.

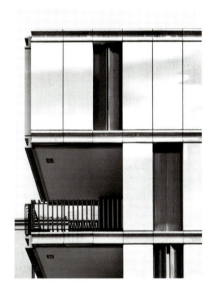

平らな鋼鉄で構成した欄干とバルコニー
Balconies with metal balustrade consisting of flat steel elements.
(Giorgio Casali, AAM, Milano).

ファサードのパネル詳細
Detail of the façade panels.
(Giorgio Casali, AAM, Milano).

劣化の調査。青にアルカリ骨材反応、黄色に苔など付着物を示す
Survey of decay: in blue mineral deposit, in yellow biological growth.
(Alessio Crespi, Accademia di architettura, USI).

屋上と入り口のスロープ
Roof floor and entrance ramp.
(Francesca Albani 2014).

Column

堀川絹江

Kinue Horikawa

タイムレスなデザイン

Timeless design

　2017年に生誕50周年を迎え、永きに渡り世界中のデザイナーやユーザーたちを魅了してきた小さなガラスのオーナメント『Giogali（ジョーガリ）』はマンジャロッティのデザインのエッセンスを詰め込んだ代表作と言えよう。

　マンジャロッティは、常々「重要なことは素材を知ること、また、それを加工する技術を知ること」と言及するモノづくりを原点とした。

　1960年に単独で事務所を開設し、精力的な制作活動を展開し始めたマンジャロッティは、デザイン業務の傍ら、1963年より64年にかけてヴェネチア建築大学の工業デザイン専門コースにて教鞭を執り、ミラノからヴェネチアに通う日々が続いた。ヴェネチアの工業製品といえばムラノガラス。もともと、地域の素材や伝統工芸と技術に多大な関心と敬意を持っていたマンジャロッティを虜にしたのは、歴史あるムラノガラスの工法であった。

　マンジャロッティは世界中の多くの大学や教育機関で教鞭を執ったが、レクチャーの基本は、1953年の最初の教員経験であったアメリカ、シカゴのイリノイ工科大学にさかのぼる。教室内でレクチャーするのではなく、地域産業を繁栄させている工場や工房を訪れ、職人や技術者や素材や製品の製造工程を見て何ができるのかを学生と探求した。ヴェネチアでも数々のムラノガラスの工房に学生を引き連れ、ガラスという素材の特質、製作の仕方や取り扱い方などあらゆる情報のヒアリングを行い、レクチャー終了後も個人的に何度もVistosi（ヴィストージ）の工房を訪ねた。

　そして1967年、マンジャロッティが誕生させたのが、照明のオーナメント『Giogali』である。ガラス職人たちは、マンジャロッティの最初のスケッチと図面を見て「ガラスをこんな風に使うなんて誰も考えもしなかった」と驚嘆したという。マンジャロッティはこう言った。

　「Giogaliはガラスだからこそ成立する。一般的にガラスは割れやすいと思われているが、強度は非常に高い。人々はガラスの『Giogali』を見て、その繊細さや洗練された美しさを感じることができる。もしプラスチックやシリコンなど壊れない素

"Giogali" is a small glass ornament that celebrated its 50th anniversary in 2017 and has long fascinated designers and users around the world. We can say that it is a masterpiece filled with the essence of design by Mangiarotti.

Mangiarotti had a starting point, always mentioning that 'important things are knowing the material and knowing the technology process of it'. He opened his own design office in 1960 and began to develop lively production activities. While working on design, he taught the industrial design course at Iuav University of Venice from 1963 to 1964 and spent days visiting Venice from Milano. A representative industrial product in Venice is Murano glass, whose historic glass construction method captured Mangiarotti, who originally had great interest and respect for local materials, traditional crafts, and technology.

Mangiarotti taught at many universities and educational institutions around the world. His lecture style was based on his first educational experience at the Illinois Institute of Technology in Chicago in 1953. Instead of giving lectures in the classroom, he and his students visited factories and workshops and vibrant local industries and observed craftsmen, engineers, materials, and the manufacturing processes of products to find out what they could design. Also in Venice, he brought students to numerous glass workshops in Murano and asked them to collect all sorts of information such as the characteristics of the glass material and how to manufacture and handle them. Even after the lecture, he personally visited the Vistosi workshops many times.

Finally, he developed "Giogali" lighting ornaments in 1967. The glass craftsmen saw his first sketches and drawings and were astonished: 'Nobody thought about using glass like this'. Mangiarotti explained, "Giogali" is completed because of especially glass. Glass is generally considered to be fragile, but its strength is very high. People can see the glass "Giogali" and feel its delicateness and refined beauty. If it was made of plastic, silicone and other materials that won't break, we cannot find these aesthetic feeling'.

To realise the brilliance and refined shape that Mangiarotti ex-

Giogali, Photo by Vetreria Vistosi srl

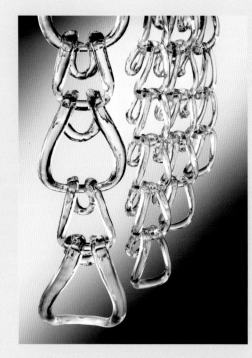

Giogali,
Photo by
Vetreria Vistosi srl

材で作られていたら、この美的感覚を見出すことはできない」

マンジャロッティの探求した輝きと洗練された形を実現するために、ガラスの強度を上げながらもその透明さを如何に維持するか、輝きを増すためにはどのような成分のガラスを作るか、職人たちと試行錯誤を繰り返し、年々『Giogali』の改良を続けた。

『Giogali』は、ガラスのポジティブなイメージである『透明』で『光を通す』性質を最大限に生かし、ネガティブな『硬さ』『割れる』『壊れる』イメージを逆手に取って『柔らかい』『繊細』『たおやか』に移り替えた、マンジャロッティならではの作品と言える。

ここで、特筆すべきモジュール性について話してみたい。マンジャロッティは、縦、横に自由に繋ぐことで線や柱や面を構成するパーツをデザインした。職人の手で一つ一つ作られる『Giogali』は、大小バラエティに富む照明を構成するパーツでもあり、ガラスのカーテンとしてのパーテーションの一部品でもある。サウジアラビアのモスクで行われたインスタレーションでは最も数多くのパーツが使われ、その数100万個であったという。

職人たちとの密接な協働を経てサイズの小さい『Mini Giogali』、透明性の高い色ガラスを使用した『Color Giogali』、横方向の繋がりを重視した『Giogali 3D』など、豊富なラインナップが生み出され、繋げる長さや位置、カラーコンビネーションをユーザー各自が自由に変更できる様相となっている。

無限の可能性を秘めたガラスのパーツ『Giogali』は、そのデザイン性や製造の歴史が認められ、ヴェネチア、ムラノ島にあるガラス美術館（Museo del Vetro di Murano）の常設展示品となった。インダストリアルデザインのプロダクトが美術館に展示されるのは極めて稀である。モノづくりへの深い思いを根底に持ち、時間を感じさせない形態を常に探求してきたマンジャロッティの秀逸なデザインの証ではないか。

plored, the craftsmen underwent many trials and errors to maintain transparency while improving the strength of the glass and to find ingredients to increase its brightness.

"Giogali" is considered the work that only Mangiarotti could make. It expresses the positive nature of the glass, it is 'transparent' and 'penetrates lights' to the maximum, and turns the negative 'hardness', 'crack', and 'broken' images to their opposite impressions of 'soft', 'delicate', and 'graceful', respectively.

Here, I would like to introduce the remarkable modularity. Mangiarotti designed these construction parts to connect vertically and horizontally to make lines, columns, and planes. "Giogali", made one by one by craftsmen, is not only made of parts that form large or small lighting but is also a part of a divider as a glass curtain. In the installation set up in a mosque in Saudi Arabia, they used an estimated one million parts, the largest number so far.

After close collaborations with the craftsmen, a wide line-up was created, such as the "mini Giogali", "colour Giogali" using transparent coloured glass, and "Giogali 3D", which emphasises horizontal connections. These allowed users to freely set the product's length, position and colour combinations.

The glass parts of "Giogali" with infinite possibilities were recognised for their design and manufacturing history and became a permanent collection in the Murano Grass Museum in Venice. It is extremely unusual for industrial design products to be displayed in the museum, so it must be proof of excellent design by Mangiarotti, who had designed with a deep thought and always pursued timeless forms.

アンジェロ・マンジャロッティ プロフィール

Biography

1921年2月26日にミラノ生まれ。1948年ミラノ工科大学建築学部卒業。1953－1954年アメリカで働きシカゴのループ地区のコンペに参加。アメリカ滞在中にフランク・ロイド・ライト、ヴァルター・グロピウス、ミース・ファン・デル・ローエ、コンラッド・ワックスマンと知遇を得る。1955年イタリアに帰国後に設計事務所を開設し、1960年までブルーノ・モラスッティとオフィスを共有。1989年東京にマンジャロッティ・アソシエイツを設立。1986－1992年コッレ・ディ・ヴァル・デルサにあるコレ・クリスタル社のアートディレクターを務める。

作品が書籍、業界誌、新聞に掲載される。建築の仕事と並行して国内外の複数の大学で教え、1953－1954年シカゴのイリノイ工科大学デザイン学科の客員教授、1963－1964年ヴェネツィア建築大学、1970年ハワイ大学客員教授、1974年スイス連邦工科大学ローザンヌ校、1976年アデレード大学、南オーストラリア大学工科大学客員教授。1982年パレルモ大学建築学部教授就任。1983年フィレンツェ大学建築学部長代理講師、1989－1990年ミラノ工科大学建築学部教授。1997年ミラノ工科大学建築学部工業デザイン科の卒業設計を指導。教育の傍ら国内外で多くの講演を行った。

マンジャロッティの設計活動はデザインならびに建築の分野で数々の表彰を受けた。1956年ドムス・フォルミカ賞、1962年ロンバルディアIn/Arch 建築賞受賞、1972 年AIP（イタリア・プレハブ工業会）賞、1979年メタリック構造ヨーロッパ賞受賞、1986年第3回ソフィア国際建築ビエンナーレ名誉賞、1994年および2007年マーブル建築賞受賞、1994年イタリア工業デザイン協会（ADI）ゴールデンコンパス賞、1998年トッレ・カラーラ・アカデミーの建築部門で金賞。2006年リマ・エディトリーチェ出版より「デザインの使徒」ゴールドメダル。

また、マンジャロッティは1988年ミュンヘン工科大学建築学部および2002年ミラノ工科大学建築学部工業デザイン科から名誉学位を授与された。

2012年6月30日逝去。

Angelo Mangiarotti was born in Milan on 26 February 1921. He was awarded a degree in Architecture at Milan Polytechnic in 1948. Between 1953 and 1954 he worked in the United States, where he participated in the tender for the "Loop" in Chicago. During the period he spent abroad, he got to know Frank Lloyd Wright, Walter Gropius, Mies van der Rohe, and Konrad Wachsmann. In 1955, after returning from the United States, he opened an architectural firm in Milan, which he shared with Bruno Morassutti until 1960. In 1989 he founded Mangiarotti & Associates Office, with a branch in Tokyo. From 1986 to 1992 he was art director of Colle Cristallerie of Colle Val d'Elsa.

Mangiarotti, whose works have been published in books, trade magazines, and newspapers, accompanied his work as a professional by teaching courses at several universities both in Italy and abroad. In 1953–1954 he was visiting professor at the Institute of Design, Illinois Institute of Technology in Chicago, in 1963–1964 he taught at the Istituto Superiore di Disegno Industriale in Venice, in 1970 he was visiting professor at the University of Hawaii, in 1974 he taught at the *École polytechnique fédérale* of Lausanne, and in 1976 at the University of Adelaide and at South Australian Institute of Technology in Adelaide. In 1982 he got a contract to teach at the Faculty of Architecture in Palermo, in 1983 he was substitute lecturer for the chair of Composition at the Faculty of Architecture in Florence, in 1989–1990 he was given a contract to teach at the Faculty of Architecture in Milan, and in 1997 he was given another contract to teach for the degree programme in Industrial Design at Milan Polytechnic's Faculty of Architecture. Over the course of his career he led many seminars and gave numerous talks the world over.

Mangiarotti's design activity was studded with many acknowledgements in the field of design as well as in that of construction, including: the Premio Domus Formica (1956), Premio In/Arch for Lombardy (1962 and special mention in 1989), Premio AIP-Associazione Italiana Prefabbricatori (1972), Prix Européen de la Construction Métallique (1979), a Medal plus Honory Degree at the Third World Architecture Biennial in Sofia (1986), the Marble Architectural Awards (1994 and 2007), Compasso d'oro ADI Career Award (1994), Gold Medal for Architecture at the Accademia della Torre di Carrara (1998), Gold Medal "Apostolo del Design" by Rima Editrice (2006).

Mangiarotti also received two honourary degrees, one in Engineering at the Faculty of Architecture of the Technische Universität in Munich (1998), and another in Industrial Design at Milan Polytechnic's Faculty of Architecture (2002).

He died in Milan on 30 June 2012.

Principal architectural works realized

1952	ビニャルディ集合住宅の一室、ミラノ	Bignardi Apartment, Milan
1955	モラスッティ社倉庫、分解可能な鉄骨構造、パドヴァ（ブルーノ・モラスッティとG. モラスッティと協働）	Modular steel structure for a warehouse, Padua (with B. and G. Morassutti)
1957	バランザーテの教会、ミラノ（ブルーノ・モラスッティとアルド・ファヴィーニと協働）	Church of the Mater Misericordiae, Baranzate, Milan (with B. Morassutti and A. Favini)
	サンマルティーノの家、カストロッツァ、トレント（ブルーノ・モラスッティと協働）	House in San Martino di Castrozza, Trento (with B. Morassutti)
	INA住宅計画のチーフ、ミラノのフェルトレ地区とフェッラーラ県	Director INA-Casa for the Feltre neighbourhood of Milan and the Province of Ferrara
	マンツォーニ集合住宅の一室、ミラノ（ブルーノ・モラスッティと協働）	Manzoni apartment, Milan (with B. Morassutti)
1958	フェッツァン通りの住宅、ミラノ（ブルーノ・モラスッティと協働）	Residential building in via Fezzan, Milan (with B. Morassutti)
	モラスッティ社倉庫、パドヴァ（ブルーノ・モラスッティ、ファヴィーニと協働）	Iron warehouse, Padua (with B. Morassutti and A. Favini)
1959	ガヴィラーテ通りの住宅、（ブルーノ・モラスッティ、ファヴィーニと協働）	Residential building in via Gavirate, Milan (with B. Morassutti and A. Favini)
	シュオブ邸の内装（ル・コルビュジエ設計）スイス、ラ・ショー＝ド＝フォン（モラスッティと協働）	Interior design for Villa Schwob (original project by Le Corbusier), La Chaux-de-Fonds, Switzerland (with B. Morassutti)

1960	クアドロンノ通りの集合住宅、ミラノ (ブルーノ・モラスッティ、ファヴィーニと協働)	Residential building in via Quadronno, Milan (with B. Morassutti and A. Favini)
1961-1964	スプリューゲン・ブロイ社倉庫、メストレ、ヴェネツィア (ファヴィーニと協働)	Splügen Bräu warehouse and office building, Mestre, Venice (with A. Favini)
1962	マルチャニーゼの工場と従業員用の集合住宅、/カゼルタ (ファヴィーニと協働)	Siag industrial/residential complex with social services, Marcianise, Caserta (with A. Favini)
1962-1963	海の見本市展示館、ジェノバ	Exposition pavilion at the Fiera del Mare, Genoa
1963-1966	ファチェプ社の構造システム、エルマグ社工場、 リッソーネ、モンツァ・エ・ブリアンツァ (A.ズブリシア・フィオレッティと協働)	FM construction system (Facep system), Elmag factory, Lissone, Monza and Brianza (with A. Sbriscia Fioretti)
1966	カザルッチ家具社の工場、ロヴェラスカ、コモ	Furniture factory for Casaluci, Rovellasca, Como
1968	ファチェプ社の構造システム、フィアット社代理店、 ドメリアーラ、ヴェローナ	FM construction system, Fiat dealership, Domegliara, Verona
	ビアンキ邸、ピアデナ、クレモナ	Villa Bianchi, Piadena, Cremona
	フォンタネージ邸、マリーナ・ディ・ピエトラサンタ、ルッカ	Villa Fontanesi, Marina di Pietrasanta, Lucca
1968	ファチェプ社の構造システム、フィアット社代理店、 ドメリアーラ、ヴェローナ	FM construction system, Fiat dealership, Domegliara, Verona
	ビアンキ邸、ピアデナ、クレモナ	Villa Bianchi, Piadena, Cremona
	フォンタネージ邸、マリーナ・ディ・ピエトラサンタ、ルッカ	Villa Fontanesi, Marina di Pietrasanta, Lucca
1968-1971	アルミタリア社の工場及びオフィス、チニゼッロ・バルサモ、ミラノ(ジュリオ・バリオ、ジョバンニ・コロンボ、アルベルト・ヴィンターニと協働)	Armitalia offices and factory, Cinisello Balsamo, Milan (with G. Ballio, G. Colombo, A. Vintani)
1968-1975	集合住宅、モンツァ	Residential building, Monza
1969-1979	構造システムU70、レマ社工場、アルツァーテ・ブリアンツァ、コモ(バリオ、コロンボ、ヴィンターニと協働)	U70 construction system, Lema factory, Alzate Brianza, Como (with G. Ballio, G. Colombo, A. Vintani)
1971	週末集合住宅、ムルロンゴ、ヴェローナ	Vacation homes, Murlongo, Verona
	ペデルツォーリ邸、バルドリーノ、ヴェローナ	Villa Pederzoli, Bardolino, Verona
	ミラ・シェーン邸、ソンマ・ロンバルド、ヴァレーゼ	Villa for Mila Schön, Somma Lombardo, Varese
1971-1978	スナイデロ社のオフィス、展示場、サービス施設、 マイアーノ、ウディネ(バリオ、コロンボ、ヴィンターニと協働)	Snaidero offices, showroom and services, Majano, Udine (with G. Ballio, G. Colombo, A. Vintani)
1972	ブリオナ構造システム	Briona construction system
1974-1978	アロジオの集合住宅、コモ	Residential building, Arosio, Como

1975	シュオブ邸の内装の完成（ル・コルビュジエ設計）スイス、ラ・ショー＝ド＝フォン	Completion of interior for Villa Schwob (Le Corbusier), La Chaux-de-Fonds, Switzerland
1976-1979	ブリオナ構造システム、フェグ社エントランス、ジュッサーノ、モンツァ・エ・ブリアンツァ（バリオ、コロンボ、ヴィンターニと協働）	Briona construction system, Feg entrance pavilion, Giussano, Monza and Brianza (with G. Ballio, G. Colombo, A. Vintani)
	ファチェプ社構造システム、フィアット代理店、ブッソレンゴ、ヴェローナ（バリオ、コロンボ、ヴィンターニと協働）	Facep construction system, Fiat dealership, Bussolengo, Verona (with G. Ballio, G. Colombo, A. Vintani)
1982	U70構造システム、ウニフォ社、トゥラーティ、コモ（バリオ、コロンボ、ヴィンターニと協働）	U70 construction system, Unifor factory, Turate, Como (with G. Ballio, G. Colombo, A. Vintani)
	イタリア国鉄のための鋼鉄指し掛け屋根、チェルトーザ鉄道駅、ロゴレード鉄道駅、ミラノ（バリオ、コロンボ、ヴィンターニと協働）	Cantilever standard steel roof for the Ferrovie dello Stato, Certosa and Rogoredo stations, Milan (with G. Ballio, C. Raffa, A. Vintani)
	ボヴィーザ鉄道駅、イタリア国鉄、ミラノ	Bovisa station, Ferrovie dello Stato, Milan
	クロスレールシステム、ミラノの地下鉄ガリヴァルディ駅、レプブリカ駅、ヴェネツィア駅（ポルタ・ヴェネツィア）、ピチェーノ駅（ダテオ）、ヴィットリア駅（ポルタ・ヴィットリア）	Cross-rail system: Garibaldi, Repubblica, Venezia [Porta Venezia], Piceno [Dateo], Vittoria [Porta Vittoria] stations in Milan
1990	U70構造システム、レマ社工場、ジュッサーノ、ミラノ（バリオ、コロンボ、ヴィンターニと協働）	U70 construction system, Lema factory, Giussano, Milan (with G. Ballio, F. Spinelli, A. Vintani)
	AEM社減ガスのキャビン、マッコナゴ、カナヴェーゼ、ミラノ	AEM gas reduction booth Macconago and Canavese, Milan
1991	IMM社オフィスと展示場棟、カッラーラ（G. パロディ、ヴィンターニと協働）	IMM office and exhibition building, Carrara (with G. Parodi, A. Vintani)
1992	クロスレールシステム、ミラノ地下鉄レプブリカ駅、ヴェネツィア駅	Cross-rail system: Repubblica and Venezia underground stations, Milan
1994	ガス測定AEM社キャビン、カッシーナ・トリウルツァ（アンナ・マンジャロッティと協働）	AEM gas measurement booth in Cascina Triulza, Milan (with Anna Mangiarotti)
1995	クロスレールシステム、ヴィッラピッツォーネ鉄道駅、ミラノ	Cross-rail system: Villapizzone station, Milan
	AEM社減ガスのキャビン、ボヴィーザ、ミラノ（アンナ・マンジャロッティと協働）	AEM gas reduction booth in Bovisa, Milano (with Anna Mangiarotti)
2006	クロスレールシステム、ミラノ地下鉄ロ・ペロ駅	Cross-rail system: Rho-Pero station, Milan
2012	ウニフォ社エントランス守衛室、トゥラーティ、コモ	Porter's lodge, Unifor factory entrance, Turate, Como

主な工業製品と彫刻 | Principal objects for industrial production and sculptures

1953	曲げ成形合板による家具シリーズ	Mass-produced furniture in bent plywood
1955	「Multiuso」(ムルティユーズ)組み合わせ家具シリーズ (ブルーノ・モラスッティと協働)	"Multiuse" modular furniture (with B. Morassutti)
	「Cavalletto」(カバレット)はめ込み家具シリーズ (ブルーノ・モラスッティと協働)	"Cavalletto" interlocking furniture (with B. Morassutti)
	「Secticon」(セクティコン)時計 (ブルーノ・モラスッティと協働)	"Secticon" clocks (with B. Morassutti)
1959	「59」椅子	"59" chair
1962	鋳型成形と旋盤加工によるブロンズの花器	Vases in cast and lathe-turned bronze
	プレキシガラスによる照明器具	Lamp with diffuser in solid plexiglas
1963	ポリスティロール成型による肘掛け椅子	Monobloc armchair in foam polystyrene
1964	ヴィチェンツァの土の花器シリーズ	Series of Vicenza clay vases
	「Barbados」(バルバドス)灰皿	"Barbados" ceramic ashtray
1965	鋼鉄管の時計「Secticon」(セクティコン)	"Secticon" clock made with stainless steel tubing
1966	吹きガラスの照明器具「Saffo」(サッフォ) 「Lesbo」(レスボ)	"Saffo" and "Lesbo" blown-glass lamps
	木製はめ込みシステム家具 「Junior」(ジュニア)「Senior」(シニア)	"Junior" and "Senior" multi-layered wooden furniture system
	インゴット角形の木製家具「4D」	"4D" furniture with solid wood angular elements
1967	「Cub8」システム	"Cub8" fitted wall system
	「Giogali」(ジョーガリ)吊り構造の照明器具	"Giogali" interlocking glass hooks for lighting
1968	磁器製の小品	Series of objects in vitreous china
	押し出しPVCによる「In/Out」(インアウト)システム	"In-Out" extruded PVC interwall unit
1971	「Eros」(エロス)重力ではめ込む大理石家具	"Eros" marble tables with gravity joint
	「Variazioni」(ヴァリアツィオーニ)切削加工による 大理石の花器	"Variazioni" milled marble vases
	「Cementa」(チェメンタ)セメントコンクリート製の 屋外照明器具	"Cementa" outdoor lamp in reinforced concrete

1973	「Tavolozzo」(タヴォロッツォ) 大理石とガラスのテーブル、テーブル用品	"Tavolozzo" marble and glass table and table accessories
1974	「Spirali」(スピラーリ) 照明器具	"Spirali" lamps
1975	「De Nôs」(デ・ヌス) 塊状の木製家具	"De Nôs" solid wood furniture
	コーヒー自動販売機	Automatic coffee machine
1978	「Incas」(インカス) 重力ではめ込むピエトラ・セレーナ石製のテーブル	"Incas" pietra serena tables with gravity joint
	「Tre 3」(トレトレ) 椅子	"Tre 3" chair
1979	「Aurea」(アウレア) モジュール編みのジュエリー	"Aurea" woven mesh jewellery
	フリーラインによるブロンズの花器	Free form bronze vases
	「Eccentrico」(エッチェントリコ) 偏心した円柱に支持された大理石テーブル	"Eccentrico" marble table with gravity joint
1980	銀製のデキャンタ、グラス、花器(ニューヨーク近代美術館に展示)	Silver carafe, glasses, and vase (on display at the Museum of Modern Art in New York)
1981	「In/in」(インイン) 化粧用突き板(イタロ・リヴェラーニ、アルピ社と協働)	"In/in" stained wood veneer panels (with Italo Liverani)
	「Estrual」(エストゥルアル) アルミニウム押出し製組み立て書棚	"Estrual" modular bookcase system made of extruded aluminium
	「Asolo」(アゾロ) 重力ではめ込む花崗岩製テーブル	"Asolo" granite table with gravity joint
1983	「Chicago」(シカゴ) 強化ファイバーグラス製の椅子	"Chicago" fiberglass reinforced chair
1984	銀製のポット一式	Complete silver tea and coffee service
	「Roto 3」(ロト3) クリスタルガラスの天板と折り畳み型木製支柱のテーブル	"Roto 3" table with crystal tabletop and folding wood support
1985	「M4」クリスタルガラスの天板と大理石の支柱のテーブル	"M4" tables with crystal tabletop and marble base
1986	「Ice stopper」(アイスストッパー) クリスタルグラス	"Ice stopper" crystal glassware
	「Forme in equilibrio」(均衡の造型) 彫刻	"Forme in equilibrio" porphyry sculptures
1987	「Loico」(ロイコ) 大理石のテーブル、書棚、コンソールテーブル	"Loico" marble tables, bookcases, marble console tables
	「Ergo」(エルゴ) クリスタルガラス製の燭台	"Ergo" crystal chandelier
	「Cono-cielo」(天空の円錐) 円錐の大理石彫刻	"Cono-cielo" marble structure with concentric elements
1988	「Casta」(カスタ) クリスタルガラス製の器	"Casta" crystal centrepiece

1988	「Bibulo」(ビブロ)クリスタル製グラスシリーズ	"Bibulo" crystal glassware
	「Aida」(アイダ)吹きガラスによる卓上照明器具	"Aida" table lamp
1989	「More」(モア)テーブル	"More" table
	「Primavera」(春)「Autunno」(秋)「Inverno」(冬)クリスタル花器シリーズ	"Primavera", "Autunno", "Inverno" collection of crystal flower vases
1990	「Touch Glass」(タッチグラス)クリスタルグラスシリーズ	"Touch Glass" crystal glassware series
	「Clizia」(クリーツィア)大理石の屋外用ベンチ	"Clizia" marble seat suitable for outdoor use
	「Ergonomica」(エルゴノミカ)ステンレス製食器、カトラリー、ボール、コーヒーポット	"Ergonomica" stainless steel tableware (flatware, ménagères, buckets, bowls, coffee pot)
	「Ebbro」(エッブロ)クリスタルグラス	"Ebbro" crystal glassware
	「Quattrotto」(クァットロット)テーブル	"Quattrotto" table
1991	「Bibulo」(ビブロ)クリスタルグラスシリーズ	"Bibulo" crystal glassware
1992	「Mesco」(メスコ)クリスタルグラス製の前菜用皿、カトラリー、チーズ入れ	"Mesco" crystal hors d'oeuvres, ménagère, and cheese dispenser
	「Gondola」(ゴンドラ)「Orà」(オラ)「Alter」(アルテル)「Nerì」(ネリ)クリスタル製燭台	"Gondola", "Orà", "Alter", "Nerì" crystal chandeliers
	オリアリ社のレバーハンドル	Handle for Olivari and Valli & Colombo
1993	「Never the same」(ネバー・ザ・セイム)組立式の着色合板のパネル	"Never the same" reassembled coloured wood panels
1994	「Vestale」(ヴェスターレ)クリスタル製酒杯とフリュートグラス	"Vestale" crystal goblet and flute
	「Italo」着色合板の彫刻(イタロ)	"Italo" reassembled coloured wood sculpture
1995	「Equilibrio di una relazione vitale」(生命の均衡)ブロンズの彫刻	"Equilibrio di una relazione vitale" bronze sculpture
	「Asimmetrie gravitazionali」(非対称な重力)「Divenire」(生成)大理石の彫刻	"Asimmetrie gravitazionali" and "Divenire" marble sculptures
1996	「Ypsilon」(イプシロン)書棚	"Ypsilon" bookcase
	「Profili in equilibrio gravitazionale」(重力均衡の輪郭)鉄の彫刻シリーズ	"Profili in equilibrio gravitazionale" iron sculptures
	「Variazioni」(変化)大理石の彫刻シリーズ	"Variazioni" marble sculptures

1996	「Futura memoria」(未来の記憶)「Stupore」(驚愕)ブロンズの彫刻	"Futura memoria" and "Stupore" bronze sculptures
1997	「At Iovis」(アト・イオヴィス) 「Sic Venus」(シク・ヴェヌス)照明器具	"At Iovis" and "Sic Venus" glass lamps
	「T-table」(Tテーブル)クリスタルガラスの天板と鋼鉄の脚のテーブル	"T-table", table with iron frame and crystal tabletop
	「Datong-simbolo」(ダトング・象徴)大理石の彫刻(カラーラ市から中国への贈り物)」	"Datong-simbolo" marble sculpture (gift from the City of Carrara to China)
	「Continuità fra pieno-vuoto」([満]と[空]の連続)鉄の彫刻	"Continuità fra pieno-vuoto" iron sculpture
1998	「DNA」「Separazione nostalgica」(郷愁の離別)アルミニウムの彫刻	"DNA" and "Separazione nostalgica" aluminium sculptures
	「Il vuoto come terza dimensione」(三次元の「空」)(1998-1999)「Energia materia-messaggio」(物質のエネルギー・メッセージ)鉄の彫刻	"Il vuoto come terza dimensione" (1998-1999) and "Energia materia-messaggio" iron sculptures
1999	「La galleria」(ギャラリー)「Le presenze」(存在)「Il percorso」(軌跡)大理石の彫刻	"La galleria", "Le presenze", "Il percorso" marble sculptures
2000	「Vera Laica」(ヴェラ・ライカ)指輪	"Vera Laica" silver ring
	「Massacro a Sant'Anna」(サンタンナの虐殺)鉄の彫刻	"Massacro a Sant'Anna" sculpture
	「Cerchia degli Idiotoi」(イディオトイの円環)ブロンズとアクリルの彫刻	"Cerchia degli Idiotoi" plexiglas and bronze sculpture
2001	「Vuoto in equilibrio」([空]の均衡) 「Omaggio a Giordano Bruno」(ジョルダーノ・ブルーノへのオマージュ)鉄の彫刻	"Vuoto in equilibrio" and "Omaggio a Giordano Bruno" iron sculptures
	「Congruenza」(合致)鋼鉄の彫刻	"Congruenza" stainless steel sculpture
2002	「Posamano」(ポーザマーノ)クリスタル製の灰皿	"Posamano" crystal ashtray
	「Strazio I」(拷問)大理石の彫刻	"Strazio" marble sculpture
2003	「Lito1」(リート1)「Lito2」(リート2)「Lito3」(リート3)大理石の洗面台	"Lito1","Lito2" and "Lito3" marble washbasins
	「La Flûte」(ラ・フルート)クリスタルグラス	"La Flûte" crystal glassware
	「Divenire 2003」(生成2003)白い大理石の彫刻	"Divenire 2003" white marble sculpture
2004	「Out-inside」「アウト・インサイド」アルミニウム製の接合システム家具	"Out-inside" aluminium joint furniture system

2004	「Psikebana」（シケバナ）クリスタルグラス製の花器	"Psikebana" crystal vase
2005	「Giogali 3D」（ジョーガリ3D）連結型ガラスフックの照明器具	"Giogali 3D" interlinking glass hooks
	「L'abbraccio」（ラブラッチョ）衛生機器シリーズ	"L'abbraccio" washbasin series
	「L'incontro」（リンコントロ）「Ad hoc」（アドック）銀製の指輪	"L'incontro" and "Ad hoc" silver rings
	「Cinque stele dialogano alle Cinque Terre」（5つの石柱がチンクエ・テッレで対話する）マナローラの石の彫刻	"Cinque stele dialogano alle Cinque Terre" stone sculpture
2006	「Balance」（バランス）「Dualità creativa」（創造的な二元性）「Divenire 2006」（生成2006）大理石の彫刻	"Balance", "Dualità creativa", "Divenire 2006" marble sculptures
2009	「Equilibrio di una relazione vitale」（生命の均衡）アクリルの彫刻、リ・エディション	"Equilibrio di una relazione vitale" sculpture, new edition in plexiglas
2011	「Equilibrio di una relazione vitale」（生命の均衡）ステンレス鋼の彫刻、リ・エディション	"Equilibrio di una relazione vitale" sculpture, new edition in stainless steel

Bibliography

The bibliography is about Angelo Mangiarotti's architectural works.

1955
In un granaio, uno studio e un alloggio, in "Domus", n. 305, aprile, pp. 13-15.
Un grattacielo italiano in cemento precompresso, in "Domus", n. 309, agosto, pp. 4-5.
Italian Skyscraper in Pre-Stressed Concrete, in "Arts & Architecture", dicembre, p. 25.

1956
Project pour un gratteciel en Italie, in "Aujord'hui", n. 7, marzo, p. 53.

1957
Milano oggi, Edizioni Milano Moderna, Milano, p. 103.

1958
Un capannone industriale prefabbricato, in "Casabella", n. 218, marzo, pp. 84-89.
Milano oggi, Edizioni Milano Moderna, Milano, p. 84.

1959
Chiesa a Baranzate presso Milano, in "Casabella", n. 224, febbraio, pp. 19-24.
Una chiesa di vetro in Lombardia, in "Domus", n. 351, febbraio, pp. 1-8.
Glaskirche in der Lombardie, in "Baukunst und Werkform", marzo, pp. 146-148.
Chiese nuove: la situazione a Milano, in "Comunità", n. 68, marzo, pp. 48-65.
Église paroissiale à Baranzate près de Milan, in "Aujord'hui", n. 21, aprile, pp. 72-73.
P.C. Santini, *Angelo Mangiarotti, Bruno Morassutti*, in "Zodiac", n. 15, maggio, pp. 170-179.
Una chiesa di vetro a Baranzate (Mi), in "Vitrum", n. 113, maggio-giugno, pp. 6-13.
Church at Baranzate near Milan, Italy, in "Architectural design", settembre, pp. 367-368.
Église de Baranzate, in "L'art sacré", n. 1-2, settembre-ottobre, pp. 9-12.
Chiesa a Baranzate, in "Chiesa e quartiere", settembre-ottobre, pp. 72-79.
Church of Baranzate, in "Kenchiku Bunka", n. 157, novembre, pp. 22-25.
Church of Baranzate, in "Progressive Architecture", dicembre, pp. 134-137.

1960
Church, in "Architecture and Building", gennaio, pp. 29-33.
Una casa in montagna, in "Vitrum", n. 18, marzo-aprile, pp. 36-36.
Due case a S. Martino di Castrozza, in "Domus", n. 365, aprile, pp. 3-22.
Sul principio della continuità dei prospetti, in "Domus", n. 367, giugno, pp. 8-9.
In una villa di Le Corbusier, in "Domus", n. 368, luglio, pp. 9-22.
Lagerhalle für Stahlprofile in Padua, in "Bauen + Wohnen", agosto, pp. 282-285.
A. Mangiarotti et B. Morassutti entrepot pour profils d'acier, Padoue, in "L'architecture d'aujord'hui", n. 91-92, settembre-ottobre-novembre, pp. 154-156.
Casa meublée a Milano, in "Domus", n. 372, novembre, pp. 11-22.
Eine Kirche aus Glass, in "Moebel Interior Design", dicembre, pp. 614-615.

1961
P. Hofer, *Baranzate*, in "Bauen + Wohnen", maggio, pp. 161-164.
C. Ceschi, *Strutture nuove per nuove chiese*, in "Civiltà delle macchine", n. 3, maggio-giugno, pp. 43-52.
Église de Baranzate près de Milan, Italie, in "L'architecture d'aujord'hui", n. 96, giugno-luglio, pp. 22-25.
Una nuova unità residenziale a Piombino, in "Domus", n. 383, ottobre, pp. 1-6.
The Editorial Commitee of Contemporary Architecture of the World (a cura di), *Contemporary Architecture of the World 1961*, Shokokusha Publishing Co., Tokyo, pp. 64-304.
G.E. Kidder Smith, *The New Architecture of Europe*, The World Publishing Company, Ohio, pp. 191-196.

1962
La casa "a tre cilindri" a S. Siro, Milano, in "Domus", n. 387, febbraio, pp. 1-10.
House at S. Martino di Castrozza, in "The Kentiku", febbraio, pp. 44-47.
A. Belloni, *Ein möbliertes Wohnhaus in Mailand*, in "Moebel Interior Design", giugno, pp. 269-271.
Struttura per un capannone, in "Domus", n. 392, luglio, pp. 5-6.
Con elementi prefabbricati, in "Domus", n. 394, settembre, pp. 1-4.
I. Kawara, *Angelo Mangiarotti*, in "The Kentiku", ottobre, pp. 81-89.
Immeuble a Milan, in "L'architecture d'aujord'hui", n. 104, ottobre-novembre, pp. 104-105.
Angelo Mangiarotti and Bruno Morassutti, in Architects' Year Book 10, Elek Ltd, London, pp. 216-225.
I. Porto de Menezes, *Arquitectura sagrada*, Ouro Preto, tav. 2, p. 44.

1963
A. Mangiarotti, *Sul principio della continuità dei prospetti*, in "Domus", n. 398, gennaio, pp. 1-10.
A. Mangiarotti, *La tradizione quale lezione di metodo nelle case del '700 in Val di Vedro*, in "Domus", n. 405, agosto, pp. 47-50.
Glazen kerk bij Milaan, in "Bouw", n. 36, settembre, pp. 1158-1159.

Casa d'abitazione in via Quadronno, in "L'architettura cronache e storia", n. 7, novembre, pp. 540-541.
XIII Triennale, L'aula Magna della Nuova Biblioteca dell'Università Bocconi di Milano, Capannone industriale a Mestre, in "Edilizia Moderna", n. 82-83, p. 163.
G. Veronesi, *Opere recenti di Angelo Mangiarotti*, in "Zodiac", n. 11, pp. 146-157.

1964
Un esempio di prefabbricazione completa, in "Domus" n. 418, pp. 8-9.
B. Alfieri, G. Veronesi, *Padiglione per esposizione alla fiera del Mare a Genova*, in "Lotus Architectural Annual", 1964-1965, pp. 124-129.
I. Kawahara (a cura di), *Angelo Mangiarotti 1955-1964*, Seidoh-Sya Publishing Co.,Tokyo.
G.E. Kidder Smith, *Chiesa "Mater Misericordiae" a Baranzate, Nuove Chiese in Europa*, Edizioni di Comunità, Londra-Milano, pp. 203-209.
L'atelier di Mangiarotti, in "L'oeil", n. 109, gennaio, pp. 50-53.
T.O. Sammartini, *The work of A. Mangiarotti and B. Morassutti 1955-1962*, in "Architectural Design", n. 3, marzo, pp. 140-151.
Un nuovo complesso industriale a Marcianise, in "L'industria italiana del cemento", settembre, pp. 843-854.

1965
B. Alfieri, G. Veronesi, *Progetto per un policentro – megastruttura*, in "Lotus Architectural Annual", n. 1965-1966, pp. 72-75.
J. Donat, *Stabilimento per la produzione di pannelli truciolari a Marcianise; Deposito industriale a Mestre*, in "World Architecture", vol. II, p. 106-111.
A. Mangiarotti, B. Morassutti, *immeuble d'appartements à Milan, Italie*, in "L'architecture d'aujord'hui", n. 117, gennaio, pp. 27-29.
Angelo Mangiarotti, in "The Japan Architect", febbraio, pp. 111-134.
F. Hiromi, I. Alane, *Angelo Mangiarotti*, in "The Kentiku", marzo, pp. 34-40.
Mangiarotti's Technical Design Method, in "Kenchiku Bunka", n. 227, settembre, pp. 94-101.
Intervista a un docente in carica: Angelo Mangiarotti, in "Marcatre. Notiziario di cultura contemporanea", Lerici, Milano, pp. 415-416.
J. Donat (a cura di), *World Architecture 2*, Studio Vista, London, pp. 99-100, 106-111.

1966
La nuova copertura del deposito della società Poretti a Mestre, in "L'industria italiana del cemento", gennaio, pp. 25-34.
E.D. Bona, *Un esempio di metodo e figuratività; Aspetti dell'opera architettonica di A. Mangiarotti*, in "Casabella", n. 302, febbraio, pp. 48-61.
M. De Santis, *Prefabbricazione integrale: valori architettonici in un edificio industriale a Lissone (MI)*, in "L'industria italiana del cemento", aprile, pp. 223-234.

G. Dorfles, *Arhitekt A. Mangiarotti*, in "Sinteza", aprile, pp. 52-54.
Prefabbricazione, una costruzione in c.a. totalmente prefabbricata in officina, in "Domus", n. 444, novembre, pp. 2-8.
Associazione Nazionale Italiana Cemento Armato Precompresso, *Realizzazioni italiane in cemento armato precompresso*, Aitec, pp. 250-263.

1967
Il sistema trilitico a struttura reticolare, in "Edilizia industrializzata", n. 1, aprile, pp. 20-24.
Wohnungen, Büros, Mensa und Garderoben in Marcianise bei Caserta, Italien, in "Werk", agosto, pp. 488-490.
A. Galardi, *Chiesa "Mater Misericordiae" a Baranzate; Deposito per materiali ferrosi a Padova; Edificio per abitazioni in via Gavirate a Milano*, in *Architettura italiana contemporanea*, Edizioni di Comunità, Milano, pp. 36-37, 88-89, 170-171.
Deposito a Mestre, in "Domus", n. 451, giugno, pp. 2-5.
Un élégant immeuble industriel en béton préfabriqué, in "Bullettin du ciment", n. 22, pp. 1-6.

1968
D. Sugden, *The anatomy of the factory: factory a Lissone*, in "Architectural Design", n. 38.
Mehrzweckhalle als Ausstellungshalle, in "Werk", n. 4.
E.D. Bona, *Razionalità sperimentale. Un padiglione esclusivamente in materie plastiche nel parco di Milano*, in "Casabella", n. 325, giugno, pp. 22-28.

1969
M. De Santis, *Integrale Vorfetigung Industriegebäude in Lissone*, in "Bauen + Wohnen", luglio, pp. 254-257.
E.D. Bona, *Cronache di disegno industriale; Struttura industriale prefabbricata in C.A.P., CUB 8 armadio parete attrezzata*, in "Casabella", n. 343, dicembre, pp. 30-37.
F. Zago, *Edificio industriale prefabbricato a Lissone*, in "Il cemento armato precompresso in architettura", Cluva, Vicenza, pp. 3-22.

1970
A. Mangiarotti conferma del trilite, in "Casabella", n. 352, settembre, pp. 40-42.
Angelo Mangiarotti: una struttura strutturata, in "Domus", n. 484, marzo, pp. 6-7.

1971
P.C. Santini, *L'avanguardia di Mangiarotti*, in "Ottagono", n. 20, marzo, pp. 76-85.
Una casa in Versilia, in "Domus", n. 498, maggio, pp. 18-22.

Analisi di un organismo prefabbricato dalle premesse progettuali alle fasi realizzative, in "Lipe", giugno, pp. 457-478.
Case in pianura, in "Domus", n. 505, dicembre, pp. 12-18.

1972
A. Mangiarotti *House in Cisano, Lake Garda, Italy*, in "Global Interior", aprile, pp. 94-101.
A.Mangiarotti *Bianchi House, Piadena, Italy*, in "Global Interior", aprile, pp. 102-107.
E.D. Bona, *Operaio sotto scocca; Mangiarotti a Cinisello Balsamo*, in "Casabella", n. 365, maggio, pp. 21-27.
P.C. Santini, *Sulla sponda veneta del Garda*, in "Domus", n. 511, giugno, p. 23-30.
Bausysteme für den Industriebau, in "Werk", giugno, pp. 336-337.
Casa di vacanza di architettura rigorosa, in "Casa Vogue", n. 15, luglio-agosto, pp. 57-61.
Silhouette des Parco Murlongo, in "Moebel Interior Design", agosto, pp. 36-41.
Briona 72 – Eine polivalente Struktur, in "Werk", n. 12, p. 683.

1973
Forum Vorfabriziertes Beton-Bausystems, in "Bauen + Wohnen", gennaio, p. 3.
A.G. Bolocan, F. Mendini, *Componente prepotente*, in "Casabella", n. 373, gennaio, pp. 8-9.
Etablessements Arm Italia, in "L'architecture d'aujourd'hui", n. 165, gennaio, pp. 80-83.
L. Patetta, *Alcune opere recenti del professionismo milanese*, in "Controspazio", n. 1, giugno, pp. 67-98.
House at Lake Garda, in "ABC", luglio, pp. 60-65.
Prefabbricazione: tre sistemi, in "Domus", n. 526, settembre, pp. 9-16.
C. Cuscianna, *Prefabbricazione ed eleganza formale in uno stabilimento industriale a Cinisello Balsamo (MI)*, in "L'industria italiana del cemento", settembre, pp. 557-572.
G. Veronesi, *Architetture recentissime di A. Mangiarotti*, in "Zodiac", n. 11, pp. 147-157.

1974
Einfamilienhäuser Plan domino 1973. Haus in Piadena, in "Bauen + Wohnen", agosto, pp. 314-316.
Angelo Mangiarotti, in "Architecture and Urbanism", settembre, pp. 67-88.
Usine Arm Italia a Cinisello Balsamo, Italie, in "Tecniques et Architecture", n. 300, settembre-ottobre, p. 94.
Macrostruttura prefabbricata 40x40: trilite più piastra, in "Domus", n. 541, dicembre, pp. 25-28.
A. Mangiarotti, *Fabbrica a Cinisello Balsamo, Italia*, in "Rivista tecnica", vol. 65, n. 1, pp. 44-45.
D. Insall, A. Chauvel, *Systèmes préfabriqués pour halls industriels. Structures en béton: usine "Arm Italia" à Cinisello Balsamo, Italie*, in "Techniques et architecture", n. 297, febbraio-marzo, pp. 94-105.
Angelo Mangiarotti: prefabbricazione, un asilo tipo, in "Domus", n. 537, agosto, p. 17.

1975
Strutture prefabbricate per uno stabilimento industriale ad Alzate Brianza (CO), in "L'industria Italiana del cemento", febbraio, pp. 75-92.
Technik unf Form. Industriegebäude in Cinisello Balsamo bei Mailand, in "Bauen + Wohnen", aprile, pp. 154-156.
I. Kawahara, M. Kawakami, Y. Sano, M. Takej, M. Tajima, *Mangiarotti's Sumptous World*, in "Space Design", n. 129, maggio, pp. 5-99.
A. Mangiarotti, *Mailand. Struktur als Form*, in "Bauen + Wohnen", dicembre, pp. 504-505.

1976
Prefabrication / Participation: gli utenti parteci-pano al progetto, in "Domus", n. 567, febbraio,pp. 5-8.
M. Rovera, *La casa trasparente di Mila Schön*, in "Vogue Italia", n. 292, febbraio, pp. 172-177.
4 Systemes industrialisés, in "Architecture pour l'industrie", n. 396, aprile, pp. 77-85.
G. Gramigna, *Un incontro: Angelo Mangiarotti*, in "Ottagono", n. 3, ottobre, pp. 76-81.
M. Rovera, *Intervento di Mangiarotti in un'opera giovanile di Le Corbusier*, in "Casa Vogue", n. 63, novembre, pp. 162-171.
G. Nardi, *Progettazione architettonica per sistemi e componenti*, Franco Angeli, Milano, pp. 134, 135, 166-168, 179, 182-184, 193-194.

1977
L. Quaroni, *Progettare un edificio: otto lezioni di architettura*, Mazzotta, Milano, p. 135.
A. Mangiarotti, *Mailand. Industrialisiertes Bauen und Nutzerbeteiligung, Wohnunghaus in Monza*, in "Bauen + Wohnen", giugno, pp. 225-227.
Angelo Mangiarotti: Prefabrication / Partecipation, gli utenti partecipano al progetto, in "Domus", n. 567, febbraio, pp. 5-8.
Sistema Briona 72, in "L'industria italiana del cemento", n. 9, settembre, pp. 791-793.
1978
Angelo Mangiarotti, in "Nikkei Architecture", n. 2-6, pp. 84-86.
M. Rovere, *A. Mangiarotti + B. Morassutti, A. Mangiarotti + C. Pampo, Refurnishing a House by Le Corbusier in Switzerland, 1959-60, 1976*, in "Global Architecture House", n. 5, pp. 69-71.
Mangiarotti Prefab Expression of Forces, in "Domus", n. 582, maggio, pp.

6-8.
Ricostruzione in Friuli, in "Domus", Milano, n. 587, ottobre, pp. 14-21.
Housing at Monza, in "Architecture and Urbanism", dicembre, pp. 56-59.
R. Janke, *Architektur Modelle*, Gerd Hatje Verlag, Stuttgart, p. 71.

1979
'28/'78 Architettura, cinquanta anni di architettura italiana dal 1928 al 1978, catalogo della mostra (Milano, Palazzo delle Stelline, 28 marzo-13 maggio 1979), Editoriale Domus, Milano, pp. 108-121.
A. Pica, *Nel Friuli uffici in campagna*, in "Domus", n. 591, febbraio, pp. 10-15.
Sei domande a otto designers: A. Mangiarotti, in "Edilizia moderna", n. 85, pp. 15-16.
Tu causes, tu causes! ...l'architettura seria continua, in "Metro3", pp. 63-66.
Collegio Tecnici Acciaio, *Giornate italiane della costruzione in acciaio*, atti del VII congresso del Collegio Tecnici Acciaio, ottobre, pp. 107-118.
A. Drexler, *Transformations in Modern Architecture*, Museum of Modern Art, New York, p. 70.
T. Koncz, M. Mazzocchi, E. Tealdi, *Prefabbricare: architettura e industria delle costruzioni*, Hoepli, Milano, pp. 57, 70, 180, 181, 199.
G. Nardi, *Tecnologia dell'architettura e industrializzazione nell'edilizia*, Franco Angeli, Milano, tavv. 4-38.
I nuovi edifici Snaidero a Majano, in "Costruzioni metalliche", n. 5.
Snaidero News Buildings at Majano, Friuli, in "IABSE structures", n. 3, agosto, pp. 6-7.

1980
Associazione Italiana Prefabbricazione per l'Edilizia Industrializzata, *Repertorio 1980*, Tipografia Ronda, Milano, pp. 104, 105, 196, 197, 226, 227.
E.D. Bona, *Angelo Mangiarotti: il processo del costruire*, Electa, Milano.
V. Gandolfi, *L'acciaio nell'architettura*, Centro italiano sviluppo impieghi acciaio, Milano, pp. 121, 170-171.
M. Grandi, A. Pracchi, *Milano. Guida all'architettura moderna*, Zanichelli, Bologna, pp. 276, 316, 317, 378.
A.M. Vogt, *Architektur 1940-1980*, Propyläen Verlag, Berlin, pp. 131, 137.
Edificio per uffici a piani appesi a Majano del Friuli, Udine, in "L'industria italiana del cemento", n. 2, pp. 101-108.
Alloggi su misura, in "Domus Prefab", fascicolo di supplemento alla rivista "Domus", n. 610, pp. 46-47.
Recent works by Angelo Mangiarotti, in "Space Design", n. 191, agosto, pp. 45-66.

1981
G. De Feo, E. Valeriani, *Architetture italiane degli anni '70*, catalogo della mostra, De Luca, Roma, pp. 90-95.
G. Nardi, *Tecnologia dell'architettura e industrializzazione edilizia*, Franco Angeli, Milano.

1982
Complesso per servizi sociali, in "L'architettura, cronache e storia", n. 320, giugno, pp. 441-451.
Strutture prefabbricate per un edificio ad uso industriale e commerciale in Bussolengo, in "L'industria italiana del cemento", n. 11, novembre, pp. 803-816.

1983
A. Mangiarotti, A. Ubertazzi, *L'immagine per le stazioni del passante ferroviario*, in "Ingegneria ferroviaria", Collegio degli Ingegneri Ferroviari Italiani, Roma.
Il passante di Milano, Janusa Editrice, Roma, pp. 96-100.
L. Galletti, *Case costruite con metodi industrializzati 11*, Over, Milano.
V. Magnago Lampugnani, *Hatje-Lexicon der Architektur des 20. Jahrhunderts*, Gerd Hatje Verlag, Stuttgart, p. 181.
Material und Form. Bauten in Bussolengo und Majano, in "Werk, Bauen und Wohnen", n. 10, ottobre, pp. 36-45.

1984
Industriebau, Deutsche Verlags Anstalt, Stuttgart, pp. 106, 107, 120, 32, 133.
P. Carlodalatri, *Percorsi di architettura italiana*, Unipress, Roma, p. 45.
Office building, Majano del Friuli, in "Detail", n. 3, maggio-giugno, pp. 246-247.

1985
I trasporti a Milano. I piani, i progetti, le realizzazioni e le prospettive, Franco Angeli, Milano, pp. 26-27.
A. Belluzzi, C. Conforti, *Architettura italiana 1944-1984*, Laterza, Bari, pp. 33, 35, 45, 52.
L. Benevolo, *L'ultimo capitolo dell'architettura moderna*, Laterza, Bari, p. 122.
R. Ostertag, *Angelo Mangiarotti, Ponte per pedoni*, Institut für Gebäudelehre und Entwerfen von Hochbauten, Braunschweig.
P. von Seidlein, *Stahlbeton, Fertigbau, Bauten von Angelo Mangiarotti*, Universität Stuttgart, Stuttgart.

1986
E.D. Bona, *Criteri generali a sei progetti*, Nuova Italsider, Genova, pp. 11, 85-94.
C. Fera, *Principi di progettazione e rassegna di interventi*, Nuova Italsider, Genova, pp. 146-147.
A. Mangiarotti, *Il linguaggio espressivo dell'edilizia industrializzata*, in O. Selvafolta (a cura di), *Industria e terziario*, Electa, Milano, pp. 114-118.

1987
A. D'Angelo, *Ferrovia d'autore*, in "Voci della rotaia", n. 4, aprile, pp. 23-25.
B. Gerosa, *Botta e risposta con Angelo Mangiarotti*, in "Costruire per abita-

re", n. 56, novembre, pp. 140-141.
C. Columba, A. D'Angelo, *L'architettura scende nelle stazioni*, in "L'Arca", n. 12, dicembre, pp. 84-91.
G.M. Jonghi Lavarini, M. De Caro, *Bruno Morassutti e Angelo Mangiarotti. Edificio in via Quadronno 1959*, in *Il condominio a Milano*, Di Baio, Milano, pp. 102-112.
W. Pagliero, *Fare l'architetto non l'artista*, in "Casa oggi", n. 160, ottobre, pp. 20-27.
E.D. Bona, *Mangiarotti*, Sagep, Genova.
Mangiarotti et al., *In nome dell'architettura*, Jaca Book, Milano.

1988

F. Dal Co, S. Polano, *Angelo Mangiarotti, Italian Architecture 1945-1985*, a+u Publishing Co. Tokyo, pp. 100-101.
G. Küttinger, H. Schöpke, *Angelo Mangiarotti. Beton im Wohnungsbau*, Verlaghaus Erdl Kg, Trostberg.
V. Magnago Lampugnani (a cura di), *Mangiarotti, Encyclopaedia of 20th-Century Architecture*, Thames and Hudson, London, pp. 210-211.
G. Muratore et al., *Italia. Gli ultimi trent'anni*, Zanichelli, Bologna, pp. 126, 129, 199, 223.
P. Musolino, *Il treno come autobus*, in P. Berengo Gardin (a cura di), *Ferrovie italiane*, Editori Riuniti, Roma, pp. 376-389.

1989

G. De Giovanni, *Acciaio come obbedienza e trasgressione*, in "Acciaio", n. 4, aprile, pp. 191-192.
S. Rossi, *Premi nazionali IN/Arch 1989: sistema strutturale per l'Unifor, Turate, nel quadro dell'opera di Angelo Mangiarotti*, in "L'architettura. Cronache e storia", n. 11, novembre, p. 814.
M. von Gerkan, *Industrie und Handelsgebäude in Bussolengo, Flache Dächer*, Rudolf Müller, Köln, pp. 73-76.

1990

C. Paganelli, *La città possibile. Nuove architetture e trasformazioni urbanistiche per Milano*, in "Casa oggi", n. 191, maggio, pp. 10-13.
Die Architektur der Serienerzeugung, in "Architektur Aktuell", n. 139, ottobre, pp. 90-93.
A. Presbitero, *Binari d'autore*, in "Costruire", n. 90, novembre, pp. 148-150.
A. Presbitero, *Le nuove stazioni di Milano Rogoredo e Milano Certosa*, in "Il giornale del fabbro e del serramentista", n. 7-8, luglio-agosto, pp. 22-27.
G. Ciucci, F. Dal Co, *Architettura italiana del '900. Atlante*, Electa, Milano, p. 204.

1991

M. Baffa, *Le stazioni del passante ferroviario di Milano: un prototipo per una struttura architettonica complessa*, in "AxA", n. 1 maggio, pp. 22-29.
A. Bonometto (a cura di), *Stazioni di acciaio*, in "Architetture elettriche", supplemento a "Quattrofili", n. 59, pp. 10-27.
A. Campioli, Angelo Mangiarotti, in "Gift", n. 39, settembre, pp. 73-88.
A. Mangiarotti, *La componente etica del progetto*, in M. Bertoldini (a cura di), *L'atto progettuale*, Città Studi, Milano.

1992

A. Campioli, M. Luchi, *Angelo Mangiarotti e la seduzione della materia. Una mostra nel Gift*, in "Gift", n. 40, gennaio, pp. 57-64.
A. Sposito, Estetica e tecnologia, in "Demetra", n. 2, giugno, pp. 8-17.
A. Mangiarotti, *Intervista*, in M. Bertoldini e M. Calloni (a cura di), *Pensare Milano. Intellettuali a confronto con la città che cambia*, Guerini & Associati, Milano, pp. 162-163.

1993

A. Mangiarotti, *Architetture tecniche*, in "Proporzione A", n. 1, giugno, pp. 26-28.
Una casa di luce, in "Chiesa oggi: Architettura e comunicazione", n. 5, luglio, pp. 74-77.
Stazione Repubblica del Passante Ferroviario di Milano, in "In costruzione", supplemento monografico a "Casabella", n. 605, ottobre, pp. 56-57.
A. Mangiarotti, *Silver House: un sistema per abitare*, in "Proporzione A", n. 1, giugno, pp. 54-57.

1994

F. Cocucci, *Angelo Mangiarotti. Tecnologia e cultura del progetto*, in "Proporzione A", n. 4, giugno, pp. 6-15.
A. Colonnetti, *Angelo Mangiarotti: la componente etica del progetto*, in "Campo", n. 8, pp. 186-187.
Regione Toscana, Internazionale Marmi e Macchine Carrara, *Marble Architectural Awards 1994*, Internazionale Marmi e Macchine, Carrara, pp. 14-21.

1995

P. Balzanelli, *Angelo Mangiarotti. Una casa e il suo camino sulla sponda del Garda*, in "Il camino", n. 58, marzo, pp. 74-77.
M. Capuani, *Angelo Mangiarotti e la materia*, in "Ottagono" n. 115, giugno-agosto, pp. 98-105.
F. Kind-Barkauskas et al., *Industriegebäude in Bussolengo*, in *Beton Atlas*, Institut für internationale Architektur-Documentation, München, pp. 258-259.
E. Mandolesi, voce *Prefabbricazione*, in *Enciclopedia Italiana di Scienze Lettere e Arti*, Istituto dell'Enciclopedia Italiana, Roma, Appendice V, p. 253, tav. XLIV.
A. Mangiarotti, *Le tecniche dell'architettura contemporanea. Evoluzione e innovazione degli elementi costruttivi*, Franco Angeli, Milano, pp. 38-45, 129-131.

C. Paganelli, *Quell'"astronave" a tre cilindri*, in "L'Unità", 11 novembre, p. 25.

1996
A. Mangiarotti, *Pensiero e materia*, in "L'Arca", n. 107, settembre, pp. 2-3.
Architect A. Mangiarotti's Homogeneity of details and the Abundance in their Variety, in Tokio. Hope and Recovery. Urban Civilization and Environment, numero monografico di "Process: Architecture", n. 129, marzo, p. 130.
O. Hamaguchi, *Angelo Mangiarotti + Alberto Vintani, Internazionale Marmi e Macchine Center*, in "The Kenchiku Gijutsu", n. 555, giugno, pp. 146-150.
A. Campioli, *Oltre l'estetica*, in "L'Arca", n. 105, giugno, pp. 82-83.
M. Arnaboldi, *Il restauro della modernità*, in "L'Arca", n. 107, settembre, pp. 4-5.
D. Premoli, *Angelo Mangiarotti, architetto e designer*, in "OFX Office International", n. 32, settembre-ottobre, pp. 56-61.
M. Nagel, *Angelo Mangiarotti Lissone, Bussolengo, Turate*, Institut für Tragkonstruktionen und konstruktives Entwerfen, Universität Stuttgart, Stuttgart.

1997
Angelo Mangiarotti, in "Zodiac", n. 16, settembre 1996- febbraio 1997, pp. 144-147.
C. Paganelli, *Via Quadronno, la casa a geometria variabile*, in "L'Unità", 8 febbraio, p. 23.
A. Mangiarotti, *Sull'oggettività del progetto di architettura*, in G. Nardi (a cura di), *Aspettando il progetto*, Franco Angeli, 1997, pp. 177-182.
G. Nardi, *Angelo Mangiarotti, tecne e progetto*, Maggioli, Rimini.

1998
F. Burkhardt, *L'aspetto artistico nell'opera di Angelo Mangiarotti*, in "Domus", n. 807.
T. Herzog, A. Mangiarotti, *Bausysteme von Angelo Mangiarotti / Construction systems by Angelo Mangiarotti / Sistemi costruttivi di Angelo Mangiarotti*, Technische Universität München, Lehrstuhl für Entwerfen und Baukonstruktion II, München.

2001
B. Finessi, *Nel segno di Angelo Mangiarotti*, in "Abitare", n. 403.
M. Giordano, *Materiale e funzione. Il progetto fra poesia e tecnica di Angelo Mangiarotti*, in "OFX Architettura", n. 63.

2002
F. Acerboni, *Angelo Mangiarotti tra tecnica e progetto*, in "Elite", n. 6-7.
B. Finessi, F. Burkhardt, L. Caramel, G. Nardi, *Su Mangiarotti*, Abitare Segesta, Milano.

2003
A. Campioli, *Modulo e coordinazione modulare nell'architettura di Angelo Mangiarotti*, in "Materia", n. 40.

2004
N. Endo, A. Mangiarotti, *Angelo Mangiarotti*, catalogo della mostra (Tokyo, Gallery-Ma, 10 settembre-13 novembre 2004),Toto Shuppan, Tokyo.

2005
D. Duva, L. Ponti, *Maestri del design: Castiglioni, Magistretti, Mangiarotti, Mendini, Sottsass*, Bruno Mondadori, Milano.

2007
M. Biaggi, *Intervista a Angelo Mangiarotti*, "Abitare", n. 473.

2009
B. Finessi (a cura di), *Angelo Mangiarotti: scolpire/costruire*, catalogo della mostra (Mantova, Casa del Mantegna, 12 settembre-8 novembre 2009), Corraini, Mantova.
2010
F. Burkhardt (a cura di), *Angelo Mangiarotti: opera completa*, Motta architettura, Milano.

2011
F. Burkhardt, *Angelo Mangiarotti*, Il Sole 24 Ore Cultura, Milano.
G. Barazzetta, I. Paoletti, *Il progetto di restauro della Chiesa Mater Misericordiae (1957-1958) / The Restoration Design of Mater Misericordiae Church (1957-1958)*, in F. Graf, F. Albani (a cura di), *Il vetro nell'architettura del XX secolo: conservazione e restauro / Glass in the 20th Century Architecture: Preservation and Restoration*, Mendrisio Academy Press, Mendrisio, pp. 395-417.

2012
A. Mangiarotti, I. Paoletti, K. Horikawa, *Architetti e designers giapponesi dallo Studio Mangiarotti*, Maggioli, Rimini.

2014
G. Barazzetta, *Il restauro di un involucro degli anni Cinquanta*, in "Archi", n. 5, 2014, pp. 96-103.
F. Graf, *Histoire matérielle du bâti et projet de sauvegarde: devenir de l'architecture moderne et contemporaine*, Presses polytechniques et universitaires romandes, Lausanne, pp. 224-241.

著者プロフィール

Authors

槇文彦
1928年東京生まれ。東京大学、ハーバード大学に学び両校で教鞭をとる。1965年槇総合計画事務所設立。代表作に「ヒルサイドテラス」「スパイラル」「幕張メッセ」「4WTC・グラウンドゼロ」等。日本建築学会賞大賞、朝日賞、プリツカー賞、UIA及びAIAゴールドメダル等受賞。文化功労者。

鈴木敏彦
建築家。工学院大学建築学部教授。黒川紀章建築都市設計事務所、フランス・ニュータウン開発公社EPA marneに勤務。早稲田大学大学院理工学研究科博士課程を経て、東北芸術工科大学助教授、首都大学東京准教授を経て現職。Atelier OPAファウンダー。2011年よりOpa Pressで建築とデザインに関する書籍を出版。

アンナ・マンジャロッティ
建築家。ミラノ工科大学建築環境科学技術学部の建築技術学科の建築技術の教授。建築環境建設工学学科で技術的な科目を教え、博士号の指導にあたる。高度な先端システム技術と部品設計に従事する設計者。2016年逝去。

フランツ・グラフ
スイス連邦工科大学ローザンヌ校卒業。1989年からジュネーヴで建築家として活動。住宅や公共施設の設計と開発、再開発および修復プロジェクトに従事。掲載多数。1989年から2006年ジュネーヴ大学建築研究所で建築と施工を教える。2005年からスイス・イタリア語圏大学メンドリシオ建築アカデミーにて設計と技術の教授。2007年からスイス連邦工科大学にて理論と設計の准教授。現代および近代の建設方式の研究、現代建築遺産の修復の研究を実施。2010年からドコモモ（Do.Co.Mo.Mo）スイスの代表、技術に関する国際専門委員会のメンバー。2012年からル・コルビュジエ財団の建築作品修復の専門委員会メンバー。

Fumihiko Maki
Maki was born in 1928 in Tokyo and studied and taught at both the University of Tokyo and Harvard University. Hillside Terrace, Spiral, Makuhari Messe, and 4WTC at Ground Zero are his representative works. Maki has been awarded with the Grand Prize of the Architectural Institute of Japan, the Asahi Prize, the UIA Gold Medal, the AIA Gold Medal, and the Pritzker Architecture Prize and has been accredited as Person of Cultural Merit.

Toshihiko Suzuki
Suzuki is an architect and a professor at the School of Architecture, Department of Architecture, Kogakuin University. He worked at Kisho Kurokawa Architect & Associates in Tokyo and EPAmarne in France. He graduated from the doctoral course at Waseda University and then taught at Tohoku University of Art and Design and Tokyo Metropolitan University. He is a founder of Atelier OPA. Since 2011, Opa Press has published many books about design and architecture.

Anna Mangiarotti
Mangiarotti is an architect and an ordinary professor of architecture technology at the Department of the Building Environment Science and Technology (BEST) of the Polytechnico di Milano. She teaches technical subjects and is head of the Faculty board of PhD programme of ABC Department with particular attention to the technologies of advanced systems and component design. She died in 2016.

Franz Graf
Graf graduated with a degree in architecture at the EPFL, Lausanne. Since 1989, he has been practicing as an architect in Geneva. He has designed and developed residential and public buildings, redevelopments, and restoration projects that are documented in various publications. He has taught architecture and construction at the Institute of Architecture, University of Geneva (1989–2006), and since 2005 has been a professor of design and technology at the Mendrisio Academy of Architecture-USI. Since 2007, he has been an associate professor of theory and design at the EPFL. Graf conducts research into modern and contemporary construction systems and restoration of modern heritage. Since 2010, he has been the president of Do.Co.Mo.Mo Switzerland and is a member of the International Specialist Committee on Technology, and since 2012, he has been a member of the Comité des experts pour la restauration de l'oeuvre of the Le Corbusier Foundation.

フランチェスカ・アルバーニ
建築家。ミラノ工科大学にて建築保存の研究で博士号を取得。建築・都市研究学科にて建築修復学の准教授。2007年からスイス・イタリア語圏大学メンドリシオ建築アカデミーにてフランツ・グラフの研究グループでの講義を担当する科学的共同研究者。建築修復の設計者として、材料や構造に関する著述多数。

堀川絹江
早稲田大学建築学科卒業後、同大学大学院理工学研究所、石山修武研究室にて建築学修士課程を修了。GKデザイングループ株式会社、GK設計勤務後、1995年よりアンジェロ・マンジャロッティ事務所およびTrust Fondazione Angelo Mangiarottiに勤務。2017年よりイタリアのAgape s.r.l.、Vetreria Vistosi s.r.l.二社の日本向けプロモーション業務を務めている。

河合俊和
1960年岐阜市に生まれる。1982年日本大学理工学建築学科卒業。1984年東京藝術大学美術学部美術研究科大学院修了。1984-91年香山アトリエ・環境造形研究所（現：香山壽夫建築研究所）勤務。1992-95年アンジェロ・マンジャロッティ事務所勤務。1996年帰国後アトリエ開設。2002年一級建築士事務所河合俊和建築設計事務所開設。

諸角敬
1977年早稲田大学理工学部建築学科卒業。1983-84年アンジェロ・マンジャロッティ事務所勤務。ミラノの駅舎設計（チェルトーザ駅、ロゴレード駅）に関わる。1985年Studio A設立。

川上元美
1966年東京藝大大学院美術研究科修士課程修了。1966-69年アンジェロ・マンジャロッティ事務所勤務。1971年カワカミデザインルーム設立。プロダクト・デザイン、家具、空間、環境デザインを手掛け、東京藝術大学、金沢美術工芸大学、多摩美術大学、神戸芸術工科大学等で客員教授歴任。公益財団法人日本デザイン振興会会長。

Francesca Albani
Albani is an architect who obtained her PhD in conservation of architecture at Politecnico di Milano, where she is an associate professor in architectural restoration at the Department of Architecture and Urban Studies. Since 2007, she has been a lecture and scientific collaborator in the research group of Franz Graf at the Mendrisio Academy of Architecture-USI. She is a designer of restoration works and an author of numerous essays on materials, construction techniques, and restoration of twentieth-century architecture.

Kinue Horikawa
Horikawa was born in Tokyo and obtained her master's degree at Waseda University under Prof. Arch. Osamu Ishiyama. She worked at GK Sekkei Inc. of the GK Design Group of Tokyo. Since 1955, she has been working for Studio Mangiarotti and Trust Foundation Angelo Mangiarotti in Milan. Since 2017, she has been working as a promoter for Japan in Agape s.r.l. and Vetreria Vistosi s.r.l..

Toshikazu Kawai
Kawai was born in 1960 in Gifu, Japan. He graduated at the Department of Architecture, Nihon University, Tokyo in 1982, and obtained his master's degree in 1984 at Tokyo University of the Arts. He worked for Kohyama Atelier in Tokyo in 1984–91 and Studio Mangiarotti, Milan, in 1992–95. In 2002, he established his own studio.

Kei Morozumi
Morozumi was born in 1954 in Kanagawa, Japan. In 1977, he graduated from the School of Architecture, Waseda University. In 1977–82, he worked for Hayashi Yamada Nakahara Sekkei-dojin. In 1983–84, he worked for Studio Mangiarotti. In 1985, he established Studio A in Tokyo.

Motomi Kawakami
In 1966, Kawakami obtained his master's degree (major in industrial design) at Tokyo University of the Arts. In 1966–69, he started his professional practice at Studio Mangiarotti. In 1971, he established Kawakami Design Office. His design work specializes in product, interior, space, and environmental design. He is a visiting professor of Tokyo National University of Fine Arts and Music, Kanazawa College of Arts, Tama Art University, and Kobe Design University, and a chairman of Japan Institute of Design Promotion.

川上元美

Kawakami Motomi

あとがき

Postscript

　イタリア建築・デザイン界の巨匠、アンジェロ・マンジャロッティは、建築、デザイン、彫刻とその幅広い活動で知られている。地中海的世界観、ギリシャの「テクネ」への憧憬が深く、その都市や建築の歴史をふまえながら、現代文明における創造的デザインに挑戦し続けてきた、その強靭にして深い哲学と独特の美学に基づく作品は、めまぐるしく変化する時代の中でも人々を魅了して止まない。

　マンジャロッティ事務所で、青春時代を長期にあるいは短期に、半世紀に渡って途切れることなく、それぞれの志をもとにスタジオに在籍する機会を得た私達20余名のアソシエイツのメンバーは、氏の仕事や人となりを通じて、建築やデザインの思想に触れ、イタリアの都市の歴史や魅力など多くを学んだ。マンジャロッティは1979年に国際交流基金の招聘で初来日を果たし、池辺陽教授の主導した箱根会議や、柳宗理館長の民芸館を始めとする各地での講演会を行って以来、しばしば来日し、ときには京都や、奈良の今井の町家を訪れて、日本建築の畳割りと柱割りの関係やモジュールの視点などを伝え、長きにわたって親交を持ち続けられたことは、日本とイタリアの文化の相互交流そのものでもあった。2004年に東京のギャラリー間に於いて「MA- un incontro展」を開催し、2012年にはイタリア文化会館で「アンジェロ・マンジャロッティの哲学とデザイン、マエストロと日本人スタッフとの協働の記録」を開催した。奇しくも展覧会の最終日を待つかのように、マンジャロッティはこの世を去った。

　2015年にスイス・イタリア語圏大学メンドリシオ建

Angelo Mangiarotti, a master of Italian architecture and design, is known for his work on architecture, design, and sculpture. The Mediterranean worldview and the Greek "techne" were his passion: considering its history of the city and architecture, he had challenged creative design in modern civilization. His works, based on strong, deep philosophy and unique aesthetics, have fascinated us in the midst of fast-changing times.

At the Mangiarotti studio, we, Japanese architects of more than 20, in turn without any breaks, had the opportunity to work as associates with respective aspirations whether for a long or short period in youth. Through his work and personality, we touched on architectural and design ideas and learned much about the history and attraction of Italian cities and so on. Mangiarotti was invited to Japan for first time in 1979 by the Japan Foundation to conduct lectures, such as the Hakone Conference facilitated by Professor Kiyoshi Ikebe, the Japan Folk Crafts Museum curated by Sori Yanagi, and all over Japan. Since then, he had often come to Japan, sometimes visiting Kyoto and the historical town houses in Imai, Nara. We told him about the composition of the Japanese traditional house based on the size of a tatami or the distance between wooden columns, and a view of modules. Having a relationship for a long time was just the very interaction between Japanese and Italian cultures. We held the "MA-un incontro" exhibition at the Gallery-MA in Tokyo in 2004 and "Angelo Mangiarotti's Philosophy and Design: A Record of Collaboration between Maestro and Japanese Associates" in 2012 at Istituto Italiano di Cultura in Tokyo. Mangiarotti passed away after the last day of the exhibition, as if he was just waiting for it to end.

This exhibition named "Angelo Mangiarotti. La tettonica dell'assemblaggio / The Tectonics of Assembly," organized by the

築アカデミーが開催した、アンジェロ・マンジャロッティの「構築のリアリティ」と銘打った展覧会は、タイムレスなシステムやモジュール、素材や工法の持つ可能性を引き出す力に焦点を当てたものだ。マンジャロッティの建築を新たな視点で解析、理解する展覧会としてスイス各地を巡回し、イタリア・ノヴァラ市での展示を経て日本でも開催の運びとなったことは、大きな喜びであり、明日を担う若者達への一助になれば幸いである。

この展覧会並びに出版を企画されたメンドリシオ大学のグラフ教授、アルバーニ教授をはじめとするスタッフの皆さま、日本の開催に協力した工学院大学、鈴木敏彦教授をはじめとするスタッフの皆さまに敬意を表する次第である。

Mendrisio Academy of Architecture of the Università della Svizzera italiana in 2015, focused on timeless systems, modules, and the potential drawing from materials and methods of Angelo Mangiarotti. After touring all over Switzerland and Novara in Italy, the exhibition to analyze and understand Mangiarotti's architecture from a new perspective finally came to Japan. It is a great pleasure, and I hope it will help young people in the future.

We express honor to Professor Franz Graf and Professor Francesca Albani who planned this exhibition and the books and all the staff. We also thank Professor Toshihiko Suzuki of Kogakuin University as the cooperator in Japan and all the people who contributed to the exhibition.

アンジェロ・マンジャロッティ 構築のリアリティ 組み立て工法による生成 展覧会

スイス・イタリア語圏大学メンドリシオ建築アカデミー………（2015年9月17日〜10月25日）
スイス応用科学大学、ヴィンタートゥール………………（2016年10月4日〜10月20日）
建築フォーラム、チューリッヒ………………………………（2017年6月1日〜7月14日）
シクリ・パヴィリオン、ジュネーブ…………………………（2018年8月31日〜9月16日）
ノヴァラ城、イタリア…………………………………………（2019年5月10日〜6月2日）
イタリア文化会館、東京………………………………………（2019年9月13日〜9月29日）

アンジェロ・マンジャロッティ 構築のリアリティ 組み立て工法による生成

発行日　2019年9月13日　第1刷

編著　　フランツ・グラフ
　　　　フランチェスカ・アルバーニ

発行所　Opa Press
　　　　〒101-0022　東京都千代田区神田練塀町55-1101
　　　　電話050-5583-6216　　press@atelier-opa.com

発売所　丸善出版株式会社
　　　　〒101-0051 東京都千代田区神田神保町2-17神田神保町ビル
　　　　電話03-3512-3256

印刷所　シナノ書籍印刷株式会社

アートディレクション　鈴木敏彦
デザイン　舟山貴士
編集　　杉原有紀（株式会社ATELIER OPA）
翻訳　　杉原有紀
監修　　堀川絹江
協力　　マンジャロッティ・アソシエイツ・ジャパン

本書の内容の一部あるいは全部を、無断で複写（コピー）、複製、
および磁気または光記憶媒体等への入力を禁止します。
許諾については上記発行所あてにご照会ください。

©2019　Opa Press
ISBN　978-4-908390-08-1